ERIC VOEGELIN'S THOUGHT

FOR OUR STUDENTS

ERIC VOEGELIN'S THOUGHT
A CRITICAL APPRAISAL

Edited with an Introduction by

Ellis Sandoz

Man is obviously made to think. It is his whole dignity and his whole merit; and his whole duty is to think as he ought.

Pascal

DUKE UNIVERSITY PRESS   DURHAM, N.C.   1982

Printed in the United States of America

Library of Congress Cataloging in Publication Data

Main entry under title:

Eric Voegelin's thought.

Includes bibliographical references and index.
1. Voegelin, Eric, 1901– —Addresses, essays,
lectures. I. Sandoz, Ellis, 1931–
B3354.V884E74   193   81-43591
ISBN 0-8223-0465-1   AACR2

CONTENTS

PREFACE

This volume of essays is intended to critically illumine Eric Voegelin's thought across a spectrum of perspectives determined by the specialized academic interests of the contributing authors. It originated as a symposium presented as a special session of the American Political Science Association's 1976 meeting in Chicago, and the papers by Jürgen Gebhardt, William C. Havard, Jr., David J. Walsh, and Eugene Webb were first presented on that occasion. Then, as now, Professor Voegelin took part and responded to the commentators.

Several of the essays published herein have been previously published in whole or part elsewhere [as follows: Gregor Sebba, "Prelude and Variations on the Theme of Eric Voegelin," *Southern Review* n.s. 13 (1977):646–87; William C. Havard, Jr., "Notes on Voegelin's Contributions to Political Theory," *Polity* 10 (1977):33–64; Dante Germino, "Eric Voegelin's Framework for Political Evaluation in His Recently Published Work," *American Political Science Review* 72 (1978):110–21; Eugene Webb, "Eric Voegelin's Theory of Revelation," *The Thomist* 42 (1978):95–110; Thomas J. J. Altizer, "A New History and a New But Ancient God? A Review Essay," and Eric Voegelin, "Response to Professor Altizer's 'A New History and a New But Ancient God?'," *Journal of the American Academy of Religion* 43 (1975):757–72.] I wish to acknowledge with gratitude the permission given by each of these journals and copyright holders to reprint these essays here. This work was made possible through the assistance of a grant from the Earhart Foundation and a research grant from the National Endowment for the Humanities, for which I wish to thank both organizations. The findings and conclusions presented here do not necessarily represent the views of the Endowment.

ELLIS SANDOZ

LOUISIANA STATE UNIVERSITY

INTRODUCTION

In 1714 Leibniz posed in these words the Question that Eric Voegelin has been asking in his own ways from the 1920s down to the present: "*Why is there something rather than nothing?* For nothing is simpler and easier than something. Further, suppose that things must exist, we must be able to give a reason *why they must exist so and not otherwise.*"[1]

The Question was not new in Leibniz in the eighteenth century but the reformulation of the one asked, and answered, in the earliest cosmological myths, in the beginning of philosophy by Anaximander and Heraclitus, by Schelling a century after Leibniz, and by Heidegger's existentialism a century later. If the Question was unoriginal, so also was the answer Leibniz gave: "This ultimate reason of things is called *God.*" While the answers of the ancients and moderns have differed widely, what Voegelin calls the "motivating structure in philosophical consciousness" as reflected in the constancy of the Question has remained the same over the millennia.[2] It is the Question in all its variety and the answers given to it that lie at the core of Voegelin's thought and that form the empirical basis and structure of his inquiry into reality, into order and disorder in politics and history, and into the formation and deformation of the human consciousness from antiquity to the present.

Voegelin's stress on asking the Question affirms not only its centrality in his thought, but also his opposition to those who prohibit asking it, namely modern systematizers and ideologists, especially Hegel, Comte, Marx, and their Gnostic epigones. Voegelin maintains the counterposition of the philosopher, i.e., of the critically self-reflective man who is open to the reality of the Whole, open to its horizon of wonder and mystery that intimates the existence of man and all that is out of nonexistence and open to the sustaining participation of the reality of nature's time and space and of man's history and mind in the divine ground that Leibniz doctrinally symbolized as "God." The counterposition is taken in an act of resistance against those who refuse to ask the Question (or to permit others to ask it), against those who resolutely reject the open horizon of reality and, therewith, their own humanity. It opposes those who perversely favor a closure against liberty and reason through the dogmatic assertion of "Answers" to the Question, "Answers"

1. *The Principles of Nature and of Grace, Based on Reason*, Sec. 7, in *Leibniz: Selections*, ed. Philip P. Wiener (New York: Charles Scribner's Sons, 1951), p. 527. Emphasis as in the original.
2. Voegelin, *Order and History*, 4 vols. to date (Baton Rouge: Louisiana State University Press, 1956–), 4:74.

which stop questioning and declare an end to history. Such thinkers impose a second reality of imaginings on the one true reality, label their whole edifice a "system of science," or a "*philosophie positive*," or "*wissenschaftlicher Sozialismus*," and, then, proceed to redefine science, reason, reality, man, and history from the perspective of the closed existence thereby asserted: an egophany of the libidinous self. Voegelin's counter is both combative and affirmative. It is a revolt against the modern revolt against reason and the "political prison culture" it imposes.[3]

Voegelin's combative posture of resistance and counterpoint, however, creates trouble for those who first approach his thought. He makes them uneasy because his work is truly at odds with all the conventions. It is contrary to the contemporary "climate of opinion" insofar as the principal characteristics of that "climate" are formed by the various ideologies. Yet in a topsy-turvy world of convention and ideology, where reason is regarded as irrationality and science as one man's opinion on subjective values, where the dream is soberly proclaimed to be reality and reality a dream, there cannot help but be difficulty in making heads and tails of the work of Eric Voegelin. It will appear at first sight, perhaps, that Robert Dahl was right when he once protested that Voegelin "has not only 'un-defined' science; he has 'un-scienced' it."[4] In fact, however, all Voegelin has done is to 'un-science' Positivism, and that is quite a different matter—except for Positivists, of course. Voegelin stands in the position of Marx's imaginary interlocutor in the Paris Manuscripts of 1844, whom Marx designated as the voice of "popular consciousness," who asks the Question of the origin of man and being in the divine Beginning (the *Entstehungsakt*; *Genesis*). He refuses to be silenced by Marx's revealing response to the Question, i.e.: "I say to you now: . . . Don't think, don't ask me. . . . [F]or the Socialist Man . . . the Question . . . has become impossible in practice."[5]

It is against the background of the modern prohibition of "metaphysical"

3. Voegelin, "Remembrance of Things Past" [1977], chap. 1 in *Anamnesis*, trans. and ed. Gerhart Niemeyer (Notre Dame, Ind., & London: University of Notre Dame Press, 1978), p. 4.

4. "The Science of Politics: Old and New," *World Politics* 7 (1955):489. This was a review of Voegelin, *The New Science of Politics* (Chicago: University of Chicago Press, 1952), the comment directed to the critique of Positivism (and its derivative, behavioralism) given at pp. 3–13. Voegelin had published a similar critique in German nearly twenty years earlier, it should be noted, when he spoke of "the dogma system of natural science superstition." Cf. *Rasse und Staat* (Tübingen: J.C.B. Mohr [Paul Siebeck], 1933), pp. 9–14.

5. Marx, "Nationalökonomie und Philosophie . . . (1844)," in *Die Frühschriften*, ed. Siegfried Landshut (Stuttgart: Alfred Kröner Verlag, 1955), p. 247; cf. "Economic and Philosophic Manuscripts of 1844," in *The Marx-Engels Reader*, ed. Robert C. Tucker, 2d ed. New York: W. W. Norton & Co., Inc., 1978), p. 92. For Voegelin's analysis of this passage from Marx, see the translation of his inaugural lecture at the University of Munich of 1958 in *Science, Politics, and Gnosticism: Two Essays*, trans. William J. Fitzpatrick (Chicago: Henry Regnery Co., Gateway Editions, 1968), pp. 22–28, which draws the inference that "Marx *was* an intellectual swindler."

questions that the Question stands at the center of all of Voegelin's work and is successively more penetratingly formulated in it over the period of the past half-century. It is the Question and not a "system" that Voegelin offers us, and the answers he gives are understood to be no more than way-stations in the process of an inquiry into man's existence as it has differentiated in history and as it mysteriously moves toward the fulfillment of time in fathomless Eternity. Hence, it is not the answer that is provided, nor the teaching, nor the doctrine, nor even the partial knowledge gained through the inquiry, but the mode of Questioning that is vital in this work of science. In some ways Voegelin's attitude is reminiscent of another scientist's toward his own great work, Sir Isaac Newton, who said: "I don't know what I may seem to the world. But as to myself I seem to have been only like a boy playing on the seashore and diverting myself in now and then finding a smoother pebble or prettier shell than ordinary, whilst the great ocean of truth lay all undiscovered before me."[6] The same sense of awe before the Whole, wonder rising to joy in the process of discovery, and humility in the face of Truth glimpsed, pervade Voegelin's thought: "Conventionally historians, philosophers, and theologians are concerned with answers to the Question. What I am trying to do here is to analyze the Question as a constant structure in the experience of reality and, since the experience is part of reality, in the structure of reality itself."[7]

Some of the complexities of Voegelin's work as viewed from the perspectives of political science, philosophy of history, and theology are explored in this volume of essays. The studied "unoriginality" of his work should not disguise the fact that in Voegelin one meets not only a thinker of the first rank but a revolution in the science of man. The main contours of his thought as viewed by knowledgeable scholars from several academic specialities, and the questions and issues raised therein, find searching exploration in the following pages. Professor Voegelin graciously agreed to respond to the essayists and does so in the Epilogue.

Gregor Sebba and Jürgen Gebhardt open the volume with two essays that address Voegelin's work from the perspective of his creation of the philosophy of history as the optimal symbolism of the new science of human existence. Both essayists draw heavily upon the early German writings of their subject to trace the lines of development from the 1920s into the present. Sebba, acquainted with Voegelin since student days in Vienna, proceeds both chronologically and topically to explore salient aspects of Voegelin's thought, from the 1928 study of the American mind through the latest volume of *Order and*

6. Newton quoted in Werner Heisenberg, *Philosophic Problems of Nuclear Science*, trans. F. C. Hayes (Greenwich, Conn.: Fawcett Publications, Inc., 1952), p. 89.

7. Voegelin, *Order and History*, 4:326.

History, with attention to the early critique of racism and National Socialism, the exhaustive study of the history of political ideas, the theory of consciousness as it evolved over a forty-year period, and the parallel concern with the problem of history, the essence of society, and the nature of modernity and the importance of Gnosticism. He critically evaluates Voegelin's truth claim and procedure and compares his theory of history with Spengler's, Jaspers', and Toynbee's, and his theory of myth and symbolization with Eliade's, Jung's, and Altizer's. Sebba concludes that the apex of Voegelin's philosophy of history is expressed in the sentence: "'History' is the area of reality where the directional movement of the cosmos achieves luminosity of consciousness."[8]

Gebhardt is especially concerned to show the genesis and progress of Voegelin's thought by tracing the various threads in a complex of motivating experiences that structure his mature interpretation of man in history and reality. He demonstrates the decisive importance of Max Weber's influence for the scientific and cognitive aspect of Voegelin's scholarly development; and he shows the pivotal significance of F. W. J. Schelling's philosophy for bringing together the theories of consciousness and history in the philosopher's personal act of recollection—Plato's *anamnesis*. The way was thereby opened for Voegelin to see that the source of meaning in history is the anamnestic dialogue that emerges to conscious articulation in the soul of the meditative. Stress is placed on the inseparability of the cognitive inquiry (empirical knowledge) and existential advance toward truth in the philosopher's development. The connection is illustrated by indicating the continuity running from Weber's demonic historiography to Schelling's account of Plato's *anamnesis* to the theory of consciousness ultimately differentiated. The essay concludes by explaining why and how the philosophy of history is the optimal symbolic form expressing the quest of man for his true humanity.

The implications of Voegelin for political science are drawn in the next two essays, one by William C. Havard, Jr., the other by Dante Germino. Havard addresses the meaning of science and political theory in Voegelin by comparing his writings with those of other contemporary political theorists, and then turns to examine the unifying elements in his principal works from the 1920s to the present. The motivation of Voegelin's discourse, he notes, parallels that of Plato, Aristotle, and Hegel: all write in response to pragmatic crises in human existence. And Havard follows the shifts and widening perspectives of especially the work from 1952, when *The New Science of Politics* was published, down to publication in 1974 of *The Ecumenic Age*. He stresses that Voegelin's substantive contributions to political science are inseparable from the process of his inquiry and the enormous body of historical materials that supply its empirical basis. He concludes with the assessment of

8. Voegelin, *Order and History*, 4:242.

Voegelin's theory as a comprehensive foundation of a new science of politics, identifies the criteria of such a science, and points to certain unresolved problems in the work to date.

Dante Germino starts from the problem of political science as an exploration of human reality. He analyzes Voegelin's revolutionary redefinition of political reality as the In-Between and examines the perspective of the new science as the participatory exploration of the tensional relationship of the In-Between of mortal and immortal—the apeirontic depth of Anaximander and noetic height of Plato-Aristotle. He next deals with the Question and the attendant issues of truth and its deformation, including the problem of second realities. After summarizing the principles of political theory, which he draws from the more recent writings, he turns to consider the continuity of Voegelin's analysis over the past quarter century as suggested by the recently published manuscripts from the 1940s and 1950s in *From Enlightenment to Revolution* (1975),[9] which he terms an "explosive work" because of its treatment of major modern political thinkers from Voltaire to Marx and Comte.

David J. Walsh next turns to the meaning of *philosophy* in Voegelin's pages and shows how Voegelin both recovers the meaning of philosophy as originally developed in Hellas and, then, places that restored understanding of philosophy at the center of his own noetic science of man and being. He finds that the principle basic to Voegelin's work, as well as to philosophy, is simply that "the psyche is the experiential center of order which radiates its meaning over society and history." The reciprocal recovery of ancient philosophy and its utilization in recovering meaning in history in the present then is related to Voegelin's understanding of Reason as itself a theophany or revelatory event in the horizon of Hellenic antiquity, one which is equivalent to the revelatory events of Israelite history and Christianity. From this perspective, then, the significance of the "derailment" of philosophy after Aristotle is considered; and Walsh shows how Voegelin puts philosophy back on the tracks, as it were, through drawing the universal implications of classical philosophy and synthesizing the strands of philosophy and revelation in a powerful new analysis of St. Paul and other New Testament materials. Walsh faults Voegelin for not indicating more clearly how the differentiated understanding of myth can concretely be employed in providing a persuasive account of the Whole in the present-day crisis of truth. But he finds it Voegelin's permanent achievement to have articulated the fundamental form of thought in terms of which we live and think and in which even his own work must finally be judged.

Eugene Webb (pp. 157–77) proffers a searching analysis of Voegelin's understanding of revelation and its comparison with that of orthodox theology.

9. Voegelin, *From Enlightenment to Revolution*, ed. John H. Hallowell (Durham, N.C.: Duke University Press, 1975.)

Webb's point of departure is to restate several of the major objections raised against Voegelin's treatment of the Christian revelation, then to provide an account of just what Voegelin means by experience-symbolization and the process of differentiation. On the basis of this analysis, Webb then shows the consistency of Voegelin's treatment of revelation in the Hellenic as well as Judeo-Christian horizons, and from that point provides responses to the objections raised by Voegelin's Christian critics. Webb, however, finds Voegelin's account of revelation may be wanting because of its exclusive preoccupation with the theoretical and philosophical dimension at the expense of the normal religious experiences and concerns of the average believer. And he is troubled by the ambiguity of the treatment given to the question of the immortality of the soul and to the central issue of the mystery of the Incarnation of God in Christ.

The volume culminates in an exhilarating exchange between Thomas J. J. Altizer and Voegelin himself concerning some of the key issues raised by *The Ecumenic Age*, an exchange already noticed by Webb in the previous chapter. To Altizer's admiring complaint that Voegelin's language is tantalizingly obscure and clear at once, making a theological exegesis of his work impossible, Voegelin responds from the New Testament, Anselm, Aquinas, and Barth by way of suggesting that his analysis moves firmly within the horizon of discourse established by Christian thinkers. Indeed, his work is consciously motivated by faith in search of rational understanding on the pattern of the Anselmian *fides quaerens intellectum*, generalized in an inquiry into the history of experience and symbolization. "Even this expansion of the *fides*, however, to all of the experiences of divine reality in which history constitutes itself, cannot be said to go beyond 'Christianity.' For it is the Christ of the Gospel of John who says of himself: 'Before Abraham was, I am' (8:58); and it is Thomas Aquinas who considers the Christ to be the head of the *corpus mysticum* that embraces, not only Christians, but all mankind from the creation of the world to its end. In practice this means that one has to recognize, and make intelligible, the presence of Christ in a Babylonian hymn, or a Taoist speculation, or a Platonic dialogue, just as much as in a Gospel."[10] To Altizer's dismay at Voegelin's abuse of Hegel, whom he finds attacked in an absurd and grotesque manner by a philosopher so akin to him that it suggests a hatred climaxing in an "attempted Oedipal murder of his father," Voegelin responds with "a few emendations." The lengthy reply traces Voegelin's difficulties in bringing Hegel's work to analytical focus until he discovered its Gnostic element, and then Hermetic and alchemistic influences, and he confirms his critical assessment of the famous German Idealist in these words:

10. Voegelin, "Response to Professor Altizer's 'A New History and a New But Ancient God?'," *Journal of the American Academy of Religion* 43 (1975):765–72, (pp. 187–97, this volume).

"At the core of Hegel's difficulties lies his misconstruction of the relation between Being and Thought, which he needs for his misconstruction of 'Christianity,' which he needs for his misconstruction of history, which he needs if he wants to place himself at the climax of history as the fully revealed and revealing Logos who completes the Revelation that was left incomplete by the Logos who was Christ."[11] To a third criticism by Altizer, that Voegelin either ignores modern thought and science or treats it negatively, the reply comes that the present "climate of opinion" (Whitehead) is, indeed, not the climate of his work, yet it is fully indebted to the remarkable flowering of the historical sciences that make the twentieth century a veritable renaissance in the study of the science of man no less than of nature. Well placed and incisive as Altizer's critique is, one is reminded in musing on the outcome of the exchange that Voegelin's debating skills were honed as a young high school teacher in the hostile environment of a predominantly Marxist workers' suburb of Vienna; and he has taken great pleasure in such exercises ever since then.[12]

11. Ibid., p. 769 (see p. 194, this volume).
12. Ellis Sandoz, *The Vugelinian Revolution: A Biographical Introduction* (Baton Rouge: Louisiana State University Press, 1981), pp. 48–49.

ERIC VOEGELIN'S THOUGHT

PRELUDE AND VARIATIONS ON THE THEME OF ERIC VOEGELIN

Gregor Sebba

Wer es sich in geistigen Dingen
leicht macht, hat nicht mitzureden.[1]

Eric Voegelin was born three days into the twentieth century, on January 3, 1901; he was twenty-one when he published his first scholarly paper, fifty-one when he turned out to be a philosopher, and past seventy-five when he began to be recognized as such, except by the philosophers.

He made his quiet philosophical debut in 1951 with the Walgreen Lectures on "Truth and Representation" at the University of Chicago; he published them in 1952 under the new title *The New Science of Politics*, and this put him on the map. Political scientists promptly mistook him for one of their own, a dangerous reactionary who fortunately was almost unreadable; only his virulent attacks on everything modern were written in all too plain language. What made him dangerous was the attempt to drag political science back to Aristotle, and this in the name of a *new* science of politics. The result was a tempest in the wrong teapot. When it finally subsided, a younger generation of American political scientists awarded the book a prize for its enduring influence on the discipline and went on with business as usual. What is nowadays called "Eric Voegelin's thought" is the philosophical thought contained in his work of the thirty years that began with *The New Science of Politics*.

The philosophical nature of *The New Science* is stated on its very first page: this investigation, when completed, "will in fact become a philosophy of history." The title of Voegelin's main work, *Order and History*, is equally declarative. The first three of the six volumes it was to comprise appeared in 1956 and 1957. In the summer of 1957 I asked Voegelin when he would publish the announced philosophy of history, which shows how much *I* knew.

The title of the present essay and some material are taken by permission from a first short version published in *The Southern Review* n.s. 13 (1977):646–76. Copyright © Gregor Sebba.

1. Erich Voegelin, *Die Rassenidee in der Geistesgeschichte von Ray bis Carus* (Berlin: Junker und Dünnhaupt, 1933), p. 23.

His answer was unexpected: he had no philosophy of history. He had said what little he knew in the introductions to the first two volumes and to the announced fourth one and was considering publishing them in one volume: "It will make a slim book." The fourth volume—an entirely different fourth volume—appeared seventeen years later, in 1974, with the promised third introduction. A reader who wants to know Eric Voegelin's thought can put the slim book together himself, reading the first two introductions and culling from the long third one those pages in which Voegelin summarizes the result of his radical rethinking of his enterprise during those seventeen years. Such a reader would be well advised to stop at these introductions. For if he ventures beyond them, an avalanche of historical analyses will descend upon him and toss him "forward and backward and sideways"[2] as he tumbles through world history. As a recent reviewer wrote, coming up for breath: "It is hardly an exaggeration to characterize Voegelin as an overwhelming author."[3]

Even the slim volume is overwhelming. From its pages rises a philosophy of God and man, world and society, of reality, divine and human, of the search for truth and the rebellion against it. Thesis fits seamlessly upon thesis to form an encompassing and consistent world view, seen in the light of "the problem of a mankind that advances in history to higher levels of truth" (2:6). He who wants to know *what* Eric Voegelin's thought is will find the most concise, most authoritative, and I dare say the most accessible statement of it in the slim book. But I wonder whether knowing what his philosophy says is the same as knowing what it is.

Of course this philosophy does not conceal its nature, to say the least. The difficulty I sense is rather one of language creating conditioned reflexes. When one hears the word "philosophy," he expects to find a body of thought, an edifice of theses he can test to see whether the roof will cave in if he leans against a pillar. Could it be that the expression "Eric Voegelin's thought" strikes a chord containing a note not in the key in which his philosophy is written? In any case it will be well to modulate from this chord to the key that wants to be heard. Take the simple question: What is philosophy?

Philosophical dictionaries and encyclopedias list answers like the knowledge of ultimates, the science of sciences, the theory of critical discussion, the study of first principles, the most general science. Voegelin's answer begins with a fact: "Thousands of years of history passed before philosophers appeared in it." In the West they rose in Greek antiquity, some 2500 years ago, not in a process of evolution but as a unique *event*: something occurred, and

2. Eric Voegelin, *Order and History*, Vol. 4: *The Ecumenic Age* (Baton Rouge: Louisiana State University Press, 1974):57. Page references to *Order and History* in the text will refer to volume and page. Italics in quotations are mine unless otherwise stated.

3. Patrick Coby in *The Thomist* 44 (1980):464.

what occurred was philosophy. The "event philosophy" (*das Ereignis der Philosophie*) was one of the epoch-making "leaps in being," a term to be clarified later. In the case of philosophy "a spiritual irruption from beyond the person" into the consciousness of representative men—the philosophers— moved the understanding of order and truth on to a higher level.[4] What had before been known "compactly" in the mode of myth now became knowable in the "differentiating" way of the philosophers who make explicit in concise, articulated concepts what had been known implicitly. The event of philosophy thus lifted into consciousness its own epoch-making division of the course of historical happenings into a "before" and an "after" this event. The epoch is still what it is, and the philosopher still does what philosophers do. And what do they do? Voegelin does not say that they produce systems or philosophies; philosophers *philosophize*. This is the note we need, and now we must identify the key. What *is* "philosophizing"? For an answer let us look at what Voegelin does rather than at what he says.

Voegelin is a great solver of problems and an even greater inventor of them, if we take the term "inventing" in the literal sense as "coming upon." Every answer produces new questions. The most important problems he comes upon are unsolvable. He calls them "mysteries." These mysteries "surround" the clearing in which man lives, acts, and strives for an understanding of the encompassing order of being. At the beginning of Voegelin's philosophizing he identified a few of these mysteries. Their number increased with every advance he made. I gave up counting them long ago, for ultimately they are but one great mystery. Only when the light that emanates from it passes through the narrow opening of a philosophizing consciousness does this one mystery diffract into a spectrum of "differentiated" mysteries shining in the surrounding darkness. This is what Voegelin's philosophy looks like, inside.

We encounter this understanding at the very beginning of his enterprise, programmatically formulated in rational language: "The ultimate, essential

4. I follow the fundamental discussion in Voegelin's "Ewiges Sein in der Zeit" (1964), collected in his *Anamnesis: Zur Theorie der Geschichte und Politik* (Munich: R. Piper & Co. Verlag, 1966), pp. 254–56; cf. also esp. 262–64. The English translation of this extremely difficult text in Eric Voegelin, *Anamnesis*, ed. and trans. Gerhart Niemeyer (Notre Dame/London: University of Notre Dame Press, 1978, pp. 116–40) should be used with the German original at hand; the text concerning the philosophers' "response" (p. 117, lines 18–20) has become unintelligible in the correction of the page proof, and English sentence structure at times shifts the intentional stress. The expression "a spiritual irruption from beyond the person" occurs already in *Rasse und Staat* (Tübingen: J.C.B. Mohr [Paul Siebeck], 1933), long before the "leap in being" was identified. Professor Voegelin told me in explanation that he had taken it from Scheler, indeed without anticipating the role it would later play in his work. [The pertinent passage is as follows: "[D]er menschliche Geist . . . ist . . . offen als Stelle des Einbruchs von Geistwirklichkeit, die jenseits der Person liegt. . . . Er ist unmittelbar verbunden mit dem Weltgrund, und er ist eingebettet in die geistigen Gemeinschaften aller Stufen: der Menschheit, der Nation bis zum Familienkreis und engen Freundschaftsbünden" (ibid., pp. 68–69). For the *leap in being*, see note 52 below and Part III of this essay generally.—Ed.]

ignorance is not complete ignorance. Man can achieve considerable knowledge about the order of being, and not the least part of that knowledge is *the distinction between the knowable and the unknowable*" (1:2). This could not have been said "before philosophy." The first sentence differentiates between "ultimate" and "essential" on the one hand, "complete" on the other. The second sentence makes the static distinction dynamic. It sets a process in motion, the process of philosophizing. What has been "compactly" known must be pursued to the very boundary between the knowable and the unknowable, in all directions, until the surrounding mystery stops the pursuit. And even this stopping is a process to be explored. What then is the status of the findings that the process of philosophizing produces?

At the end of *The Ecumenic Age* (1974) where the historico-analytic avalanche slows down toward a temporary halt, Voegelin notes that history has a long breath: "It will always be a wholesome exercise to reflect that 2500 years from now our own time will belong to as remote a past as that of Heraclitus, the Buddha and Confucius in relation to our present." The wholesome exercise is a safeguard "against the human weakness of elevating one's own present into the purpose of history" (4:331). For the process of history is not a story to be told from its happy, or unhappy, end; it is "a mystery in process of revelation" (4:225), and Voegelin's findings emerge from a philosophizing that is itself part of this process. Philosophizing yields only such insights into flowing reality as a thinker in his own time can attain. Voegelin marks the status of these findings, and the process that engenders them, in one sentence: "Our present, like every present, is a phase in the flux of divine reality in which we, like all men before us and after, participate" (4:331). One last step, from "participation" to "response," would disclose the innermost nature of philosophizing in Voegelin's sense. But this step cannot and need not be taken yet. This modulation from one key to another has already established what needs to be established at the outset: the distance that separates this philosophical enterprise from what the conventional terminology would lead us to expect. It has also made it possible to characterize the nature of the enterprise itself, for in this modulation I found myself forced to go beyond the immediate purpose toward what I venture to call "the theme of Eric Voegelin."

This expression, too, is off key. The theme is indeed Voegelin's *theme*. But is it *his* theme? The question brings his massive historical analyses into focus. In these readings of the vast historical core we hear the theme in variation upon variation, never in its purity.[5] These variations are not playful exercises;

5. "The interpretation is not a reproduction but merely a more or less insufficient means of making more accessible what is difficult to understand; it is . . . itself merely the variation of a motif which is always given in its variations, never in its purity." Erich Voegelin, *Über die Form des amerikanischen Geistes* (Tübingen: J.C.B. Mohr [Paul Siebeck], 1928), p. 40, speaking of Charles S. Peirce whose philosophizing he brilliantly analyzed.

one might call them "variations in pursuit of the theme." Voegelin's own work is an advance within the advance and not its end point. The title of the final volume of *Order and History*, now in the making, "In Search of Order," says it plainly; for, according to Voegelin, this search has no appointed end.

Now we can turn to what Voegelin's philosophy *says*, without fear of misunderstanding its nature. What we find are issues, innovatively grasped and explored. These issues are fundamental, and I shall take them up one by one later in this essay, not to introduce the reader to Eric Voegelin's thought but for their own sake. Not being a philosopher in any sense of the word, I have no business offering myself as a guide for the perplexed. But the issues he raises are another matter. They concern everyone who lives in awareness of the fact that what little we know of reality points beyond itself. I say that as a hard agnostic who knows what ultimate, essential ignorance is and who does not conclude from ultimate unknowability to nonexistence. This is enough for a start. But before we get to the issues I want to take the reader back to where Voegelin was in his beginnings and to the five unduly forgotten books from his Vienna years. Of these years I can speak from personal knowledge. Meet then Dr. Erich Voegelin, Privatdozent for Government and Sociology at the University of Vienna[6] during those years of a depression which Europeans called "the world crisis" until they turned into the Hitler years.

I

Vienna. "Crises bring out greatness," said Jakob Burckhardt, adding grimly as always, "but it may be the last." Vienna in the 1930s was the enormous head of a tiny, mangled country which did not want to live and was not allowed to die. Impotent and hypersensitive, Vienna reacted like a seismograph to every political or economic tremor abroad. This shabby, sardonically cheerful city was an invigorating cultural center of the first order, teeming with talent, ideas, experiments, hospitable to every kind of intellectual venture from the stiffly orthodox to the wayward. In 1930–31 I found it still possible to bring together scholars and politically engaged people of every persuasion for informal debate on the burning current issues—probably the last group where Liberal and Marxist, Jew and antisemite, Socialist and Monarchist sat down together until civil war ended all that in 1934. The largest group among the nearly forty participants were scholars like Felix Kaufmann, Aurel Kolnai, Fritz Machlup, Oskar Morgenstern, Maria Jahoda, Karl and Ilona Polányi, Eugen Kogon, Otto Neurath, Heinrich Gompertz, and Eric Voegelin, young theologians like Father Johannes Oesterreicher,

6. *Privatdozent* indicates a scholar with doctorate and qualifying book on whom the university bestowed the privilege of teaching unrequired courses without salary, receiving only the nominal fee paid by the students who registered for the course.

and several unknowns who during and after the troubles of 1934 unexpectedly rose to play a political role in an effort to stem the Nazi tide. Among the scholars, Voegelin had a reputation for fiendish erudition and for his ability to take off vertically from any question whatever and to disappear within minutes in the theoretical ionosphere, leaving only a trail of recondite references behind, a slim young man with blonde hair and sharp eyes behind his glasses, his Pascalian nose jutting out in a metaphysical curve.

Voegelin has always defied departmentalization. Since he rarely speaks of himself, his real concerns during his formative period became known only very recently, although he stated them in a few little-read pages published in 1966:[7] the nature of the experiences that motivate philosophical thinking, the theory of social action and of political order, the problem of ideology. I took him at the time for a sociologist of the Max Weber, Simmel, and Scheler type, Weberian in his comprehensive grasp of wide-ranging empirical fact and literary sources, philosophically oriented like Simmel and Scheler. But even in his early beginnings he had already a vague notion (*eine Ahnung*) of how it might end, as he told me a few years ago. He evidently also knew from the beginning that he was to take the philosophical road. Sociology, still an as yet undefined, unspecialized academic discipline, offered the greatest freedom for development, and "government" offered him the only chance of a salaried professorial position. There was no "political science" in the American sense; German *Staatslehre* was a much broader field, the right one for a theoretician of political order who was able to master constitutional law, if needed. But philosophy was Voegelin's central concern, and within it, the theory of consciousness. His own first contribution went almost unnoticed, since it was imbedded in a book on America where nobody would look for it.[8]

What I learned from him came from personal contact. One day he asked me what I was working on. I had just discovered the enormous expansion of our perceptual and experiential range produced by technological advances such as the new technique of the "close-up" which expands a human face to fill a movie screen. "So what?" he asked. As the eye wanders over that face, it reveals itself as a landscape. At that, a beatific smile slowly spread over his face; he began to exude a sense of well-being and benevolence—a sure sign that I had once more made a complete ass of myself. And sure enough, it came,

7. "In memoriam Alfred Schutz," in Eric Voegelin, *Anamnesis* (1966), pp. 17–20, omitted in the English version. An English translation will be found in the documentary appendix to the international Festschrift honoring the philosopher on his eightieth birthday: Peter J. Opitz and Gregor Sebba (eds.), *The Philosophy of Order: Essays on History, Consciousness, and Politics* (Stuttgart: Klett-Cotta Verlag, 1980), henceforth cited as *Festschrift Voegelin*.

8. It is discussed in technical detail by Aníbal A. Bueno: "Consciousness, Time, and Transcendence in Eric Voegelin's Philosophy," *Festschrift Voegelin*, pp. 91–109. On Voegelin's critical concern with phenomenology, see Helmut R. Wagner, "Agreement in Discord: Alfred Schutz and Eric Voegelin," ibid., pp. 74–90, based on the correspondence of the two friends after their emigration to the United States, now being edited by Professor Wagner.

kindly: "Dr. Sebba, a human face is not a landscape. It is a human face. Don't start wandering over human faces, it leads to bad things. Stay with *rrreality*." Disregarding the human measure in the encounter with reality did indeed lead to bad things. Voegelin's five books of the Vienna period assert the fundamental human experience in the face of a new technology. I shall discuss these books in chronological order.

1928: America. A Laura Spelman Rockefeller Memorial Fellowship had taken Voegelin to the United States for two years of study and research, chiefly at Columbia, Harvard, and Wisconsin. The outcome was his first book, *The Form of the American Spirit*.[9] Nothing about skyscrapers, Wall Street, Henry Ford's assembly line, Spanish moss, or stock yards. The book opens with an exploration of existential and symbolic being, of consciousness, of time, to seek the spirit of America in the understanding of self, God, society, in the history of the labor movement, in the Federal Reserve System, Santayana, Jonathan Edwards, the Anglo-American theory of law. Let me focus on two issues of importance to Voegelin's mature work: his method, and his results.

Voegelin himself calls the vast mass of detail he discusses—from metaphysics to "the $22.50 suit made of a fabric we do not use in Europe" (the seersucker?)—"an apparent chaos." In fact it is the product of a radical process of selection and exclusion. Nothing is admitted that does not find expression in *language*, and a particular language at that: theoretical language that rationally orders a field to make it intelligible. This rules out music, the arts, literature (not enough rational substance), the film, schools, business organization, technology, etc. What remains are *die selbstsprechenden Erscheinungen*, literally: those "self-speaking phenomena" that will one day be called symbolisms. The natural sciences, too, are out. They speak about objects, not about themselves as does philosophy in the process of *Selbstbesinnung*, a meditative recovery of its self-understanding. Under this aspect even the history of the labor unions, or the principle of giving "due weight to all facts," turns out to be part of the American mind's *Selbstbesinnung*. These are still principles of Voegelinian method, especially the principle that the selection of the material must follow the selection history itself has made: "*The historical line of meaning runs like a rope across the abyss into which everything plunges that cannot stay on the rope.*" This sentence somehow belongs with the beautifully expressed characteristic of the unquiet tension between "symbolic and existential being," which he will one day identify as the Platonic In-Between of existence, the *metaxy*.

9. See note 5 above. None of the nine reviews it received appeared in a philosophical journal. The publisher of the book also published the work of Max Weber and other leading sociologists of the period. This book deserves translation into English.

The American spirit, Voegelin finds, is grounded in "the open self," the "central experience of intimacy." Socially it manifests itself in "the escape from the mystery of the self, the dissolution of its solitude into intimacy." It seeks intimate communion with a God who is like man, only more so; intellectually it produces a metaphysics of rationalism which wants to master and order reality. Why then the two figures that take central place—Santayana the aloof neither-nor philosopher, and John R. Commons, the least metaphysical of practical reformers? I would venture that the choice reflected an unconscious decision concerning Voegelin's own way in life. The figure of Santayana is, in Jungian terms, Voegelin's "shadow," the kind of sterile thinker he *might* have become.[10] Commons, "whose greatness one must love to defend oneself against its superiority," is by contrast what Voegelin could never be: the nonreflective man who, in all simplicity and modesty, has experienced life so fully that "almost not knowing what he is doing, he merely has to say what he sees to give highest philosophical expression to the meaning of the society in and for which he lives." The quotation from Commons, in the original English, which closes the book, is Voegelin's own declaration of faith in the spirit of America:

> I do not see why there is not as much idealism of its kind in breeding a perfect animal or a Wisconsin No. 7 ear of corn, or in devising an absolutely exact instrument for measuring a thousand cubic feet of gas . . . as there is in chipping out a Venus de Milo or erecting a Parthenon. . . . Of course a cow is just a cow, and can never become a Winged Victory. But within her field of human endeavour she is capable of approaching an ideal. And, more than that, she is an ideal that every farmer and farmer's boy— the despised slaves and helots of Greece—can aspire to.

1933: Racism. The Preface to Voegelin's second book bears the ominous date, "January 20, 1933." Two days later, Adolf Hitler became chancellor of the German Reich, the head of a parliamentary government. In March 1933 he made himself the sole master of Germany. Within days, Karl Polányi wound up a discussion in our research group with a warning and a stunning prediction. Hitler, he said, was no wild rabble rouser but a dangerous political genius of the Lenin type, though not of Lenin's caliber, ruthless and cunning, who would systematically outplay the democratic West. The Nazi horrors we had seen were nothing yet; we were rushing down cataract after

---

10. In *Anamnesis* (1966) Voegelin describes those earliest recollections which, he feels, were determinants of his philosophical development. Of one, called "Cloud Castle," he says that its meaning is not clear to him. It concerns an inaccessible mountain called "Cloud Rock," with a legendary "Cloud Castle." He thought of the knight there as "a vague, mournful, lost figure" who sometimes travels on mysterious business, then returns to his lonely habitation. I take this Cloud Knight as a symbol of intellect lost in pure speculation, divorced from the ground of reality—the "shadow" philosopher, *Anamnesis* (1966), pp. 66–67. "Die Wolkenburg", English version (1978), pp. 41–42.

cataract toward the final plunge into the Second World War. The date? September 1938; if not then, *early September 1939.*

Polányi was a master analyst of the political chess board; Voegelin was struggling to understand the demonic nature of the new political mass movements. He had his own analysis of the Hitler phenomenon ready: a study of the race idea in three parts. Hitler's "theoreticians" were looking forward to the book; they needed someone to make their racism scientifically respectable. The "Nordic" *Privatdozent* in Vienna seemed to be just the man. There was a chair in Berlin waiting for him, no doubt. The work appeared as two separate books. The last part came out first, in the summer of 1933, under the title *Race and the State;*[11] the first two parts, a study of the idea of race, appeared a few months later. When I read these two books, I knew that Voegelin would be on the Nazi list when Austria fell. I still wonder how he had the nerve to publish both books in Hitler's Germany, and how two German publishers could accept them.

Race and the State maintains its stance of theoretical objectivity only with the greatest difficulty. Voegelin savages the leading German race biologists; he cannot bring himself to use the word "National Socialism" even when he refers to it, yet he attempts to write his way around the censor without budging from the truth.[12] For me the book still evokes the nightmarish atmosphere of these crucial years when it first dawned on us that the freedom of expression was becoming lethal to its practitioners.

The History of the Race Idea, by contrast, is one of Voegelin's best books,[13] magisterial in its calm, uncompromising stance: "The knowledge of man has come to grief. . . . The present state of the race theory is one of decay. . . . Race theory today is unauthentic thinking about man." Individuals are "living entities and not the jigsaw puzzle of hereditary factors which genetics makes of them." From the genetic race theories "a malignant trait of fatalism radiates out, foreign and deadly to life and spirit." Then he adds the ultimate insult: Nazi racism and the Liberalism and Marxism it abhors are brothers under the skin. Not only that, he underlines the sentence to make sure it will not be overlooked in Berlin. It worked: by the end of the year both books were suddenly "unavailable."

The study is grounded in the Greek and Christian hierarchical conception of man as a unity of body, soul, and spirit; no natural science can grasp his

11. Erich Voegelin, *Rasse und Staat.*

12. There is, for example, a list of what is bad about Jews in German life. But these socioeconomic facts are not presented as racial traits; Voegelin calls them *Erregungsanlässe*, meaning things that allow Germans to get hot under the collar. A Nazi reader would hardly catch the irony of it. [Cf. ibid., pp. 184–91.—Ed.]

13. For the full title see note 1 above. For Voegelin, the history of the idea of race begins with Francis Willughby and John Ray, 1676 and 1694, and ends with Gustav Carus, 1849, who gave final form to the "Urbild"—Voegelin would now say "symbol" of the perfect spiritually and bodily well-formed man (p. 10). Carus thus initiated a profounder conception of race, defined

nature. This leads to the central attack on all racism: genetic endowment can never determine the spiritual and moral character of an individual or group. There are no superior or inferior races, no good or evil ones. The German racist hates the Jew as the "anti-idea," the metaphysical opposite of the German who needs to overcome his feeling of political inferiority.[14] This casts the Jew into the role of the Devil in the flesh, the genetic carrier and spreader of the evil seed. It follows that the Jew can be overcome only by physically exterminating every carrier of Jewish genetic material. Since even Hitler had not yet arrived at that conclusion, Voegelin carefully avoids stating it explicitly, but the implication is horribly clear: Racism begins with the impermissible application of a natural science to areas beyond its competence; it must by its very logic end in mass murder.

1936: The Authoritarian State. Just before Hitler became dictator, in March 1933, the Austrian government declared that the elected parliament had "eliminated itself." Again, it was Karl Polányi who explained the mystifying proclamation. There would be a new regime, unlike any other, faceless, undefinable, nondictatorial, nondemocratic, unsupported, impossible to bring down, and unable to fall "because there was no place it could fall into." The name which this regime adopted in the event was "the authoritarian state." In 1936 Voegelin published a monograph on this conception,[15] still important for its theoretical part.[16] Here he tackles the problem of the contemporary state and nation as a political scientist, theoretician, and constitutional lawyer. Here too is his most detailed critique of positivistic liberalism, a harsh, open break with his teacher Hans Kelsen. The harshness reflects the expe-

---

at the end of the book (p. 159) as that of a political idea that is community-forming (*gemeinschaftsformend*), not an object of study but "body-soul-spirit reality" (p. 160).

14. The idea was much discussed at the time. My friends Eugen Kogon and Ernst Karl Winter had the ingenious idea that the German hated the Jew with a passion because the Jew was too much like him. This political anti-idea has, however, an important philosophical counterpart which came to the fore in the essay-length critique of *The New Science of Politics* that Alfred Schutz sent to Voegelin in 1952 and in Voegelin's two answers of January 1 and 10, 1953. The exchange is published in my English translation, *Festschrift Voegelin*, Documentary Appendix, pp. 434–62. Schutz points out that every position gives rise to a counter-position; how then can Voegelin maintain that only one position represents the truth, since both of them are justifiable? (pp. 446–47). Voegelin answered by raising the question to the highest philosophical level (Letter to Alfred Schutz on Gnosticism, January 10, 1953, ibid., p. 461–62; cf. the preceding Letter on Christianity, January 1, 1953, pp. 450–51 and my introduction to the exchange, pp. 431–33).

15. Erich Voegelin, *Der autoritäre Staat* (Vienna: Springer, 1936). Almost the whole edition was destroyed during World War II, and the book is very rare.

16. The second half of the book is a meticulous legal study of the new "authoritarian" Austrian Constitution of 1934. Its studied objectivity was mistaken for an advocacy of the authoritarian regime, while the theoretical stress on protecting a state against revolutionary ideologies that use the constitution to overthrow it raised dark doubts concerning Voegelin's political stance among his liberal friends.

rience of having watched the German liberals work straight into Hitler's hands. When the Nazi Party first entered federal and state elections to participate in that democratic process which it had sworn to destroy, a reporter asked Dr. Goebbels ironically how he could defend this betrayal of the Party's principles. Goebbels replied coldly: "If the calf offers us the knife for cutting its throat, we would be fools not to take it." Voegelin drew the lesson: "Playing the freedom-of-thought game is the opposition's business; for the ruler it is suicidal."

Voegelin defines the "authoritarian" state as an institution legitimized by the founding act of its supreme organ, the act of establishing, preserving, and developing the state. This is essentially the American notion of the "Founding Fathers." Revolutionary decrees, Voegelin finds, are not unconstitutional; rather, "the constitution has changed." Ironically, the Austrian case was that of a "fatherless society," as the Freudian Paul Federn had called it in 1919.[17] But then the revolutionary American founding act is still the law while the Austrian "founding act" of 1933 merely postponed the inevitable. Why?

The modern state and the modern nation are not collections of individuals held together by a legal and organizational framework. They are realities, "substances," in their own right. What turns a population into a body politic is a permeating feeling of what Voegelin would now call "participation." Yet such is the complexity of contemporary society that even in an established, living nation any factor—economic, psychological, ideological, ethnic or whatever—any element of power or leadership, can become distorting and may paralyze the organizing power of the state. The fascinating historical and theoretical material on which Voegelin draws may now seem remote, but the problems he studies are much timelier today than they were in 1936. Creating regimes by revolutionary action is now the rule, not the exception. And their stability and viability still depend on the degree to which they are able

17. The rise of totalitarian mass movements in the interwar period was not the only problem forcing a rethinking of the foundations of political society. There was also the failure of even the best-made new democratic constitutions, proving that political science engineering alone can not resolve the problem of holding such a society together. The very nature of civil obedience was in question. The answer had to be sought at levels much deeper than hitherto envisaged, as the work of Carl Schmitt and Friedrich Smend indicates. Austria was a veritable test case on which Federn shed a sharp sidelight, but psychology could not penetrate to the depth of the troubling problems. The Third Conference of the League of Nations Institute for International Intellectual Cooperation in Paris, 1937, had a memorandum on the Austrian case before it, three papers—by Eric Voegelin, Otto Brunner, and myself—dealing with the constitutional, historical, and ideological aspects respectively. The common issue was the lack of that self-understanding of a political society which renders it capable of "action in history," as Voegelin puts it in *The New Science of Politics*. The problems of the interwar period, 1918–39, have not gone away; they live on, seemingly undetected; only their names have changed. In *Der autoritäre Staat* and also in *The New Science of Politics*, one may find an instrumentarium for the study of dangerous internal and international problems that transcend empirical analysis. That these theoretical tools of analysis remain unused and indeed undiscovered would be surprising were it not that the turn which the social sciences have taken is itself part of these dangerous developments in our century.

to weld tribes, peoples, nations, or would-be nations into a stable body politic. The ills of the old multinational Austro-Hungarian monarchy plague the Western democracies as they plague Soviet satellites and the new African states. The principles of incompatibility that Voegelin found analyzed in the 19th-century work of Baron Eötvös need only be brought up to date to become applicable to a world in vehement and violent transition. Theory once more anticipated events.

1938: The Political Religions. Voegelin's last book written in Vienna, just before the storm broke, carries a foreboding motto: *Per me si va ne la città dolente*—the first words above the gate to Dante's *Inferno*. Its Epilogue is a muted lament *per la perduta gente*, for the lost hosts about to perish in the holocausts, for no sin of their own:

> Neither knowledge nor the Christian decision resolves the mystery of God and Being. Divine creation contains Evil; the glory of Being is obscured by the suffering of the creation; the order of the community is being built out of hate, blood, heartbreak, in defection from God. Schelling's ultimate question: *"Why is there Something? Why not Nothing?"* is followed by the other one: *"Why is it the way it is?"*—the question of theodicy.[18]

Voegelin's third attempt to understand the demonism of the age fails as the earlier attempts had failed. This time he links and confronts State and Religion, seeking for a common existential root—a false track, as he later said, unjustly, I think. The construction is indeed untenable—explaining, for example, the Nazi-Fascist idolization of *Blutrausch*, murderous orgiastic blood lust, as a variant of religious ecstasy. But in this short essay for the general reader the horizon opens for the first time on Akhenaton, Paul, Augustine, Joachim of Flora, Hobbes; the chilling analysis of a hymnic poem on God-Hitler bares the abysses of the ecstatic murderer's lonely soul. Above all, symbolism has become thematic. This is an emotion-laden rapid pencil sketch, a first intimation of what will ripen into *Order and History*. When the foreseen becomes actual event, passion and compassion must yield to detachment. Add the shock of sudden exile and the strains of cultural transplantation, and the ground is laid for an inner development which eventually led to a philosophical breakthrough. It was not just a philosophical one either. Even if we did not have Voegelin's own guarded hints in his *Anamnesis* of 1966, *Die politischen Religionen* would tell us.

18. Voegelin, *Die politischen Religionen*, p. 65. In the second edition (Stockholm: Bermann-Fischer, 1939), which contains a new preface, the passage is on p. 67.

II

In the summer of 1938, emigration to the United States suddenly brought Voegelin's formative years to a close. A period of transition followed, ending in 1952 with the publication of *The New Science of Politics*. During this period Voegelin labored, as professor of political science, on a *History of Political Ideas*, a commissioned textbook which grew into a multivolume manuscript and was abandoned about 1950, just short of completion.[19] Beneath the surface, the philosopher Eric Voegelin was struggling with problems so increasingly difficult that he later called the years 1945 to 1950 "a period of indecision, if not paralysis, in handling problems which I saw but could not intellectually penetrate to my satisfaction."[20] These problems arose from the source material for the "History of Political Ideas," a work whose genesis sheds light on Voegelin's pattern of seemingly moving in fits and starts, abandoning whole volumes and unexpectedly changing direction. For here the great issues that dominate his mature work can be viewed *in statu nascendi*, while *The New Science of Politics*, though still transitional, is already grounded in the new philosophical insights. In this section I shall take up the problems that created difficulties: the concept of "ideas," the theory of consciousness, the problem of history, the essence of political society, and the nature of modernity.

The History of Political Ideas. The title reflects the rise of A. O. Lovejoy's conception of a history of ideas to the status of an established discipline.[21] Voegelin accepted this conception, just as he accepted the conventional historical framework of the leading textbooks, but rising doubts about both approaches soon forced him on to a radically different road. What struck him first was the fact that the conventional histories began with the Greeks, as if there had been nothing before them—and this despite the tremendous recent advances in the understanding of the ancient Near Eastern civilizations, especially through the work of the Chicago Oriental Institute. Something was wrong with the whole conventional understanding of history.

19. The publisher commissioned a modest book of 200–50 pages. Of the enormous manuscript that resulted, only the part dealing with the eighteenth to the middle of the nineteenth century has been published, skillfully edited by Professor John H. Hallowell: Eric Voegelin, *From Enlightenment to Revolution* (Durham: Duke University Press, 1975). This part alone runs to some 300 printed pages.

20. This quotation, and others followed by page numbers in the text, are taken by kind permission of Ellis Sandoz from Voegelin, "Autobiographical Memoir," (1973), a transcription of unpublished, tape-recorded interviews, copyright Ellis Sandoz.

21. In 1938 Lovejoy published a programmatic paper on the historiography of ideas, now the first chapter in his *Essays in the History of Ideas* (Baltimore: The Johns Hopkins University Press, 1948). In 1940 he founded the *Journal for the History of Ideas*.

Something was wrong with the concept of "ideas," too. Lovejoy had established the history of ideas on the premise that ideas are existent and effective.[22] But ideas are products, not independent entities; they are effective not as interacting entities in a world of such entities but as expressions of something that "engenders" them. In his "Autobiographical Memoir" Voegelin writes: "The methodologically first—and perhaps most important—rule of my work is to go back to the experiences which engender symbols." He had always done this, but only in retrospect could he formulate the principle underlying his suspicion that the history-of-ideas approach falsifies history from the ground up: "On the occasion of the chapter on Schelling it dawned on me that the conception of a history of ideas was an ideological deformation of reality. There were no ideas unless there were symbols of immediate experiences," he says in the memoir. Furthermore: "No language symbol today can simply be accepted as a bona fide symbol, because the corruption has proceeded so far that everything is suspect" (p. 64). And further still: ideas are merely "a secondary conceptual development, beginning with the Stoics"; they transform experiences and their symbols into concepts that refer to a "reality" other than the true, experienced reality. "Hence, ideas are liable to deform the truth of the experiences and their symbolizations." He had begun by accepting the conventional assumptions: "I had humbly worked through the materials, and a manuscript of several thousand pages was in existence" but had to abandon it in the end as "a senseless undertaking, incompatible with the present state of science" (p. 75).

A senseless undertaking in the end, yet a great achievement in itself and by no means incompatible with the present state of science, judging from the one published volume and the two brilliant unpublished chapters I have seen. What led into the years of agonizing indecision and "paralysis" was the fact that the historical material raised momentous problems that defied theoretical resolution because Voegelin was traveling on the wrong highway and could not leave it without wrecking the project. But even as he was stubbornly pursuing it, the right trail was widening out to become the highway on which *Order and History* could proceed. What were the roadblocks that held up Voegelin's decision for years and the problems he could not theoretically resolve to his satisfaction?

Only a conjecture is possible. In extending the scope of the projected textbook, Voegelin introduced material of a very different kind—"ideas" embodied in mythical, not conceptual language. The work of the Chicago school makes this very clear. In 1946 this work was summarized in an Institute report which appeared under the telling title *Before Philosophy.*[23] The in-

22. George Boas, art. "Lovejoy." *Encyclopedia of Philosophy*, ed. Paul Edwards, 8 vols. (New York & London: Macmillan Pub. Co., 1967), 5:96.
23. Henri Frankfort et al., *The Intellectual Adventure of Ancient Man* (Chicago: University of

troductory chapter by the Frankforts states the ensuing problem under the equally telling heading "Myth and Reality," and the concluding chapter identifies the problem as "The Emancipation of Thought from Myth." Why then worry about the nature of myth and the sudden rise of philosophy? Because the Frankforts' explanation merely described the event without answering the question: Why? Voegelin would have to go back from myth, thought, and philosophy to the experiences that engender these symbols, but he had not as yet identified the nature of such experiences or, for that matter, the nature and function of the symbol. This was one roadblock. The other was the problem of political society raised by the radical difference between the divine kingdom, the Greek *polis*, and the modern forms of that society. Let us begin with "ideas" and "engendering experiences," i.e., the theory of consciousness.

Experience and Reality. Voegelin's first book turned to English and American theories of consciousness to determine the "form" of the American spirit (*Geist*), moving back from what the philosophers *say* about consciousness to what shapes their life and thinking. But the experiences of self as "closed" or as "open"—the British and the American form—still fall into the "personal category," even if these experiences characterize the spirit of the two societies. For the way in which a self experiences itself and the world tells us only that this is the way this self experiences itself and the world.[24] It tells us nothing about the connection between experience and reality.

Around 1948 we find the search for the engendering experiences turning up "sentiments" which "crystallize" into "ideas" that engender their "formulation," where "idea" is not a concept but "a symbol that draws its life from sentiments."[25] This product of perplexity born of indecision is the more remarkable since some five years earlier an event had occurrred which Voegelin rightly calls an unexpected "critical breakthrough" in his understanding of consciousness, experience, and reality.

The event can be precisely timed: September to November 1943. During a visit to New York early in September Voegelin had long discussions with the phenomenologist and social theoretician Alfred Schutz (1899–1959), his closest intellectual friend and critic since their student days in Vienna. The

---

Chicago Press, 1946), repeatedly republished since then under the main title *Before Philosophy* (Baltimore, Md.: Pelican Books, 1949).

24. Ibid., pp. 16–17, on "personal and peripheral categories." As to the concept (rather the symbol) of the closed versus the open self, the stress lies not so much on the conception of the self (*das Ich*) as on the *movement* toward and away from it. He finds British philosophers moving from the problems of the universe to the personal, private self, while their American counterparts reject this "crawling into oneself, the miseries of solitude and skepsis in Hume"; they pay hardly any attention to this origin but move away from self to the "unmysterious, public, unsceptical areas of thinking" (p. 44).

25. *From Enlightenment to Revolution*, p. 68.

subject was Husserl's *Krisis der europäischen Wissenschaften*, of which the first two parts had been published in the Yugoslavian journal *Philosophia* in 1936, a rare issue which Voegelin had only recently seen. The dialogues initiated an intensive period of meditative *Selbstbesinnung*; its results were published in *Anamnesis* in 1966, twenty-five years later. They form the first part of the book, prefaced by an autobiographical memorial to his friend, in which Voegelin expressly speaks of his reason for abandoning the "History of Political Ideas": his new insight into the connection between experience and reality had shifted the accent from symbols to the engendering experiences, i.e., "toward the philosophy of consciousness" and investigations into "experiences of order and its symbolic expressions, into the institutions that establish it"— the political societies—"and finally into the order of consciousness itself."[26]

The memorial is followed in *Anamnesis* by three capital documents written during this meditative period: a critique of Husserl's *Krisis* in the form of a letter to Schutz, a fundamental essay "On the Theory of Consciousness," and a set of twelve "anamnestic experiments." The essay marks the new direction in one phrase: ". . . all philosophizing [is] an event within the consciousness of the philosopher."[27] Voegelin's anamnestic experiments trace this event back to his earliest memories of "irruptions of reality" into this consciousness, identified, by the remembered *frisson*, as experiences of transcendence and as roots of the philosopher's "radical philosophizing."[28] Let us look more closely at this meditative process.

"Philosophy of order is the process in which we as human beings find the order of our own existence in the order of consciousness." Plato placed this process under the symbol of anamnesis, of remembrance. "We remember what has been forgotten, and we remember it—at times with considerable difficulty—because it should not remain forgotten."[29] What the philosopher had to remember in mid-life was the "biography" of his own philosophical consciousness. Until then he had regarded the relation between consciousness and the experienced world as a relation between the observer and the world *outside* him, as Husserl did. But when Husserl in his last work explicitly stopped the investigation of consciousness at this point, Voegelin rebelled

---

26. "In memoriam Alfred Schutz," *Anamnesis* (1966), pp. 19–20. This memorial to Schutz (1899–1959), a remarkable summary of the research enterprises of the two friends, states the main result of the New York dialogues: "Phenomenological philosophizing à la Husserl is in principle oriented to the model of the experience of objects in the external world; classical philosophizing about the political order is equally in principle oriented to the model of noetic experience of transcendent divine being" (p. 19). An English translation of the memorial appears in the *Festschrift Voegelin*, pp. 463–65. In the English version of *Anamnesis* it is replaced by an introductory chapter, "Remembrance of Things Past," which sheds great light on the "dead-end" of 1943 and succinctly sums up the results of the *Selbstbesinnung*.

27. *Anamnesis* (1966), p. 57; English version, p. 33.

28. See *Anamnesis*, p. 61 (English version, p. 36) and note 80 below (p. 54).

29. *Anamnesis*, Preface, p. 11, omitted in the English version.

against the limitation. Yet how could he move beyond Husserl without changing position? For Husserl was right: if consciousness is considered from without, then the world this consciousness experiences is outside it. But the only
consciousness a philospher can directly study is his own. There was only one
way to do that: *rentrer en soi-même*, re-enter into oneself, beginning with
the "remembrance of things past." Hence the delving into earliest childhood
memories in search of the structure and order of one's own consciousness,
a meditative process analogous to the search for *dikē*, the ground for just
judgment, for which Aeschylus in his *Suppliants* had created the symbol:
". . . descending to the depth, with keen eye and not too much perturbed."[30]

The descent brought up immediate evidence beyond Husserl's ken. It
showed that consciousness is a *process* of experiencing, that consciousness has
a "biography," that "consciousness finds in the order of the world no level
which it does not simultaneously experience as its own foundation."[31] So that
not only the philosopher's own life but also the history of his society and civilization and that of mankind and the cosmos as well are experienced as foundations of his own philosophizing consciousness, not as something outside it.
Moreover, *Selbstbesinnung* reveals that this immediate experience of the
world, which Voegelin calls *the primary cosmic experience*,[32] transcends at the
high point of meditation toward the world-transcendent ground of being itself. Finally, the experienced process of reality *in* the world points to a process
within the divine ground of being. In one leap the meditation thus rises from
the newly found position *within* to the awareness that reality in process is
reaching up toward a truth of being which is not unmoving, unchanging,
static; it is itself *in process* as man experiences it, as it reveals itself to him, and
as it shapes history.

The essay "On the Theory of Consciousness" formulates all this in the rational language of the philosophy and theory of consciousness. But this language is a language not of concepts but of symbols engendered by experience
of the descent into the depth. And this descent is the breakthrough of 1943.

History. Voegelin called Husserl's advance in theory of consciousness magnificent except for the limitation, but Husserl's new *Geschichtsbild* shocked
him. According to this view of history, philosophy had begun with the Greek
Urstiftung or primordial founding act; it had just entered the final stretch

30. *Order and History*, 2:249–51. For the full development of the symbolism of "the depth"
see "Equivalences of Experience and Symbolization in History," in: *Eternità e storia. I valori permanenti nel divenire storico* (Florence: Vallecchi, 1970), pp. 215–34.

31. *Anamnesis*, p. 52; English version, p. 28.

32. In ibid., p. 52, Voegelin speaks of this "'Fundamentalerfahrung' des Bewusstseins als
eine Epitome des Kosmos, als ein Mikrokosmos." The terms "kosmische Primärerfahrung" and
"primary cosmic experience" can be misleading. They do not refer to a primary experience that
is "cosmic" but to the *primary* experience being that of the world (*cosmos*).

with Husserl's *Endstiftung*, the irreversible beginning of the philosophy of all future. This view of "world" history from the Greeks to modernity, skipping only "an insignificant period of a mere two thousand years" and treating Western man as man per se, Voegelin called "Victorian."[33] In 1977 he used harsher language as he recalled his encounter with *Krisis*: "I remember the shock when I read this 'philosophy of history.' I was horrified. . . . I recognized it as one of the violently restrictive visions of experience that, on the level of pragmatic action, surrounded me on all sides with [their] tale told by an idiot"—a reference to the political ideologists from the extreme left to the extreme right. But this "apocalyptic construct" was the work of a philosopher who wanted to abolish history "to justify *the exclusion of the historical dimension from the constitution of man's consciousness.*"[34]

In this statement Voegelin's own position becomes clear. What he rejects is not a restricted time frame but a restrictive "vision of existence." History, for him, is not just a course of events to be observed from the outside; the historical dimension is part of the very structure of consciousness. Only much later, in *Order and History* (1:11), will he find that "existence in historical form" is a late type of experience. The essay on "The Theory of Consciousness" still lacks the cornerstone of his mature philosophy of history, the conception of the "leaps in being," irruptions into the course of events that divide it into a Before and After and thus open the horizon of history.

Even so, Voegelin's theoretical thinking was far ahead of his study of the historical material. The ensuing tension was broken with the invitation to deliver the Walgreen Lectures at the University of Chicago in 1951. "Here I was forced to formulate in comparatively brief form some of the ideas that had begun to crystallize."[35] The result, a first synthesis confined to one major problem, was *The New Science of Politics*.

The Political Society. Voegelin suspects conventional language of being corrupted; his reader may suspect conventional language in Voegelin's work of meaning something else. In *The New Science* it does. This science is neither science nor new in the conventional sense. As a science it is that *epistéme theoretiké* which Aristotle also called *philosophia* and which Voegelin defines as "a truthful account of the structure of reality,"[36] not new but renewed by taking into account what has become known since the Greeks. "Politics" refers to the Greek conception of society in the sense of Aristotle, who said that a man without a *polis* is either a beast or a god, a lost chessman. *The New Science of*

33. "Brief an Alfred Schütz über Edmund Husserl," *Anamnesis*, p. 22. Cf. the sharp detailed critique of Husserl's view of history and philosophy, pp. 23–29. The essay is omitted in the English version.

34. "Remembrance of Things Past," *Anamnesis* (English version only), p. 10.

35. "Autobiographical Memoir," p. 65.

36. *The New Science of Politics* (Chicago: University of Chicago Press, 1952), p. 5. The following page references in the text refer to *The New Science*.

Politics deals with "Truth and Representation"; if it is also a book about the new science of politics, this is only because the truth and order of a political society is oriented toward the truth of being and because the society constitutes itself as the representative of this highest truth. Representation is thus "the form by which a society gains existence for action in history" (p. 1).

"The political society" is Voegelin's term for the encompassing human society in the *philosophically relevant* sense,[37] a participatory whole which transcends the individual's existence. Seen from outside, it is a society among others; in itself it is "a little world, a cosmion, illuminated with meaning from within." Its self-understanding finds expression in symbolisms that render its internal structure "transparent for the mystery of existence" (p. 27). The manifold of these symbolizations in their historical sequence discloses a pattern of advance toward higher levels of truth so that an inquiry into truth and representation "will in fact become a philosophy of history" (p. 1).

In this conception we can see what the "renewal" of classical philosophy entails. The foundations are Greek, but the conception of the historical dimension of consciousness breaks open the field of the history of transcendent truth in the world. The whole theoretical structure of the work is grounded in the new theory of consciousness, down to the hint that "the order of history emerges from the history of order," as the very first line of *Order and History* will say. "The political society" is not a classificatory term but a symbol for the historical interplay between truth and the order of society, here pursued across the mere two thousand years that Husserl had skipped.

Modernity. If truth and representation is the theme, modernity is the topic of *The New Science.* The analysis begins with the struggle between three competing truths for representation in the Roman Empire, where the Roman state cult represented the dying truth of "the cosmos filled with gods," Greek philosophy the truth of world-transcendent being, and Christianity the revolutionary truth of Redemption and of the ultimate salvation of man's soul as his supreme goal in this life. Christianity won, and its victory laid the ground for the existential crisis in Western modernity, since the order of the political society could no longer remain unified:

> The spiritual destiny of man in the Christian sense cannot be represented by the power organization of a political society; it can be represented only by the church. The sphere of power is radically de-divinized; it has become

37. *The New Science* speaks of "theoretical relevance," attacking the Positivistic "perversion of relevance through the shift from theory to method" (p. 10). "Relevance" is a cornerstone of Schutz's theoretical work, which may account for Voegelin's use of the term here. Schutz discusses it in the light of his own theory of relevance in his critique of *The New Science* (Letter to Eric Voegelin, November 1952, *Festschrift Voegelin*, pp. 435–36). Cf. also the detailed analysis of the issue of relevance "brought up by Voegelin in the discussion [with Schutz] in 1943," by Helmut R. Wagner, in *Festschrift Voegelin*, pp. 80–85.

temporal. The double representation of man in society through church and empire lasted through the Middle Ages. The specifically modern problems of representation are connected with the re-divinization of society. (p. 106)

In *Order and History* 1:11 Voegelin will speak of the split as "a dualistic structure of existence" symbolized by the distinction between civil and supranatural theology, temporal and spiritual power, state and church. "Re-divinization" would then mean overcoming this existential dualism and grounding the order of society again directly in the full spiritual truth which the society will then represent.[38]

The interaction of three elements—political order, Christianity, and the understanding of history—forms the theoretical framework for Voegelin's analysis of the transformations through which modernity came into being. The argument, summed up in reverse historical order, from modernity back to its roots, is as follows: (1) In modernity two components struggle for the representation of the political society. One is the traditional order that represents "the truth of the soul" (*The New Science of Politics*, p. 189), the other a revolutionary "Gnostic" component striving for the transfiguration of man and society here and now. (2) The history of this revolutionary promise is the history of the Gnostic component in modernity. "Modernity" is the name of the period in which Gnosticism becomes a contender for the existential representation of society. (3) The point of origin of the revolutionary component is a tension within the first Christian communities between the expectation that the kingdom of God is at hand and the growing awareness that history would continue as before until the end of the world. The history of the belief in the imminent transfiguration of man and world is the history of modern Gnosticism.

Before tracing the course of this history we must clarify two terms in Voegelin's analysis. "Christianity" refers to *Western* Christianity, and to only two of its basic variants: the Christianity of the Church up to the end of the Middle Ages and the Gnostic millennial variant. Voegelin's use of the term "Gnos-

38. "Re-divinization" is a stumbling block. "*De*-divinization" refers to a specific historical *fact*, while "*re*-divinization" suggests a (necessary?) *process*. Schutz already recognized that "the processes of dedivinization and redivinization occur on fundamentally different levels" (*Festschrift Voegelin*, p. 442, with my note 4). Furthermore, "redivinization" is applied exclusively to the *Gnostic* component (cf. note 42 below). The deeper difficulty lies in the underdeveloped conceptions of the political society, existential representation, and especially of the double truth of the society and of being. Schutz found the distinction "outstandingly good" (ibid., p. 440) because he accepted the notion of the "self-interpretation of society," which is a makeshift concept (a society is not an entity having a consciousness, a sensorium of its own). In my summary survey of the "two truths" conception (ibid., pp. 229–30), I therefore added the missing factor, "the truth of being as understood by the presumptive knower." Only with the first analysis of the leap in being in *Order and History*, 2:6, will things begin to fall into place: "The revelation comes to one man for all men," though "the order of being is the same for all men at all times." But this does not yet resolve the problem of the order of society. In his reply to Schutz, Voegelin merely amplifies what he means by *Gnostic* redivinization (ibid., p. 460).

ticism" in this sense differs from the conventional scholarly usage.[39] With this clarification, we can sum up in five points his analysis of the transformations of Gnostic expectation in the West.

1. Uncertainty about the scriptural promise of the Second Coming created two radically different understandings of history after Christ. The Revelation of John promised that Christ would come to reign on earth with his saints for a thousand years until Judgment Day. The repeated disappointment of these "eschatological" hopes led to the "apocalyptic" interpretation that Christ was already reigning with his church on earth and that this reign would last until Judgment Day.[40] The present age would continue indefinitely, growing old in the waiting. Man would be transfigured in eternity, never on earth.

2. Around 1200 A.D. the orthodox conception of the *saeculum senescens* was revolutionized by the mystic speculation of the Cistercian Abbot Joachim of Flora, who divided spiritual history into three ages: those of the Father, the Son, and the Holy Spirit. The Third Age or Realm was to begin in 1260, an age of "spiritual men" living in mystic contemplation, apart from the secular world. With one stroke this speculation relegated the age of Christ to the past. A new conception of history was born and Joachim's description of the Third Age created "the aggregate of symbols which govern the self-interpretation of modern political society to this day" (*The New Science*, p. 111 ff.).[41]

3. After Joachim came the slow but decisive transformation of his mystic speculation into a secular, immanentist conception of history. In this process of "secularization" Gnosticism gains its modern form. Its essence is "the im-

39. Present-day scholarship treats Gnosticism as a religious phenomenon which ended in essence in the sixth century. In the introduction to *Wissenschaft, Gnosis und Politik* (1959), American edition entitled *Science, Politics and Gnosticism*, trans. W. F. Fitzpatrick (Chicago: Regnery, 1968), Voegelin went back to the literature culminating in Ferdinand Christian Baur's great work of 1835 which already recognized the Gnostic nature of modernity. What he took from contemporary scholarship was the existentialist interpretation represented by Hans Jonas; but even in Voegelin's reinterpretation it does not fit his own analysis. For the underlying conceptions of history and historiography, see my detailed study in *Festschrift Voegelin*, esp. pp. 191–96 (Baur), pp. 201–6 (Jonas), pp. 213–21 (the present state of scholarship), and the closing section on Voegelin.

40. For "eschatological/apocalyptic" Voegelin refers to Alois Dempf, *Sacrum Imperium* (Munich: Oldenburg, 1929; reprt. Darmstadt: Wissenschaftliche Buchgesellschaft, 1962), chap. 1. Dempf applies the term *apocalyptic* to the doctrine that the divine will reveals itself in history, in the world, in the Christian communities and in their members, creating a new historical consciousness (p. 72), in opposition to the "eschatological" proclamation of the millennium in the *Apocalypse of John*, chap. 20. This should clarify the compacted opening of p. 108 in *The New Science*, where the missing comma after "the Kingdom of God" (line 3) adds to the difficulty.

41. The basic outline of this transition from the two-age to the three-age conception and its subsequent secularization already appears in Oswald Spengler's *Untergang des Abendlandes* (Munich: Beck, 1923). Voegelin had overlooked this minor strand in an otherwise totally different conception of history. Spengler had found the connection between the two theological periodizations and the changing understanding of history in Wilhelm Windelband's *Lehrbuch der Geschichte der Philosophie*, first published in 1892. Cf. note 49 below.

manentization of the Christian eschaton": the belief in salvation beyond world
and time becomes a belief in the transfiguration of man and society in *this*
world and in *our* time. Voegelin offers two explanations for this transformation. A new spirit of activism chafes against confinement in the dedivinized
social order; spiritually the Christian life in uncertainty of ultimate salvation
becomes too hard to bear, and the Gnostic promise of salvation here and now
offers a way out.

4. With the Renaissance and Reformation, roughly, the new Gnosticism
grows strong enough to strive for social dominance and for the creation of
unified societies that represent a Gnostic truth. Since Gnostic truth deforms
the truth of being by denying transcendent reality, it is not the existential
truth of man's position in the order of being; it is a deliberate lie.

5. Today "the truth of the soul," eminently represented by the Anglo-
American type of democracy,[42] is in danger of succumbing to the Gnostic advance. Totalitarianism threatens it from without, but the more dangerous en-
emy is the insidious Gnosticism within the Western world which weakens
and could paralyze its will to resist.

With this analysis of modernity Voegelin has spanned the range of the philosophy to come, from the theoretical foundations to the crisis of our time.
The theory of consciousness is implicitly present; the conception of history,
still in nuclear form, is brilliantly applied to a concrete problem; and the crucial identification of modern "Gnosticism" is made in almost definitive form.
The New Science is the end of a long development and the energetic if hasty
beginning of a new one. I shall conclude this section with a retrospective look
at this exciting and inevitably misunderstood book, the result of a second
breakthrough which was to lose its impetus not many years later when its
conception of history proved to be inadequate.

New Science, New Philosophy. The first readers of *The New Science* were its
best readers: philosophical friends and foes who knew the theory of consciousness that stands behind it. The best of them was Alfred Schutz. In an
essay-length letter to Voegelin of November 1952 he wrote: "And now . . .
for your book! It is a marvelous book, over-rich and difficult to read because it
is written in double counterpoint. Although I have been studying it continuously ever since it reached me, I am by no means certain that I have truly
understood it in its full content."[43] Even he could hardly have understood it
in its full content because essential parts of that content are not in the book.

42. If "the truth of the soul" represents "the truth of being," Western civilization with its civil
theology has been redivinized. If this "truth of the soul" falls short of what a redivinization of
society requires, the fact that a great dedivinized political society has survived for 1500 years
casts doubt on the proposition that the order of the society receives (must receive?) its justifica-
tion and legitimacy from the attunement to the highest truth.

43. Letter to Eric Voegelin, November 1952, *Festschrift Voegelin*, p. 437.

But he unfailingly recognized *The New Science* as a philosophical work (he read the text, not the title), and analyzed it accordingly. Had this review appeared in 1953, it would at once have set the discussion on the right track— to the philosopher's detriment, I think, for this philosophy needed quiet years for its maturation.[44]

It was Schutz too who at once raised the ultimate critical question whether the truth claim Voegelin makes is philosophically tenable, and it matters little that the question came out skewed. Schutz claimed that this philosophy is grounded only in its author's personal Christian faith; that experiences of transcendence do not prove the existence of supranatural reality; that immanent interpretations of these experiences can be made with equal validity; and that the conception of Gnosticism (which he basically accepted) was too broad and contained "three components, if not more, that I find it very hard to bring together."[45] Voegelin responded with two essay-length letters, on Christianity and Gnosticism. His very specific replies are indispensable for the clarifications, the background, and the contexts they offer.[46]

The critique of the truth claim was independently made again in 1959 by the political scientist Arnold Brecht from the standpoint of his Positivistic conception of "Scientific Method and Scientific Value Relativism."[47] I shall briefly deal with the objection in this form, to get one obstacle to critical discussion out of the way.

Brecht placed Voegelin among the leaders of a "revolt" against contemporary political science, in the name of a metaphysical or religious truth—lead-

44. In *Über die Form des amerikanisches Geistes* Voegelin spoke of "theoretical objectivity" as "a typical solitudinal value" (p. 9). He was clearly referring to philosophical distance.

45. *Festschrift Voegelin*, p. 447. Cf. p. 444: "Can there not also be non-Christian experiences of transcendence, just as there are non-Euclidian geometries?" Voegelin's answer: "Quite obviously"—but the Christian experience is the maximally differentiated one (ibid., p. 450 et passim). Helmut R. Wagner's discussion of the two friends' disagreement over Christian transcendence and Gnosis (ibid., pp. 85–89) rightly reads Voegelin's replies as an explanation of his most fundamental philosophical orientations which Schutz could not accept since he did not share "the ultimate, ultimately religious convictions of his friend." Schutz could hardly have avoided this still common misunderstanding, *The New Science* being silent on the foundations from which it springs. In his replies Voegelin insistently demonstrates that his position is a radically *philosophical* one. The real issue was that of the philosopher versus the social theoretician, of the view of society from within versus the view from without, as I tried to show in my brief introduction to this exchange (ibid., pp. 431–33).

46. *Festschrift Voegelin*, pp. 449–61. The Letter on Christianity distinguishes "essential" Christianity from its "gnostic and eschatological components," spells out four "very significant achievements" of Christian theology and philosophy (Christology, Trinitarianism, Mariology, and "the critical understanding of theological speculation and its meaning"); it closes with a critical look at the question to what extent "essential" Christianity and Catholicism can be identified. The analysis of the Trinity symbol was resumed in recent years in connection with the as yet unpublished Thomas Aquinas Lectures at Marquette University entitled "The Beginning and the Beyond: A Meditation on Truth."

47. Arnold Brecht, *Political Theory: The Foundations of Twentieth-Century Political Thought* (Princeton, N.J.: Princeton University Press, 1959), chap. 7, esp. pp. 267–68.

ers such as Leo Strauss, Jacques Maritain, and John Hallowell. But can this kind of truth be demonstrated to those who differ in good faith? The leaders evade the issue, Brecht finds. Voegelin in particular treats it "cavalierly" (perhaps a reference to the fact that he attacks Positivism as a Gnostic deformation of the truth instead of proving his own thesis.) Brecht's point is of course valid. A scholarly truth claim must be able to convince unbelievers and believers alike. His complaint, too, is justified. Voegelin did have an answer, but it was not to be found in *The New Science*. And since Brecht's question keeps troubling serious readers, it will be useful to state where the answer is to be found: in Voegelin's analysis of consciousness.

What this analysis arrives at is not Christianity or a conception of God or a metaphysical truth in Brecht's sense but the structure of reality as a constitutive element of the structure of the experiencing consciousness itself. Now experiences of reality cannot be "proved," any more than sense experiences. Nonetheless there is nothing arcane or esoteric or exclusive about such experiences. Every human being experiences reality. Voegelin's claim is that the philosophizing consciousness experiences reality as *transcending*. This is the ground from which his philosophy rises, and no belief of any kind is needed to test that ground. No belief is needed to test the speculative structure either, step by step; Voegelin himself insists on the rational nature of all philosophy. He does not condemn philosophers for arriving at different conclusions, unless they deny what they cannot deny in good faith: the easily ascertainable fact that experienced reality is experienced as *transcending*. This is the point at which any critical testing of Voegelin's speculative edifice must begin.

What remains to be examined is the curious fact that Voegelin's best philosophical reader and one of the best Positivistic methodologists in political science both grounded their critique on something understandable only in the light of Voegelin's work since 1966 and of the documentary evidence surfacing in 1980. *The New Science* results from a kind of leapfrogging procedure: the historical analysis jumps over the unstated theoretical foundations; in doing so, the theory leaps beyond the analysis to problems and solutions that will surface only very much later. This relation between theory and material needs to be elucidated.[48]

Procedure and Process. The Walgreen Lectures allowed the philosopher to break out of an impossible situation, and *The New Science* made the most of it. The book is a veritable blitzkrieg, designed to occupy strategic positions to be consolidated later. Swiftly crossing treacherous ground,[49] it races

48. On this subject, see Thomas Hollweck, "Gedanken zur Arbeitsmethode Eric Voegelins," *Philosophisches Jahrbuch* 88 (1981): 136–52.

49. The attempts to use Christianity "for bolstering the political theology of the [Roman] Empire" (*The New Science*, pp. 102–6) are an example. The analysis of their failure closely follows Erik Peteron's *Der Monotheismus als politisches Problem* (1935), an authoritative work

through the Middle Ages in one short paragraph, to reach and demolish the Gnostic stronghold, leaving the critical press corps far behind. One would call this a brilliantly conceived maneuver were it not that necessity was once again the mother of invention. In his "Autobiographical Memoir" (p. 82) Voegelin states: "I always ran into the problem that in order to arrive at the theoretical formulations, I had first to present the materials on which the theoretical formulations were based as an analytical result." In plain English, the cart had to be presented before the horse could be hitched to it. Is it surprising that critics should have had the dark suspicion that an invisible hand was pushing the cart from behind?

The fact is that the historical analysis is impossible without a theoretical basis and that the analysis inevitably moves beyond this basis as it reveals new theoretical problems. The "material" as such is inert; Voegelin unhesitatingly uses (and appreciates) the findings of current state-of-the-art scholarship in every pertinent field, regardless of methodological or even ideological grounding, provided the technical work is sound. But the material he presents has already undergone a theoretical transformation, critically secured by the principle that if the facts established by specialized scholarship conflict with his theory, it is the theory that must yield. The order of history must *emerge* from the history of order; it must not be *imposed* upon it.

Outwardly Voegelin's procedure may appear circular—the theory shapes the material that shapes the theory. But this is a misunderstanding. A philosophy of process becomes a philosophy *in* process when the philosophical consciousness relinquishes the observer's position to participate in the process to be studied. But this does not yet explain how the intimate *unity* of experience, theory, and material is safeguarded in the leapfrogging movement. For this we have to go back to the experience that generates the symbols out of the analysis of the material. It is an experience *of the whole*, of reality. What the procedure divides is at one in the process; analysis *differentiates* what has been *compactly* experienced: the whole.

Voegelin's truth claim and his procedure are the two chief obstacles to an

---

which applied the history of ideas method to the history of political theology in the Empire. Since "the one person of an imperial monarch could not represent the triune divinity," these attempts had to fail and dual representation ensued (*The New Science*, pp. 105–6). But did they have to fail? The question is irrelevant in the case at hand, yet it shows once more that the interaction between historical material and theory can prematurely cut off the theoretical questioning when the material to be analyzed points in only one direction. The deeper reason for this particular cut-off is of course that the theory was far ahead of the limited material: the Letter on Christianity makes it clear that Voegelin had recognized the trinitarian symbolism as the philosophically perfect expression of "essential" Christianity; its Western victory over Arianism and monophysitism therefore appeared as the logical outcome of the controversy. A radically different view in which Western Christianity is dislodged from the center was developed by Spengler. I discussed it in the *Festschrift Voegelin*, pp. 196–201, esp. p. 198, and will come back to it in the next section of the present paper.

understanding of his thought. If the foregoing discussion has succeeded in placing the two problems in the right context, our way to the later work is finally open.

III

From "Symbol and Experience" to "Mankind and History." The philosopher Max Scheler, a convert to Catholicism, was a womanizer, to the chagrin of the Archbishop of Cologne, who once pointedly asked why the professor did not practice what he taught in his admirable ethics course. Scheler answered: "Has His Eminence ever seen a signpost walking down the road it points to?" Womanizing apart, there is a question in this question. Voegelin addressed the problem in his first book.[50] He discovered that signpost and road, pointing and walking, cannot be as neatly separated as Scheler might have wished. You can lay a cut through being and put all symbols on one side and all that they symbolize on the other, trying to divide symbolic being from existential being. But the attempt fails. The symbols are "full of existence," existence is "full of symbolic being": we do not possess an independent reality beneath this "irreal" superstructure. "Existence" is merely an expression for the pointing, transcending character of the symbols; existence is just as "irreal" as the symbols, for symbols and existence are only events in the consciousness, related to one another in a perturbing way. Unquietly the relation weaves back and forth between symbol and existence, making the one express the other and vice versa, vainly trying to find something that is beyond the play of signifying and being signified, some firm hold in this "edifice of unrealities." But as soon as the desired resting point is reached, the movement reverses itself to seek the firm ground at the other pole. The harder one pushes, the more does existence "thin out to a dusky boundary which elastically recedes but never splits to grant us a glance beyond itself." Whatever we grasp of existence turns out to be merely symbolic. But, conversely, existence penetrates the symbols, draws them down to the maternal ground and gives them life, just as the sap rises in the plant, giving it existence in the sun, "never letting it forget in waxing and wilting that its blossom is of the earth." There is no duality between symbol and existence, but neither is there oneness; the relation would have to be called "Two-in-Oneness."

Being has no firm foothold without, and it is not a closed system within; its transcending into existence allows no closure. Being is therefore never an assured, absolutely certain "having"; it is always a movement beyond, symbolizing a tension within: "We can believe in symbolic being, for it promises

---

50. *Über die Form des amerikanischen Geistes*, pp. 19–20. This is the introduction to the examination of the concept of self in British and American philosophy. My summary occasionally interprets the text in the light of Voegelin's later writings.

us more than it gives us; and we can doubt it, since it never gives what it promises—but we can not know it."

This gleaming Husserlian *Wesensschau* ends on a note of apparent (but only apparent) resignation, which makes one wonder how volume after volume came to be filled with analyses of symbolic being, considering that we cannot know it. But these volumes deal with symbolic being in historical action and passion; they analyze the symbols that did stay on the rope across the historical abyss. It is true that "history" does not appear among the symbols emerging in this analysis, which are, first, the symbol *symbol* itself; then *order* (the mass of symbols reaches from fairly solid symbolic orders like art, religion, eroticism, the state, political action, down to the simple single sense perception); *existence*; *transcendence*; and finally the tension between the poles, the In-Between or *metaxý*, as it will later be called. But *reality* is already there, if only negatively: it is that which the analysis finds absent, "ungraspable, an 'X' or a transcendental task," the firm something that will not turn out to be "merely symbolic" when one tries to "possess" it.

There is nothing wrong with that. A meditation on being as the "Two-in-Oneness" of symbol and existence cannot go beyond what consciousness experiences as symbolic being. The analytical description of this experience is in fact outstandingly good; it already shows *where* reality enters, if it enters at all: not in symbol, not in existence, not in being, but in the existential tension—the one place where one does not look for it, since this tension is neither sign nor signified. But this tension is a place of entrance, not an exit that could lead analysis out of the isolated consciousness into the community of being. The first sketch of Voegelin's theory of symbolization begins therefore with the statement that God and man, world and society, form a primordial community of being. This community "is, and is not, a datum of human experience." "Is, and is not" refers to man's "participation in the mystery of its being." Man does know this community by virtue of this participation; he cannot know it as an object in the external world. Here, "existence" is not irreal: participation involves man "with the whole of his existence, for participation is existence itself."[51]

One consequence of this must be stated at once. If the whole is not "given in the manner of an object in the external world," then nothing can be said about it in language created to fit such objects. The language of participatory knowledge is not "objective" and it is not literal. It is the language of symbols, engendered by participatory (but also by deliberately nonparticipatory) experiences. Such language symbols do not point outward to external objects, they point back to the experiences themselves; they try to make intelligible the meaning of man's existence, of passing and lasting, of the orders of

51. *Order and History* I:I.

existence and of being. But the early analysis of the "edifice of irrealities" applies also to the two types of language: they transcend toward one another. The language of an income tax form is technical, external language, yet it is "full of symbolic being," despite the intent of its framers; conversely, the symbolisms of participatory language are "full of existence."

The Leap in Being. This incipient theory of symbolization and language becomes a research tool of the first order with the discovery of the "leap in being." In *Israel and Revelation*, the opening volume of the main work, the term appears for the first time as "the leap upward in being" which the soul experiences "as a passion, as a response to a revelation of divine being [in world transcendence], to an act of grace, to a selection for emphatic partnership with God" (1:10). The introduction to the second volume, summing up the theoretical results that emerged from the first one, treats the "leap in being" (as it will henceforth be called) under the title "Mankind and History."[52] This is the decisive step, for now the phenomenon of the epochmaking breaks in the course of historical events can be brought under theoretical control: the leap in being is "the epochal event that breaks the compactness of the early cosmological myth and establishes the order of man in his immediacy under God," an event that "transforms the succession of societies preceding [it] in time into a past of mankind" (2:1, 3). With the leap in being, the horizon of history opens; man and society enter into existence in historical form, and man will come to know his nature in the new mode of explicit, differentiated symbolization. "For history is the process in which man articulates his own nature." This nature has not changed; the historical dimension is "an essential component of man, [but] its presence rises to the level of consciousness only through the leap in being" (2:2).

This last statement shows how difficult it is even for the discoverer to grasp at once the extent of his discovery. For how could this historical dimension have risen into consciousness before that consciousness became conscious of itself as a consciousness? Can one apply the differentiated symbol "consciousness" to the compact mode of understanding in which even the difference between "I" and "we" may be uncertain? Can a highly differentiated consciousness speak of a compactly experiencing one except by differentiating the as

52. I once suggested that the term *leap in being* was coined as a parallel to *quantum jump* (*Quantensprung*). In both cases there is no gradual transition from level to level. However, Voegelin states in his "Autobiographical Memoir" that he took the term *leap* from Kierkegaard, "in order to characterize the decisive transition from compact to differentiated truth in the history of consciousness" (p. 50). The "leap into emphatic partnership with God" (1:11) indeed has Kierkegaardian overtones, but in "Mankind and History" the existentialist overtones disappear; the emphatic leap becomes a special case of theophanic experience and no longer characterizes the phenomenon as such. Cf. the chapter on Paul in *Order and History*, 4:241–44, where "noetic" theophanies are distinguished from the "pneumatic" ones like that of Paul, whose emphatic leap almost went too far.

yet undifferentiated, by reading compact symbolisms the way it reads differentiated ones?

These were difficulties at the experiential end. Historically too the global statement of an emphatic leap upward in being needed adjustment. For there were differences between the actual leaps in being. Three of them—the revelation of divine being as transcendent in Israel, the rise of philosophy in Greece, and the Christian revelation of grace meeting man—coalesced into one "complete" form in Western civilization. But there were also "incomplete" leaps in being in China and India, which the expression "emphatic partnership with God" does not fit. They were not experienced as epoch-making events either, that is, as incisions that turn all that happened before them into a past and mark the beginning of a new age.

In modern Western historiography and scholarship the three Western breaks did not go unobserved, but too many interpretations gradualize them into "transitions" from polytheism to monotheism, from myth or religion to philosophy or thought, etc., without recognizing the "transitions" as epoch-making breaks. This is not true, of course, of the work of historical thinkers like Spengler, Jaspers, and Toynbee. But recognizing the break as a break does not in itself prevent misinterpretation. Thus Jaspers claims that a view of universal history in which the epiphany of Christ is the central event can be valid for Christians only. To this Voegelin replies: "Leaps in being, to be sure, have occurred elsewhere; but . . . only the Judaeo-Christian response to revelation has achieved historical consciousness" (2:22). Voegelin (2:7−24) concludes: "The origin and historical structure of Western order were better understood by the men who created the form than by their late successors who live in it without remembering the conditions of tenancy. It should be clear why our study had to begin with Israel; and why it had to move from Israel to Hellas." It is clear indeed. But it is equally clear from what precedes this statement that the order of *Order and History* is one thing, and the order of history is not quite the same thing. This is the source of difficulties at the historical end.

Order and History begins with a sketch of the compact cosmological order before the leaps and follows the triple "Western" leap from Israel to Hellas, while the canceled three last volumes were to conclude with "Empire and Christianity," "The Protestant Centuries," and Modernity as "The Crisis of Western Civilization." In this straightline sequence there is no systematic place for the parallel Far Eastern leaps. This is not accidental. It is true that "the intolerance inspired by the love of being" should be balanced by a new tolerance that respects man's "tortuous ways" in moving closer to the true order of being. But even if Plato is right and "every myth has its truth," (1:11), the balance still tips heavily to the side of differentiated truth.

Even within the Western order a difficulty arises when the analysis reaches

Modernity. For here the history of order turns into a history of disorder. One understands that "a critical study of the authoritative structure in the history of mankind" cannot "systematically accept on an equal footing" all the "authoritative communications of truth about order as they have sprung up in the course of history" (2 : 7). This applies of course to the parallel Far Eastern leaps in being, but the modern case is different. Those "authoritative" communications that Voegelin characterizes as modern Gnosticism are not on the level of "revelations"; they arise on the level of the speculative understanding of history and fall under the heading of philosophy of history.[53] (This, by the way, is one explanation for Voegelin's insistence that the Gnostic *knows* the truth he rejects; he *knows* existence in historical form because it is the inner form of his own existence, within his own society and civilization.) But if philosophy itself is a leap in being, and if philosophy of history is the currently most advanced knowledge of the truth on this higher level, what justifies treating "the gnostic fallacy of declaring the end of history" as a fallacy? (2:7). Might this "rebellion against God" not signify another irruption into history?

These difficulties can wait. The question is rather how Voegelin arrives at the position that creates them. What do we have to concede in order to accept that position, if only for the sake of understanding it? Two points, I think: that the multiple Western leap in being has raised the knowledge of the truth to the highest level yet; and that philosophy, culminating in the philosophy of history, has advanced toward the maximally differentiated understanding attainable in our time, Voegelin's philosophy at present leading the advance. This position is grounded in the proposition: "Man participates in the process of reality" with all that this implies. Voegelin does not ask that this proposition be accepted on faith; its validity "can and must be tested in the historical field of experiences and their symbolizations," that is, by the historical material. I am quoting from the fundamental paper on "Equivalences of Experience and Symbolization in History" (1970), which I can discuss only so far as the matter of proof requires.[54]

The Truth Test. The history of philosophy abounds with propositions concerning the nature of reality, "each claiming to be the only true one, but none

53. Voegelin notes that the problem of successive and parallel leaps in being became acute twice, first in antiquity, as the historical and the philosophical forms were absorbed in Christianity, then through the rapid expansion of the historical horizon beginning with the Enlightenment. The ancient period produced "indigenous histories whose writers tried to understand the new order whose rise they were witnessing. The second occasion arose with the collapse of the Augustinian conception of history. Modern attempts at revising it (Voltaire, Hegel, Spengler, Jaspers, Toynbee) are those of "late successors" to the early writers; to them, the whole thing is merely "history."

54. "Equivalences of Experience and Symbolization in History," in *Eternità e storia. I valori permanenti nel devenire storico* (Florence: Vallecchi, 1970), pp. 215–34. Italics in quotations are mine.

of them commanding the universal acceptance it demands in the name of truth" (p. 217). The historian has no choice but to treat them as being on the same level. So do those philosophers who believe that "existential truth is a doctrine to be universally accepted," a belief which makes "deformed existence the model of true existence"—the hallmark of the "age" of modern man, c. 1750 to 1950, with its overtones of "an apocalyptic new age . . . of the perfect and therefore last age of man" (pp. 218–19).

Voegelin does not demand universal acceptance. His proposition symbolizes a truth experienced in philosophical consciousness when it meditatively reflects upon its own structure. There was no such philosophical consciousness before the leap in being; this consciousness is "*the new historical consciousness*." It experiences existence and reality as it could not be experienced before and cannot be experienced today except in openness toward the reality of existence in historical form. The claim for the new insight into reality is not that it is generally acceptable but that it is true.

With this claim the relation between the history of philosophy and the philosophy of history is reversed. Instead of allowing itself to be placed in the amorphous collection of philosophies that constitute the history of philosophy in the usual sense, this philosophy of history imposes its order upon the field of propositions concerning reality. What the history of philosophy treats as artifacts the philosophy of history treats as symbols whose trail reveals the history of truth advancing in tension to untruth, a history of formation and deformation, of acceptance and rejection.

Two difficulties at once come to mind. The first is the seeming circularity of the argument: the sequence of symbolizations demonstrates the advance of that truth which turns the artifacts into a sequence. Voegelin resolves this difficulty by recourse to an extended theory of consciousness which does not concern us here.[55] But the second difficulty does. The leap in being divides the sequence of symbols into two parts: compact and differentiated, and these two types are by no means directly comparable. We need only think of the Babylonian creation myth on the one hand, of Aristotle's highly differentiated analysis of "principles and causes" on the other. How then can one speak of a history of mankind, of a search which continues unbroken across the break?

---

55. The differentiating consciousness which discovers the advance of the truth from compactness to the leaps in being is itself a late product of the leaps in being. Compact myth could not have anticipated this kind of consciousness, but then the differentiating consciousness cannot compactly experience reality any more either. Yet both modes of understanding grasp the same truth. How did compact understanding grasp it? This is the first difficulty, given that Voegelin limits the symbol *consciousness* exclusively to the differentiating consciousness created by the leap. The difficulty is met by an exegesis that probes into what lies "beyond" consciousness, to discover "psyche"—a symbol for what "surrounds and includes the area of conscious experience." Psyche extends down to "the depth," here, a reality deeper than consciously experienced reality engenders the symbolizations of compact myth. The sequence of symbolizations advancing in history is therefore not produced by manipulation ex post facto; the sequence does articulate reality in history as experienced at the depth, then in consciousness.

Voegelin replies that the new truth "is not a truth about a reality hitherto unknown, but a differentiated and *therefore* superior insight into the same reality that had been compactly symbolized by the old truth" (p. 226). The old and the new symbols are not homogeneous but *equivalent*, and so are the experiences that engender them. This enables Voegelin to formulate the test: "Are the propositions [to be tested] recognizably *equivalent* with the symbols created by our predecessors in the search of truth about human existence?" These predecessors are not the unknown creators of compact myths but the thinkers whose cognitive efforts let the new truth gradually emerge in the process of reality itself. If Voegelin's philosophy were a singularity in the history of these cognitive efforts, then it might be a mere flight of the imagination; hence "*The test of truth, to put it pointedly, will be the lack of originality in the propositions*" (p. 222).

Voegelin's claim to be an innovative thinker rests therefore on his claim that he is *not* an original one. It is the strongest claim he could make. Only errors are original, inasmuch as they have their origin in men's minds and souls, and even the great errors could not be made were they not grounded in the tension between truth and deformation within reality itself. Voegelin can therefore point for proof of his innovative propositions to "ancient, medieval and modern predecessors: to Plato and Aristotle, to St. Augustine and St. Thomas, to Bergson and Whitehead"—not because they are in agreement but because their philosophies are milestones in the process by which knowledge about reality and existence advances. All these thinkers were innovators, participants in the advance; all of them, Voegelin finds, gave "equivalent symbolizations of the central issue, i.e., the experience of participation, and the consequent identity and non-identity of the knower and the known." [56]

If the central issue, participation, was already known to the Greeks, why then the restless striving for ever more, ever finer differentiation? What is gained by it? How secure is even the foundation? How can consciousness reflecting upon its own structure find the structure of reality?

Voegelin's answer to the last question is the clue to the others as well. Phil-

56. "Equivalences of Experience and Symbolization in History," p. 223. The formula "identity *and* non-identity" refers to the two aspects of participation. When Parmenides says that thought and being are the same, he expresses the participatory identity of the knower and the known; but the knower, Parmenides, is not identical with what he knows. If it were not for this understanding, propositions about reality based merely on a descent into one's own consciousness would be open to the fundamental doubt for which Descartes created the symbolism: the inner certainty could be the work of a *Dieu trompeur*, a deceiving God who so created man that even his most certain knowledge is necessarily false; and even if God were a true God, a *malin génie*, an evil spirit, might slip into the very process of cognition between immediate experience and articulation, and make the false appear true. Descartes could never dispel the shadow of this doubt. It surfaces at the very end of the *Meditations* when he makes a last inconclusive attempt to distinguish illusory dream from true perception of reality. What began with a triumphant *cogito ergo sum* ends in resignation: ". . . man's life is often subject to error in particular matters, and in the end we must acknowledge the weakness of our nature."

osophical self-reflection springs from the process of reality; consciousness is part of that reality; the meditative event is part of the process and therefore real. The event occurs in the confrontation between an older and a newer truth. It is "recognizably related to a less reflected experience of participation and its less differentiated symbolization. . . ." (p. 222). The earlier insights are felt to be unsatisfactory; the new symbols engendered by the effort are superior but recognizably equivalent with the earlier ones. The philosopher is thus forced to go forward, and his every step—if it is the right one—[57] is an advance in the history of mankind. This is the gain: a gain in knowledge. The price paid for it is another matter; I shall come back to that.

The whole philosophical advance remains, however, within the fundamental form and range of what the leaps in being have opened up. It was otherwise at the rise of philosophy as such: "A descent into the depth will be indicated when the light of truth has dimmed and its symbols are losing their credibility; when the night is sinking on the symbols that have had their day. . . ." (pp. 225–26). Philosophy rose when the night was sinking on the world of myth. Can philosophy understand myth?

Myth and History. It has been well said of myth that those who do not live in it cannot know what it is, while those who live in it do not know that it is myth. We cannot relive the past as people of the time experienced it. Yet they too were human beings like ourselves. Human nature has not changed. Had there been a change, men before the change would be as foreign to us as animals. This is the ground on which Voegelin stands: man is man. His problem is not that of understanding the past, but the problem of a reality in process, which revealed to differentiated understanding what was not revealed to earlier compact understanding.

The terms *compact* and *differentiated* as such are descriptive. What the music lover hears in a concert is "compact"; the conductor hears the same music in the "differentiated" manner. But reality is not a symphony performed for us, and we are certainly not conducting the performance either. The man who lives in myth participates in reality no less than the one who does not. Yet something is closed to him which the others experience as the very form of their existence. Can we say that both participate in the "same" reality?

The leap in being is far more than a change in the mode of symbolization:

57. The step is right if the truth of reality thereby becomes "luminous" in consciousness: the newly differentiated symbols will be true if the philosopher's consciousness is not deformed; "[They] are 'true' in the sense that they intelligibly articulate the experience of existential unrest in the process of becoming cognitively luminous" (*Anamnesis*), English version, p. 112). "Luminosity," a mutating descendant of Husserlian *Selbsterhellung* (self-illumination) of consciousness, is a participatory symbol. Truth becomes "luminous to itself" in the consciousness that becomes "luminous to itself." What forces the philosopher to go forward is his existential unrest: "The life of reason in the classical sense is existence between life and death" (Voegelin, "Reason: The Classic Experience," ibid., p. 103).

the change is "in the order of being and existence itself" (1:10). Such changes plunge those who experience them into a turmoil of fear and hope, of uncertainty, disorientation and insecurity. To us in this time of trouble these are no mere words. Nowhere perhaps has Voegelin spoken more poignantly and profoundly of the impact of the leap in being than in his exegesis of the great symbolism of the leap, Israel's exodus from Egypt: "When the spirit bloweth [John 3:8], then society in the cosmological form becomes Sheol, the realm of death: but when we undertake the Exodus and wander into the world, in order to found a new society elsewhere, we discover the world as the Desert. The flight leads nowhere, until we stop in order to find our bearings beyond the world" (1:113). For Canaan, the promised land,

> is as far away today as it has always been in the past. Anybody who has ever sensed this increase of dramatic tension in the historical present will be cured of complacency, for the light that falls over the past deepens the darkness that surrounds the future. He will shudder before the abysmal mystery of history as the instrument of divine revelation for ultimate purposes that are unknown equally to the men of all ages. (1:129)

If, in the leap in being, society in the cosmological form becomes Sheol, the realm of death, what was life in myth before it became Sheol? Is "before philosophy" the same as "before history"?

Between Myth and History. The parallel leaps in the Far East are imperfect by comparison with the three leaps that occurred in Israel and Greece. As these multiple leaps coalesced in the Western form, a summit was indeed reached. In what respect did the Far Eastern leaps fall short?

They achieved personal existence under the cosmic *tao* or Way (China) or in acosmic illumination (India), but they did not attain existence under God in historical form. They never attained understanding of the community of being. Their differentiating philosophy never found its grounding in the structure of reality which Aristotle accomplished (2:22–23). Moreover, it remained ahistorical: "History is made wherever men live, but its philosophy is a Western symbolism." The philosopher of history has no choice. He must judge the Far East by the standards of his philosophy "because there is nothing he could put in its place" (2:23). By this standard the Eastern leaps in being were imperfect. No Eastern society has constituted itself as "the carrier of a new truth in history," as Israel did (1:123). And since "the process of human history is ontologically real" (1:129), they did not participate in the advance: they moved beyond myth and fell short of history.

Voegelin's philosophy of history is one of god-given advance: *vexilla regis prodeunt.* The advance is real—a change in the order of being, in the form of existence. The measure and indeed the nature of the advance so far as man is concerned is in the *knowledge* of reality, a profoundly Greek insight. This advance cannot possibly be mistaken for that "gnosis of a progress in time" which Voegelin brands as a deformation of the truth. Man is conscious of an unfolding mystery but knows nothing about its goal in the future (2:5). In the light of philosophy the new truth stands as a shining rock; in the shadow of the abysmal mystery of history it is shrouded in ultimate uncertainty. Only man's search for the meaning of his existence and for the truth of the whole is a certainty, because this search for his own humanity is what makes him what he is: man. The certainty with which this philosophy advances is therefore grounded in the ultimate uncertainty of the human condition; we know only what the search yields: the truth, for us, in our time. We cannot go farther and we must not stop short.

Let us now hear the other side. An ancient Chinese sage, for example, might answer, in his own symbolic language and form: "How very Western! The truth was simple; now it is complex. Does the complex explain the simple? Does the simple explain the complex? If the old truth is the same as the new truth, where is the advance? If it is not the same, is it truth? The One is the same and not the same. Is this not enough? Is the search more perfect than the attainment? Is the knowledge of attainment less perfect than the knowledge of the search?" As the *Chuang Tzu* says: "If the Way is made clear, it is not the Way. If discriminations are put into words, they do not suffice."[58] And: "Forget the years; forget the discriminations. Leap into the boundless and make it your home."[59]

The Eastern leap is an upward leap into the boundless where being is non-being and nonbeing is being, so much so that the sacred Sanskrit can put it into one single word: *satasat*, "beingnonbeing." The leap does not reach transcendence, since nothing is transcending toward anything. Only in the bounded is there history, the history of bondage: eternal return, giant cycles rising from beingnonbeing and coming to rest in beingnonbeing, no one can say for how long, for there is no change and no time between the cycles. There is no tension between life and death, only the minute life cycles from birth to death through which all that comes into existence is driven again and again until the giant cycle ends.

The cyclical conception of history will not die. Spengler's and Toynbee's conceptions replace the great cosmogonic cycles with the shorter cycles of the rise and fall of civilizations. Voegelin comments: "The conception of history as a sequence of civilizational cycles suffers from the Eclipse of God, as a Jewish thinker [Martin Buber] called this spiritual defect. Spengler and Toynbee return, indeed, to the Sheol of civilizations, from which Moses had led his

58. *The Complete Works of Chuang Tzu*, trans. Burton Watson (New York: Columbia University Press, 1967), p. 44.
59. Ibid., p. 49.

people into the freedom of history" (1:126). The Far Eastern leap into the boundless is the personal attempt to attain freedom *from* history. But this history is not the same as the other.

Voegelin's philosophy of history thus stands against those conceptions of myth and history that take no account of the differentiations of truth through philosophy and revelation (2:22) or take it into account in a different way. Let us examine some of them.

IV

Morphology. Historians articulate world history into prehistory, antiquity, the Middle Ages, and modernity. It is like counting beads on an unending rosary. This is "a view of the 'present' as a kind of machinery that grinds out an ever lengthening past. I call it the 'sausage view' of history." So Voegelin in *The Ecumenic Age* (4:332). Oswald Spengler did not call it the sausage view, but he did not think much of it either. How did this view originate?

Spengler already saw what Voegelin came to see later: the rise in Near-Eastern antiquity of a vision of history, from the creation to the annihilation of the world, split into two ages by a divine soteriological act; then, a millennium and a half later, Joachim's speculative transformation of this static, balanced two-age scheme into a dynamic three-age scheme suddenly fills the present with meaning. But here the parallel with Voegelin ends. According to Spengler, the subsequent secularization of Joachim's vision merely turns his mystical third age into a time shell to be filled with whatever a deep thinker or shallow *Incroyable* might fancy to be history's ultimate goal, meaning, or purpose. Spengler brushes all these linear constructions of history aside. What *he* sees in Joachim's bold mystic speculation is the insatiable spirit of a great new civilization shaking off the yoke of inert history, giving history a forward thrust and making it the symbol of its metaphysical urge toward the infinite. This is Western civilization remodeling history in its own image, the image of Goethe's ever-striving Faust.

As the sun of this civilization is setting, its historian—Spengler—discovers the true structure of world history. In close parallel to Voegelin he sees "history" not simply as the course of events in linear time but as an experience. Out of the mass of ahistorical peoples, great high civilizations spring up to act out their inner life in awareness (*Wachsein*), each of them unique, taking the road of all higher life, from birth to death. Spengler might well have used Voegelin's formula for the political society: a culture articulates itself for action in history. But, again, the parallel ends here. For there is no advance in this drama of history, no universal rise and fall, no meaningful time except life time passing through its stages, from birth to childhood, youth, maturity, old age, and death.

Spengler is not a philosopher, whatever he himself may say. He is a mor-
phologist.[60] His uncanny physiognomic eye sees in everything the *morphé*,
the *Gestalt*, an outer form whose "inner form" has to be identified and understood. For a Goethean like Spengler there is no "without" separated from a
"within." As Goethe himself puts it: "Ort für Ort, / Wir sind im Innern"—
whatever the place, we are *within*. Like Goethe, Spengler trusts the senses,
provided "thy mind keeps thee wide awake":

> Den Sinnen hast du dann zu trauen;
> Kein Falsches lassen sie dich schauen,
> Wenn dein Verstand dich wach erhält.

Spengler's second master, after and far below Goethe, is Nietzsche, from
whom he took the notions of decadence, destiny, nihilism, the will to power—
notions Spengler calls "deeply grounded in the nature of Western culture,
and simply decisive for its analysis." Yet in the very next sentence he puts
Nietzsche down as a provincial who mistakes his province for the world: "But
how does his notion of the Dionysiac relate to the inner life of a highly civi-
lized Chinese of the time of Confucius, or to that of a modern American?"
Each historical culture has a unique "soul" of its own, and only those who live
in this culture can understand this soul unerringly and to the full, from
within.

What the conception of *Kulturseele* can do is splendidly shown in the long
chapter on the "Arabic culture," a great discovery or invention of Spengler's—great even if mistaken. For this is a veritable phenomenology and psychology of the *Kulturseele*, reaching its climax in the memorable pages on
Jesus and Paul.[61] What is the innermost nature of a *Kulturseele*? Spengler
answers: deepest religiosity, unique yet universal. Unique in its perception
and conception of reality, universal in that every *Kulturseele* creates a self-

60. Voegelin rejects Spengler's and Toynbee's "cycle theories" of history which break up the
course of history into an assembly of independent units of study. This type of historiography runs
into "self-annihilation" (2:16). Cf. Gerhart Niemeyer, "Are There Intelligible Parts of History?"
Festschrift Voegelin, pp. 302–15. Voegelin's latest critique of Toynbee's "intelligible field of
study" is in *The Ecumenic Age* (4:173–74). The main argument, however, is that neither
Spengler nor Toynbee accepts "the principle that experiences of order, as well as their symbolic
expressions, are not products of a civilization but its constitutive forms" (1:126). For an ex-
cellent summary and critique of the work of Spengler and Toynbee as philosophies of history, see Helmut Kuhn, "Periodizität und Teleologie in der Geschichte," *Festschrift Voegelin*,
pp. 285–300.
61. The "Magic" culture is that of the Near Eastern religiosity which manifested itself in
Judaism, in the "Jesus religion," and in Islam, which was blocked and suppressed in Europe by
Pauline Western Christianity, though it resurfaced again and again in monophysitic, Gnostic,
and mystical Jewish movements up to quite recent times. Spengler moved this Eastern religiosity into the historical limelight. Even though the construction is untenable, it raises legitimate questions concerning the dominant interpretations of the history of Judaism, Christianity,
and Gnosticism. On this see my "History, Modernity and Gnosticism," especially the section on
Spengler, *Festschrift Voegelin*, pp. 195–201.

understanding in response to the mystery of existence. These unique responses, confined to higher, historical *Kulturen*, have three elements in common: first, a deep, all-encompassing *response* to the mystery of existence; second, *Wachsein* or existential consciousness; third, *symbolism* as the form in which each culture expresses its self-understanding and its truth. For each culture has its own truth, and each culture takes its own to be *the* truth. Only in the great historical overview are these truths episodes in the drama of mankind. The "magic," "Arabic" culture that created the symbolism of world history as the opposition between the new and the old age was an episode. The "Faustian" Western reach for the unattainable, its dream of the impending age of perfection, is an episode too, no more. Deeper than all these episodes is the universality of human questioning in the face of a reality that passes human understanding. This is Spengler's unspoken, unanalyzed, ultimate position.

Wachsein, "awakeness," corresponds to the leap in being, inasmuch as history begins with it. Aside from that, it is the opposite of the spiritual irruption that creates the philosophizing consciousness. The unique soul awakens to itself in a world wholly its own, the world as only this unique soul experiences it. "And therefore there are as many worlds as there are awake beings and hosts of beings that live in felt unison"—the *Kulturseelen*. The unique, independent, eternal world that everyone believes he shares with everyone else is in fact "an ever new, singular, never repeated inner experience." Only this uniqueness, and the belief that it is not unique, is universal—and even that only in history, when the soul is awake.

Every stirring within the soul is expressive, every foreign stirring makes an impression. Hence everything we are conscious of has a *depth* beyond and beneath consciousness itself. "The only and the extreme way of making this unattainable, ultimate meaning comprehensible is a kind of metaphysics for which *everything*, whatever it be, possesses the meaning of a symbol." The world, the experienced reality of the *Kulturseele* is one encompassing symbolization; whatever the culture creates is a symbol of itself at "the depth."

Spengler defines symbols as "sensory signs, ultimately indivisible and above all unwilled impressions which have definite meaning. A symbol is a trait of reality which, for men whose senses are awake, marks with immediate inner certainty something that cannot be rationally communicated." Everything becomes sign and symbol as the physiognomic eye catches it: cathedrals and castles, dervishes and Darwinists, grammar and gladiator games, newspapers, slaves, steam engines, pogroms, popes, logarithms—the list looks familiar. It corresponds in fact to the list of what Voegelin, in his first book on the American spirit, eliminated from his material, leaving only *die selbstsprechenden Erscheinungen*—phenomena that tell us about themselves in analyzable language symbols. What these symbols tell does not have the mark of immediate inner certainty, but it is rationally communicable. The Spenglerian symbols, by contrast, are not cognitive; they belong to what Husserl calls the *Lebenswelt*, what Voegelin subsumes under the symbol of the primary experience.

The unique symbolic worlds created by these civilizations are responses to the mystery of existence, but they do not reveal a truth that is universal to mankind. They are modes of experiencing. Spengler stops at the modes, Voegelin begins with the mystery that moves in the process of history. In missing the process, Spengler misses history. In missing history, he discovers the differentiated modes that reveal the inner life and the character of the high civilizations. To Voegelin's philosophy of history these individuations are as little relevant as are the individual differences between thinkers. For this philosophy, the procession of great cultures across the Spenglerian stage is no more history than the river of multitudes passing from birth to death. History is a process, not a procession.

Had Oswald Spengler (1880–1936) lived to see Voegelin's philosophy of history, he would have hailed it as the ultimate manifestation of the spirit of the dying West, rising as Plato's philosophy rose when Athens was falling. He would have recognized it as the pure philosophy of the unreachable for which the Faustian soul yearns, a philosophy which imperiously casts all history into its own mold, never doubting that its truth is the truth of man, God, and history. He would have placed this philosophy with Beethoven's Great Fugue and modern quantum theory—Faust's deepest metaphysical statements before the clock stops and the Western episode is over. He would have heard this philosophy as music, but he would not have called it a philosophy of *history*.

Voegelin stands on the other side. Wherever a great theophanic event occurs, even in a forlorn corner of the world, there history is made. What does not participate in the advance of truth sinks to provincialism. The theophanic events do not occur in the soul of a culture but in the consciousness of representative men, "for the revelation comes to one man for all men, and in his response he is the representative of mankind" (2:6).

Once the process comes into view, Spengler's colorful, dramatic world of *Gestalten* fades; its great rhythms, which he called a "tremendous music of the spheres which wants to be heard, which some of our profoundest minds *will* hear," becomes inaudible. In the silence of meditation, consciousness hears another rhythm, another sound: the rhythm of spiritual advances and deformations, of obsolescence and renewal, of questions and responses, the sound of a movement toward the eschaton. One of Voegelin's anamnestic experiments brought up a boyhood memory of that sound:[62] "Und schliesslich verschwand auch das Wehen, und es blieb nur ein Rauschen; manchmal leise,

---

62. *Anamnesis* (1966), pp. 74–75; English version, p. 49.

hoch oben; manchmal stark und nahe, so stark und nahe, dass es kaum noch zu unterscheiden ist von dem Rauschen des Meeres, in dem wir versinken."

I leave this sentence just as Voegelin wrote it down in the course of his anamnestic experiment. It is untranslatable into English because it contains two untranslatable words, *Wehen* and *Rauschen*, the sound of the wind and that of the sea, the breeze that is breath and spirit, *atman, ruach, pneuma*— but this a boy not yet ten years old would not know or sense; he thinks of the ship going down, its flag still flying. In this early experience of transcendence the flag dematerializes and vanishes and only a sound remains, *ein Rauschen*, sometimes gentle, high above; sometimes strong and near, "so strong and near that it can barely be distinguished from the sound of the sea into which we sink." "History, it appears, has a long breath," Voegelin will write in his patriarchal age. "It will always be a wholesome exercise to reflect that 2,500 years from now our own time will belong to a past as remote in relation to our present as that of Heraclitus, the Buddha, and Confucius" (4:331). In this long perspective, it is Spengler's morphological panorama that appears episodic, perhaps the last great self-expression of a declining civilization which attempted to create a reality in its own image and conceived of a history without a mankind.

The Terror of History. November 3, 1960. Mircea Eliade records in his diary: "Eric Voegelin comes to see me. I had just finished reading the first volume of *Order and History*, surprised by the affinity of our positions. He is still young, looks barely fifty. . . ." Voegelin, he writes, can hardly believe that nobody ever recognized the "gnosticism" of the Hegels, Heideggers, Bultmanns, or Jungs. In a conversation three years later, Thomas Altizer wants Eliade to enter into a dialogue with the representatives of modern consciousness. Eliade replies that "they are all *Westerners*," that their cultural horizons are "provincial," their problems and crises obsolete. "For my part, I try to open up windows on other worlds for Westerners. . . . I try to understand a paleolithic hunter, a yogi or a shaman, an Indonesian peasant, the Africans, etc., and to communicate with each of them."[63]

Eliade has indeed opened windows upon the world of archaic myth and Oriental understanding. Looking out of the window is of course not the same as being out there yourself. Those out there spoke myth; Eliade speaks about myth. Myth "defines itself by its own mode of being. It can only be grasped . . . in so far as it reveals something as having been fully manifested." The titles and subtitles of Eliade's two best known books are the formulations of

63. Mircea Eliade, *Fragments d'un Journal*, trans. from the Romanian by Luc Badesco (Paris: Gallimard, 1973), entries for November 3, 1960, and January 3, 1963, pp. 349 and 413–14 English trans. from the French by F. H. Johnson, Jr.: *No Souvenirs: Journal, 1957–1969* (New York: Harper & Row, 1977), p. 116.

his great themes: "The Sacred and the Profane: the Nature of Religion" and "Cosmos and History: the Myth of the Eternal Return."[64] The sacred and the profane are "two modes of being in the world." Only in the sacred mode is man "real," whole, human, and safe; only then is his being in the world intelligible to him, his suffering bearable. In the world of myth the sacred fully manifests itself. The man looking out of the window can grasp this because the sacred is not foreign to him, even if he grasps it only as an absence. If Eliade can open windows on archaic myth, it is ultimately because he sees modern man from out there, in the perspective of archaic myth.

The sacred is "the foundation of a structure of reality as well as of a kind of human behavior." Man maintains himself in the sacred mode by the periodic re-enactment of the original act of creation. This myth of the eternal return protects him from "the terror of history," the terror of meaningless, endless suffering in profane time. The eternal return reveals "an ontology uncontaminated by time and becoming"; it is the "ontology of religious man."

Eliade knows that life in myth can become degraded, savage, inhuman. But all this pales before the consequences of the break with myth. What Voegelin identifies as an upward "leap in being" Eliade abhors as the Fall. Western man has been taken out of the sacred circle into an increasingly desacralized world; his irreversible commitment to profane history and progress is "the final abandonment of the paradise of archetypes and repetition."

We understand why Eliade calls the crises and woes of Western intellectuals, from Hegel to Freud, Joyce and beyond, provincial. The fundamental fact for him is that "almost the whole of humanity" now lives in the "continuous terror" of historical tragedies without meaning. Only by "presupposing the existence of God" can modern man arrive at a new mode of being that is "unique in the universe." Eliade, who must have been very close to peasant life in his native Rumania, understands the self-revealing symbols engendered by hierophanies, irruptions of the sacred into profane time and existence, as he understands the theophanies that transform ancient rhythmic life into the hovering of the soul in the In-Between, the Metaxy, of divine-human reality. But these revelations leave man's spiritual life dangerously exposed. The exodus from civilization into eschatology is an exodus from the security of myth. It leaves a civilization unprotected against the shock and threat of historical tragedies. And when this exodus becomes an exodus into profane

64. The pertinent texts will be found in Eliade's *The Sacred and the Profane: The Nature of Religion*, trans. Willard R. Trask (New York: Harper & Row, Harper Torchbooks, 1961), pp. 96–100, 213; and especially in *Cosmos and History: The Myth of the Eternal Return* (New York: Harper & Row, Harper Torchbooks, 1959). pp. vii–xiii and chap. 4 ("The Terror of History"). See also Thomas J. J. Altizer, *Mircea Eliade and the Dialectic of the Sacred* (Philadelphia: The Westminster Press, 1963), pp. 23–26 and 41–47, esp. p. 44 on the archaic mode of understanding which Eliade sees as "a human mode of participation in the sacred" which is "reality itself." Altizer interprets Eliade from his own theological viewpoint.

time and existence, the consequences of revelation horrify the historian of archaic myth.

Voegelin, with the philosophers, sees the drama of mankind within the great frame of coming into existence and passing out of it, set against the unfathomable ground before and beyond existence:

> The Mystery of the historical process is inseparable from the Mystery of a reality which brings forth the universe and the earth, plant and animal life on earth, and ultimately man and his consciousness. Such reflections are definitely not new, but they express, in differentiated form, the experience of divine-cosmic order that has motivated the oldest cosmogonic symbolisms; and that is precisely what they should do, if universal humanity in history is real and not an illusion. (4:335)

Voegelin's philosophy of history breaches the gap between the archaic symbolizations and the new understanding of the truth opened up by the revelations. But history is not exactly joyful for the philosopher either. He, like Eliade, notes with deepest concern that the peak of the leaps in being, the epiphany of Christ, is also the beginning of the "Gnostic" countermovement, which Eliade characterizes as an exodus from sacrality into profane time and existence. The history of events casts a dark shadow on the history of the truth: Voegelin sees a gigantic civilizational cycle rising from the age of myth through the leaps of being to its peak, the epiphany of Christ. From then on it *falls*. In its falling it encompasses the whole of Western civilization, from its beginning to its decline.

The Unacceptable East. Voegelin has tried hard to do justice to the East, but his heart is not in it. Perhaps the breakthrough that fell short of the goal is more of a scandal than no breakthrough at all. As we have seen, Voegelin characterizes his philosophy as "Europocentric." The philosophy of history arose in Europe and nowhere else. To find out what Voegelin's Europocentrism is *not*, let us consider the strange case of C. G. Jung, the explorer of Eastern symbolizations who also had trouble in dealing with the East.[65]

According to C. G. Jung there are two Jungs: Jung No. 1 and Jung No. 2. Each has his own style. Jung No. 1 is a respectable Swiss academic with a nineteenth-century notion of scientific rigor, a practical, steady mind, who can turn in a moment into a berserker. Jung No. 2 is a pneumatic visionary whose eruptions fling out chunks of flaming insight for Jung No. 1 to

---

65. The following discussion of Jung sums up my detailed documented analysis in *Festschrift Voegelin*, pp. 206–13, which is based on the autobiographical *Erinnerungen, Träume, Gedanken von C. G. Jung*, ed. Aniela Jaffé (Oldenburg und Freiburg i. B.: Walter Verlag, 1971), English trans. by Richard and Clara Winston: *Memories, Dreams, Reflections by C. G. Jung* (New York: Pantheon Books, 1972).

make scientific sense of. Jung No. 1 sails through life, leaning like a galleon's figurehead into the rush of a dark future; Jung No. 2 dwells in the inner light of mythical images and visionary events. According to C. G. Jung, the coexistence of a No. 1 and a No. 2 is normal, present in every human being, whether he is aware of it or not.

The prelude to Jung's encounter with India, an initiatory crisis, occurs at age twelve. Long-growing doubts about the religiosity of his father, a pastor, and the church he serves lead to a vision in which the boy literally sees God delivering his very explicit verdict on both. Returning from school, the boy sees before him the Basel cathedral, its many-colored tile roof gleaming in the sunshine. He mentally intones a hymn: "The world is beautiful and the Church is beautiful and God has created it all and he sits above it, high in the blue sky on a golden throne, and. . . ." Terrified, he stops. One thought more, and he will be damned forever. For this thought, irrepressibly rising in him, will be the one unredeemable sin, the sin against the Holy Ghost. This thought must be suppressed at all cost. For two days and two nights the boy fights down the urge, not knowing what God wills him to do. Does God himself want him to *sin*, as he wanted Adam and Eve to sin? In the end he musters all his courage and decides to do God's will and disobey his command. At that moment he *sees* the dreaded thought. From beneath God's throne a gigantic turd drops on the cathedral and crushes it. The boy experiences an indescribable sensation of joy and liberation; he is free of father, Church, and the threatening old Creator God.

In 1938, at age sixty-three, Jung goes to India, "deeply convinced of the value of Eastern wisdom" and deeply suspicious of it. Jung No. 1 is to receive three honorary degrees. Jung No. 2, foreseeing the worst, brings along, in lieu of bell, book, and candle, an old Latin tome on alchemy. India is overwhelming. It receives him with open arms, but in Calcutta India finally becomes too much for him. A massive attack of diarrhea—symbolic as well as physical—sends him to the hospital for ten days. The hospital is "an island of salvation in the inexhaustible sea of impressions." Back at his hotel, purged in body and soul, he has a dream about the Holy Grail. He understands it to be posing the question: what are *you* doing in India? What indeed? The dream tells Jung No. 2 that he must at all cost preserve his "European personality" intact—as once before in Africa a dream had warned him not to risk "going black."

Jung No. 1 explains Jung No. 2's reaction to India: he must stay away from all "saints" because he must not accept "their truth"; he has to find his own. For Easterners do not seek moral perfection; they are "outside good and evil." The boy's vision sheds light on the strange statement. Without knowledge of good and evil there is no ordeal of choice, no moral dilemma, no initiatory *decision* that turns the ego into the individuated self. Truth is not knowledge of something; it is that realized selfhood which cannot be gotten ("stolen," he says) from anyone else. And since this realized self "includes the world," a spiritual search for "the imageless void" would rob that self of its marvelous possessions—fellow human beings, himself, nature. He must choose, not the knowing truth of the "saints," but "the living contemplation of nature and of the psychic images." But whenever Jung No. 2 in dream or vision approaches the rock temple in outer space where the meaning of his existence is to be revealed to him, he sees a yogi sitting in the lotus position before the entrance, the guardian of ultimate knowledge. One yogi bears his own features, and he knows: this yogi is meditating him and when he stops meditating, Jung will cease to exist.

The symbol of the yogi expresses what Jung feared: *knowledge* beyond compact truth. His case is not that of a "Gnostic" but of a genuine shamanic visionary in a scientific society, a tribal seer without a tribe.[66] Unable to make his visions socially effective by ritual enactment, yet feeling himself to be representative of his society and responsible for it, he develops the symbol of the "European personality," the individuated self that encloses outer and inner world within itself, expressed in the only form possible in that society, the incongruous form of a "scientific" analytical theory of the psyche. His efforts to save this society from itself can only consist in healing individuals who suffer from the Western malaise that Eliade calls the fall into profane existence. But the mere "presupposition of God's existence" will not heal them; they need religion, plain and simple. That religion is not a hovering between time and eternity, a Christian life in uncertainty of salvation. Jung heals by taking his patients back into the world of the luminous archetypes of the collective unconscious, into the world of myth.

The state of consciousness sought by the Far Eastern "saints" transcends civilization, whether European or Eastern. This transconsciousness, as Eliade calls it, still knows the mythic relationship between "all sentient beings" which precludes the conception of universal humanity. It is "the most incisive expression that can be of a wholly ahistorical soul" (Spengler). The Far Eastern leaps in being forced Voegelin to ask whether there are two mankinds, each independently going through the disintegration of compact symbolisms, each with a consciousness of its own. Only a consciousness centered on man's existence in eschatological tension could ask this question, and it can do so only because it already knows the answer: all symbolizations of the truth are responses to a questioning which is a "constituent of humanity," the re-

66. This assessment of Jung as a shamanic type is in seeming conflict with his own Gnostic self-identification, G. Quispel's attempt to link him to ancient Gnosticism, and Voegelin's classification of Jung as a modern Gnostic. The conflict resolves itself when we consider the difference between what Jung No. 1 says and what Jung No. 2 reveals.

sponses stop at differing points, and the connection between these points marks the path of truth through history.

Jung fears the imageless void. As the yogi bearing his own features meditates him, his "European" self dissolves in that void. For Jung's is a fully individuated self in time, space, society, and person. Voegelin's thinking, grounded in his own time, space, society, and life, is not that of a European or Western self; what we hear is a *philosophizing consciousness* which, in participating in the exodus from civilization, participates in the process that has passed beyond archaic man and yogi to the revelation of universal mankind.

The Solitude of the End. "Does a man really have to make a virtue out of the misery of his condition, which he perceives to be the graceless disorder of his soul, and set it up as a superhuman ideal? Does his deficiency entitle him to perform Dionysian dances with masks? Let us, with the brutality that the times compel if we are not to fall victim to them, ask whether he is not rather compelled to be silent. And if his lament were more than a mask, if it were genuine, if he suffered from his condition, would he not then be speechless? But Nietzsche is not in the least speechless." In probing the soul of this "murderer of God" Voegelin finds his speech to come from the "deepest reach of persistence in the deception," the "demonic mendacity" of a Gnostic rebel against God.[67] Comte, Hegel, Marx, and Nietzsche are the thinkers of the "Gnostic-Satanistic movements" that are now one step away from supremacy. This is the long historical and philosophical view. For contrast, here is what a very contemporary view sees, looking out of itself.

Hegel, Kierkegaard, Marx, Nietzsche are the great figures of the modern revolution in consciousness, society, and history, a revolution that answers Meister Eckhart's prayer: "We pray to God to be free from God"—"a mystic call to full redemption in full continuity with the proclamation of Christianity." So Thomas J. J. Altizer in his most recent book, *Total Presence.*[68] Altizer's "apocalyptic theology of history" is a super-Hegelian antithesis to the Voegelinian philosophy of history. It has to be a theology: philosophy after the death of Hegel "is virtually dead." In Hegel and Nietzsche a totally new consciousness has arisen; with its rise, history too has come to an end. It has become "a museum in our time, a graveyard of dead societies and cultures. . . . Whatever future can appear before us is a future wholly dissociated from

67. Eric Voegelin, *Science, Politics and Gnosticism,* trans. William J. Fitzpatrick (Chicago: Henry Regnery, 1968), pp. 32–34.

68. Thomas J. J. Altizer, *Total Presence: The Language of Jesus and the Language of Today* (New York: The Seabury Press, 1980), pp. 49–50. "There are only three great modern historical thinkers—Hegel, Marx and Nietzsche. . . . Pure historical thinking begins with Hegel and already comes to an end with Nietzsche, but in that brief period the full actual meaning of our history was established" (p. 75). Cf. the exchange between Altizer and Voegelin in this volume.

the past. Knowledge itself is now the knowledge of death," of what is most remote from anything manifest to us as movement or life.[69] God has become manifest as the center and ground of both silence and speech. For speech is born in the pure silence of total emptiness, and its genesis is the apocalypse: "Genesis and apocalypse are one, but they can only be one by way of the realization of exodus, the exodus of the speaker from the source and ground of speech. That exodus is speech itself, and it is ultimately the speech of God."[70] Nietzsche would indeed have been compelled to be speechless, had his consciousness remained the consciousness of identity, of the "I." But this consciousness passed into silence with Hegel and reversed itself in Nietzsche's *Zarathustra*.

Hegel had understood "the death or the self-negation of God as the advent of modernity." In the Calvary of the Spirit, consciousness knows itself as pure negativity, as a radical No-saying. The Nietzschean "ecstatic vision of the dance and joy of Eternal Recurrence" is an act of total Yes-saying: "now all identities and all events flow into one another" in an actualization "in which everything whatsoever is totally present." This "reversal of consciousness then becomes manifest as the full realization of the death of God,"[71] revealing "a total presence, a pure immanence." This is the exodus that is speech itself, and ultimately the speech of God. The speech is heard and spoken only in "the solitude of the end," in a silence marked by "the absence of every center of selfhood."

How would the new consciousness, in which all identities and all events flow into one another, know itself as new? The answer, unfortunately, is that it can know this only by knowing itself as something other than what it has been: the end of history cannot be known except by knowing history. And thus the devil sneaks in by the apocalyptic back door. Altizer must rewrite history. He cannot let all identities and events flow into one another. He must differentiate, but he must differentiate differently. He must begin by differentiating the mystery, the unknowable, and rewrite the history of consciousness from the Greeks to the present as the history of God.

The mystery and unknowability of God can be understood and has been understood in two ways. Either the unknowability of God is a consequence of the radical transcendence of God "which can only truly be known in faith," or else it is "an unknowability which is simply and only unknowability." There is "an overwhelming and uncrossable distance" between these two kinds of unknowability. The first gives God a transcendent identity; it makes God

69. Ibid., pp. 91–92.

70. Thomas J. J. Altizer, *The Self-Embodiment of God* (New York: Harper & Row, 1977). The quotation is taken from the author's summary on the book jacket.

71. Altizer, *Total Presence*, pp. 79–80. Further page references to this book will be given in the text.

preexistent; it makes unknowability an attribute of God, and it names God negatively, saying what God is not. But "a mystery which is wholly and only a mystery cannot be spoken or evoked as such, and must therefore perforce remain silent" (pp. 45 ff., 25 ff.). Apocalypse reveals the wholly unknowable, the anonymous God, as totally present in pure immanence. It reveals "the Kingdom of God beyond God" in silent manifestation.

In the parables of Jesus the Kingdom is silently present, rejected by all, and especially by the disciples of Jesus; "for it is precisely [the] faith in the transcendent God which most diverts attention from the actual presence of the Kingdom" (pp. 46–47, 8–10). The present Kingdom was rejected by historical Christianity, "the only religion in the world which historically established itself by effecting a pure negation and reversal of a visionary world" (p. 37), the world of the Greeks whose discovery of man was the advent of a fully human consciousness. Two polar consciousnesses clashed; Christianity won, and fully human consciousness was destroyed, never to rise again. The God of historical Christianity is the transcendent, preexistent God of the Old Testament, the Creator God whose preincarnate identity is not a final, an ultimate identity. "So it is that in an eschatological situation a partial identity of God can become a demonic identity of God and a preincarnate God can be identified as Satan. This identification was made in the ancient world by the Gnostics and again in modernity, from Milton to Melville" (pp. 53, 68–72).

The new consciousness negates *all* identity; its "radical iconoclasm [negates] all our given images of both deity and humanity." In Nietzsche the negation of all meaning and identity is "a Yes-saying of triumphant joy"; to Mallarmé it is a mystical plenitude of grace (p. 29). Its purest expression is the total anonymity of contemporary poetry, art, and music in which every center of selfhood is absent. As the apocalyptic theologian listens to the new silence released from the background noise of jazz, whose embodied power "hurls us into a new and posthistorical universality," he participates in "a movement which leaves self-consciousness and ego behind" (p. 105). It is a movement into the solitude of the end. "And we rejoice when confronted with this solitude, for the only true joy is the joy of loss, the joy of having been lost and thereby wholly found again. Not only is the only true paradise [the one] that we have lost, but the only regained paradise is the final loss of paradise itself." [72]

Voegelin would ask: "Does a man really have to make a virtue out of the misery of his condition?" Altizer would answer: "Is there still such a thing as 'a man'? Is there any condition he can call 'his own'?" But the joy is no longer triumphant. These closing pages of *Total Presence* remind us of Beckett's *The Unnameable*; they remind us even more forcefully of the closing pages of

72. This is the close of *Total Presence*, pp. 107–108.

another book, where the revolutionary composer Adrian Leverkühn, alias Friedrich Nietzsche, faces the solitude of the end. His masterwork, the atonal oratorio which "takes back" Beethoven's Ninth Symphony and the Hymn to Joy, is the *Apocalypsis cum figuris*, composed in the house of Mrs. Silence (Frau Schweigestill).

Altizer's identification of modern art as pure anonymity, a descent into a depth deeper than any conscious individuality, is brilliant. I prefer to treat it as an observation rather than as revelation, for this brings us to the point. Every apocalypse is a revelation of the end. There have been many of them since the Apocalypse of Daniel. Something is indeed coming to an end in our day. This, too, is not exactly new. Plato knew that something was coming to an end as he was writing, not an apocalypse, but a philosophy which still lives. Is the end we are witnessing that of the consciousness of which Plato's Third God, the divine *Nous*, is a symbol? *Total Presence* raises the question whether this consciousness is changing in a reversal which, in Eliade's language, would be a return to the sacred mode of existence, if it were a mode of existence and not a retreat from existence into pure inwardness. Certainly the night is once again falling on symbols that have had their day. Is transcendence, is history, one of them? Or is this reversal another manifestation of "Satanistic Gnosticism" deforming consciousness and dreaming up a second reality?[73]

Being hurled into posthistorical universal humanity does not take man out of the reality of a world which is what it is; neither does the joy of loss (commonly called resignation) remake man. But something is hanging in the balance. It has been hanging there for a long time. As Voegelin says: "If one realizes that we are still grappling today, and still inconclusively, with the problems set by the differentiations of consciousness in the Ecumenic Age, one may feel that nothing much has happened during the last 2,500 years" (4:331).

73. Total otherness and unknowability of divinity characterizes what I call ancient "radical Gnosticism" (*Festschrift Voegelin*, pp. 222–27). This world then becomes existent nothingness and its existence becomes an eschatological scandal. In a letter of July 2, 1980, from which I quote by permission, Altizer responds to my paper by pointing out that this eschatological scandal "is an essential ground of all truly modern Christian theology. The utter *Otherness* of reality can have an apocalyptic as well as a Gnostic mythical identity." The absence of a bridge from the wholly Other to this world and the need to explain the existence of the nonexistent by de-absolutizing the Absolute (my formulation) "is a uniquely Western problem and necessity." Radical Gnosticism "was reborn in modernity, and perhaps never so comprehensively as in our world. . . . And why is the death of God not a modern analogy to the experiential upheaval caused by the felt withdrawal of divinity in the axial period of the leaps in Being?" In *Science, Politics and Gnosticism* Voegelin identified the death of God as the murder of God, taking the word out of the mouth of Nietzsche's new Diogenes ("Der tolle Mensch," *Die Fröhliche Wissenschaft*, Aphorism 125) who on a bright morning comes running into the marketplace, carrying his lantern: ". . . the philosopher is search of man has become the madman in search of God" (p. 60). Are we witnessing the murder of God or the "taking back" of the leap in being? God alone knows, and he is not telling yet.

V

The Ecumenic Age. In 1974, after a break of seventeen years in the series, the fourth volume of *Order and History* appeared under the title *The Ecumenic Age*. This is Voegelin's "Book of Exodus." The itinerary crisscrosses the desert of pragmatic history, station after station, ending with the long look from the last mountain. Yet the book has unity—the unity of the exodus: *Incipit exire qui incipit amare*—he begins to love who begins to leave, as Voegelin translates the first words of the Augustinian text that invisibly governs the work.[74] The god who guides the journey is the God "revealed in the cosmos and in man," Plato's Third God, the Nous (4:230, 232).

"Exodus" is the title under which the index to *Anamnesis* records the two emigrations Voegelin experienced, one in childhood, the other in maturity.[75] Exodus from his own society is the condition any philosopher must accept if he is to be a critic of that society and a healer—to the extent that philosophy can heal. The leap in being initiates the exodus from myth and from civilizations. The exodus of Israel begins with the exodus of Abraham, the first Patriarch, from Ur of the Chaldees, followed by the exodus from Egypt. The anguish of its third exodus begins with Isaiah and Jeremiah. It is the "exodus of Israel from itself": in the symbolism of the suffering servant (Deutero-Isaiah) "Israel as the representative sufferer has gone beyond itself and become the light of salvation" (1:419, 515).

In the "Ecumenic Age"—roughly from the rise of the Persian empire to the fall of the Roman one—pragmatic history becomes the battlefield between spirit and civilization. New types of imperial society rise, clashing with the older cosmological societies and subjecting the two centers of revelation,

74. "Eternal Being in Time," *Anamnesis* (1966), p. 280; English version, p. 140: ". . . the dynamism and direction of the process stem from the love of eternal being. The exodus in the sense of *incipit exire qui incipit amare* is the classical formulation of the material principle of a philosophy of history." On Augustine's *amor Dei* "as the existential exodus from the pragmatic world of power" and his intermingling of *civitas Dei* with *civitas terrena* "as the In-Between reality of history," see *Order and History*, 4:172.

75. The last of the anamnestic experiments of 1943 recorded in *Anamnesis* is entitled "First Emigration"—the family's move from the Rhineland to Austria. "What had happened to me dawned on me only several weeks later, when I first went to school in Vienna." The second exodus was the emigration to the United States. There is an implicit hint at yet another, unidentified, exodus in the record of Voegelin's anamnestic experiments. No. 3 is called "Cloud Castle," and he says that its meaning is not clear to him. It concerns an inaccessible mountain called Cloud Rock, topped by a legendary Cloud Castle (*die Wolkenburg*) which is invisible from the foot of the mountain. The castle and its knight "were firmly ensconced in my soul." The place was dank, surrounded by rags of clouds. He thought of the knight as "a vague, mournful, lost figure" who would often travel on mysterious business, then keep house again in his lonely habitation. I take this Cloud Knight as a symbol of intellect lost in pure speculation, divorced from the ground of reality—the "shadow" philosopher who loomed as a possibility in the boy's future until the exodus from childhood and home ("my own revolutionary change of location to Austria," No. 8) confronted him with a different kind of reality (*Anamnesis*, English version, pp. 41–42).

Israel and Hellas, to the power of empire. Conflict and strife is the condition into which philosophy is born, in which it still remains; only when embattled, in a *Kampfposition*, does it advance, differentiating the truth. "We therefore dare to generalize empirically that the philosophical investigation of the field of phenomena has always received its dynamism from contemporary situations of struggle."[76]

In the Ecumenic Age, ethnic societies are overrun by conquerors representing "the new type of empire, this peculiar power shell which apparently has no substance of its own." A new expansionism drives them forward, for now the *ecumene*, the dwelling place of man in the Old World, is coming into view "not [as] a subject of order but [as] the object of conquest" (4:117). But the Ecumenic Age was also the age in which the great world religions, above all Christianity, originated. Christianity above all because the theophanic irruptions that make history reached their peak in the appearance of Christ and in the vision of Paul. "There is no history other than the history constituted in the Metaxy [the 'In-Between'] of differentiating consciousness; and if any event in the Metaxy has constituted meaning in history, it is Paul's vision of the Resurrected" (4:243).[77]

Experientially, a theophanic event is "a turbulence in reality." Those who "cut themselves loose from the theophanic event" transform "the encounter between God and man into the violence of an encounter between man and man," most violently in the modern revolutionary intoxication of bloodshed, Marx's *Blutrausch*. "The magic of the *Blutrausch* is the ideological equivalent to the promise of the Pauline vision of the Resurrected" (4:253–54). For the Gnostic worm sits at the very root of the advance. "Considering the history of Gnosticism, . . . I am inclined to recognize in the epiphany of Christ the great catalyst that made eschatological consciousness an historical force, both in forming and in deforming humanity" (4:20).

In the Ecumenic Age, the exodus from civilizations has its correlate in a variety of forms of exodus from reality. "Beyond the concupiscential exodus of the conquerors into the vision of an imperially unified mankind, [beyond] the spiritual exodus of prophets and apocalyptics into a vision of a mankind under God, and [beyond] the noetic exodus of the philosophers into immortalizing participation in the Nous and the cosmos, the Ecumenic Age has also produced the Gnostic imagery of an exodus into ecumenic death" (4:235).

The fourth volume of *Order and History* breaks with the linear sequence of the series, chronologically as well as thematically and philosophically. The main theme, "the Beginning and the Beyond," places the analyses between the poles of the experienced process of reality. Time, instead of providing the

76. *Anamnesis* (1966), p. 277; English version, p. 138.
77. "The theophanic events do not occur *in* history; they constitute history together with its meaning" (4:252).

chronological thread, becomes part of the problem to be analyzed, and history, released from the form of simultaneity and sequence of events, becomes "a movement through a web of meaning with a plurality of nodal points." This is "the form which a philosophy of history must assume in the present historical situation" (4:57).

Time and History. "The order of history emerges from the history of order." So it did, but not for long. *Order and History* moved comfortably forward on the straight line laid out for it, from the Ancient Near Eastern empires to Israel and Hellas. But when the Western civilization came into view, the history of order became complex beyond expectation. The original program broke down at this point, as Toynbee's program for *A Study of History* had done. Spengler's conception of pseudomorphosis can explain what happened.[78] Voegelin's new philosophy of history found an old traditional shell to grow into, assuming a false form. Then the pressure of the historical material forced the thinker to recognize what he had sensed but not acknowledged before: that the Western conception of history and time is not natural, self-evident, and inescapable, that unilinear chronological time is a fact which hides a problem, and that a philosophy of order and history must assume a form which allows the order of history to emerge, not from a rigged "course of history" but from the historical material itself. What triggered this insight was Voegelin's discovery of a symbolic form of historical speculation to which he gave the name *historiogenesis.*[79]

The unfamiliar word is easily explained. Historiogenetic speculation carries "history" back to "Genesis," to the myth of the Beginning. Hence its definition: "a mytho-speculative extrapolation of pragmatic history toward its cosmic-divine point of origin" (4:101), a form midway between cosmological myth and noetic differentiation. It appears in the historical material from

78. Spengler took the term from mineralogy. A mineral, crystallized inside the shell that has formed around a now leached-out crystal of quite different shape, will be forced to grow into this false shape. This, according to Spengler, happened to the "Magic culture" which filled the shell of Hellenistic culture with its own spirit; only with the Arab conquests did it assume its own outward form. Spengler's discovery bore unexpected fruit when it enabled Hans Jonas to identify ancient Gnosticism as an autonomous spiritual movement. Cf. his *Gnosis und spätantiker Geist*, Vol. 1, *Die mythologische Gnosis*, 2nd ed. rev. (Göttingen: Vanderhoek & Ruprecht, 1954), pp. 73 f.

79. Voegelin identified the Europocentric constructions of history as "the gnosis of progress" (2:5), which robs history of its "lateral dimensions." Though Jaspers and Toynbee overcame this defect, they showed "a sometimes surprising disrespect" for phenomena—the parallel leaps in being—that would not fit into their own constructions. Only later did Voegelin himself run into the difficulty they had encountered. The problem of the "parallel outbursts" in fact became manageable only when he discovered the reason for their failure: both thinkers "treated hierophanic events on the level of phenomena *in time*, not letting their arguments reach into *the structure of experiencing consciousness*" (4:5). But this insight was attained only through a philosophical effort of the first magnitude, encompassing the structure of history, time, consciousness, and reality.

the Ancient Near Eastern empires to Hellenistic times chiefly in the form of chronologies that take a present order of society back in direct line to ever longer-lived and more heroic predecessors and finally to the mythical founder or ruler "who was lowered from heaven," to quote the Sumerian King List, the most ancient of these ancient chronologies, written over 4,000 years ago.[80]

What Voegelin discovered in this seemingly unpromising material was a conception of history which "implacably places events on the line of irreversible time, where opportunities are lost forever and defeat is final" (4:65). What historians see as a rudimentary type of historiography lapsing into unhistorical fabulation Voegelin sees as the result of unrest and anxiety caused by the rise of a new imperial order—unrest among the more ancient city states that fell under the rule of imperialistic upstarts, existential anxiety created by the change of order and not assuaged by the traditional rituals of foundation and renewal. Historiogenesis legitimizes the new rule by letting it descend in unbroken line from the mythical beginning; it sublimates the new order to "the timeless serenity of the cosmic order itself," at the price of violating historical reality. For there must be only one line of descent, the one that leads to the imperial conquerors who, by reconstructing history, appropriate even the ancestry and independent existence of the conquered.

The procedure looks strangely familiar, almost Orwellian. Historiogenesis in fact "displays a curious tenacity of survival—from cosmological societies proper to contemporary Western societies" where from the Enlightenment on it has "proliferated into a bewildering manifold of progressivist, idealist, materialist, and positivist speculations on the origin and end of history." Hence the conclusion: "Historiogenesis is one of the great constants in the search of order from antiquity to the present" (4:67). Only the focus has changed, from the problem of the origin of specific ancient societies to that of the genesis of world history itself (4:113). And so, ironically, the form in which Voegelin's *Order and History* began to grow, unilinear history which forces the plurality of lines of meaning into the strait jacket of chronological sequence, now stands exposed as a half-mythical, half-differentiated manip-

80. The discovery of historiogenesis is ultimately grounded in one of the childhood experiences which Voegelin recognized as shaping his philosophical consciousness. This is No. 15 in the anamnestic experiments, entitled *Das Realienbuch*, the "fact book" used in the five-grade elementary school he attended. Here the history of the Hohenzollern dynasty was presented in reverse, beginning with the reigning Emperor Wilhelm II, a man of ordinary stature, then going back to his increasingly more impressive and heroic ancestors; behind them loomed "the gigantic shadow" of the Great Elector known as "the Bear." To this reverse history Voegelin ascribes the development of "whatever capacity I have today [1943] to understand mythical images. . . . I have always taken it for granted that the present was to be measured . . . in human terms, that with increasing distance men grew to the size of a Solon and Lycurgus, that before them there capered the heroes, and that the horizon was securely and dependably closed by the gods." In the English version of *Anamnesis* (pp. 47–48), *Das Realienbuch* is translated as "The Book of Realities," which is what the "fact book" became in the conception of history of *The Ecumenic Age*.

ulation of historical reality intended to raise modern Western man to the apex of history.[81]

The importance of the discovery can hardly be overrated. It forced a re-thinking of the very structure of history and the time of history. When the history of order is no longer a story to be told from the beginning to whatever the end may be, how does the truth advance within the time of history? Did myth disappear when, in the wake of revelation and philosophy, the intra-cosmic gods disappeared? And "what exactly was modern about modernity" if the great struggle between modern historiogenetic constructions of history is, like the ancient struggles, a battle between "imperialist speculators in the best cosmological style" (4:8)? But is there no truth at all in this type of spec-ulation, ancient or modern? No lasting truth of the cosmos?

The questions are not new. Voegelin asked the decisive question from the outset: "Why did we start with Israel . . . and not rather with China and In-dia? Are we not indulging a 'Western prejudice' in the choice of the starting point and the mode of procedure" (2:6)? Now the question becomes central and answerable: the *philosophy* of history can finally turn into what it was meant to be from the beginning, a material philosophy of *history*. The histor-ical material itself testifies to "the richness of the spirit as it reveals itself all over the earth in a multitude of hierophanies" (4:3), creating a pluralistic field of meanings. China and India enter on equal terms. "There are indeed two ecumenic ages, a Western and a Far Eastern, both unfolding parallel in time." Are there then "two mankinds, each having a history of its own and each developing an Ecumenic Age" (4:300)?[82]

This, not the problem of fitting ecumenic ages into a postulated evolution-ary sequence, is the crux of the matter. There can be, there are indeed, many

81. Exactly 100 years before *The Ecumenic Age*, in 1874, Nietzsche had already identified the historiography of his century as a product of hybris on the part of epigonal latecomers—*Erdflöhe*, mere fleas on earth, as he called them—who presumed themselves to be the apex and the very goal of world history. Nietzsche recognized the purpose of this historiogenesis in re-verse. Cf. "Vom Nutzen und Nachteil der Historie," Nietzsche: *Werke in drei Bänden*, ed. Karl Schlechta (Munich: Hauser, 1954), 1:266. Spengler recognized this historiography as a West-ern symbolism and tried with his morphology to break the implacable unilinear direction it im-posed on the phenomena. Jaspers and Toynbee identified the parallel leaps in being as the prob-lem that made constructing a meaningful unilinear history impossible. The final insight is Voegelin's: the conception of history must emerge from the historical material; it cannot be im-posed upon it without distorting known fact.

82. What dissociates is the compact order of the early empires, not compact myth. The order splits into "indefinitely expanding power organizations without spiritual meaning" and "hu-manly universal spiritual movements in search of people whose order they could form" (4:145). This places the split between empire and church in the European Middle Ages in the context of the Ecumenic Age (the age of dissociation) which outlasted the Ecumenic Age that ended with the Roman empire. What made the multicivilizational power organizations "ecumenic" was their striving to expand to the limits of the then known ecumene. The spiritual expansion, on the other hand, transformed the geographical ecumene into the ecumene of men past, present, and future, symbolically understood as "universal mankind" (*The Ecumenic Age*, chap. 7).

lines of meaning running through history, but there can be no independent histories whose existence and coexistence is meaningless. The final understanding of history and time arises when the notion of a course of history is abandoned altogether and the historical dimension of *humanity* is grasped as a dimension within reality in process. "History is not a merely human but a divine-human process. Though historical events . . . have a calendar date, they also partake of the divine lasting out-of-time. The historical dimension of humanity is neither world-time nor eternity but the flux of [divine] presence in the Metaxy," the In-Between, experienced in the differentiating consciousness (4:304).

There is a "calendar date" for the event that breaks the unilinear concept of history. It is the date of the Ecumenic Age of the dissociation into power and spirit. "In the Ecumenic Age, the process of reality is discovered as a spatially and temporally open field." In "the new center of consciousness" of men "widely dispersed in space and time over a socially and culturally diversified mankind," this process of reality is concretely experienced as the process of history moving toward transfiguration (4:314–15), as "the Mystery that has no end in time" (4:333). What then is "the time of history"?

History does not happen in time, but things happen in history. More precisely, "what happens 'in' history is the very process of differentiating consciousness that constitutes history" (4:331–32). Hence there is no "length of time" in which things happen; "there is only the reality of things which has a time dimension" (4:333). This reality of things is stratified, and each stratum has its time dimension, its own mode of lastingness. What we call "time" is the measurable mode of lastingness of the astrophysical universe by which we measure the lastingness of all things. But even this ultimate lastingness is not a "time" in which things happen. It is the time dimension of a thing within the Whole that includes "the diverse reality whose mode of lastingness we express by such symbols as 'eternity.' Things do not happen in the astrophysical universe; the universe, together with all things found in it, happens in God" (4:334). This happening is a movement of which we can only say that it is "the Mystery that has no end in time."

The Beginning and the Beyond. When, in the Ecumenic Age, the cosmological order of empire disintegrated, the truth of revelation and philosophy was to become fatal to the intracosmic gods. Their disappearance from the cosmos "set a de-divinized nature free to be explored by science" (4:8). Science so thoroughly isolated "nature" that the terms "cosmos" and "universe" have become synonyms. The only cosmos we know is the astrophysical universe with all that is in it. Our dictionaries define "cosmos" as "the universe as an ordered whole or system." This fits the original Greek meaning of "cosmos" as "order" and especially "world order," but the modern conception lacks what the ancient one had: the view that this order is divine and divinely created. For us, the presence of the universe is a fact, no more. Only some philosophers still ask why there is anything at all and not rather nothing, why things have to be the way they are and not different. Leibniz was the first to make the question explicit, but the problem is as old as myth, if "a myth is an intracosmic story that explains why things are as they are" (4:224).

One does not bother to explain unless there is something that needs explaining. What needs explaining is the sheer fact of existence, since existence is imbedded in nonexistence. Things come into existence and must go out of existence; their lasting is a passing. To exist in passing lastingness is "the primary experience of reality as a tension between existence and nonexistence," "the tension of existence out of non-existence" (4:73–74). The problem thus has two aspects. One is the aspect of existence, and the question is why things are as they are. The other aspect is that of the coming into existence, and the question is why and how things came to be in the first place, in the Beginning.

In Voegelin's early conception of the progress from compact myth to the symbolic forms of history and philosophy (1:13–14) the symbolic form created by societies rising above the order of tribal organization was cosmological myth, the myth explaining the order of the divinely created cosmos. "To establish a government is an essay in world creation"; the cosmological myth gives expression to the society's participation in its own order, "in the divine being that also orders the cosmos" (2:16, 27). To create government is to create an order modeled on the order of the divine cosmos. This is the symbolic form of order that dissolved in the Ecumenic Age. How then could it be that "the meaningful advances of differentiating consciousness were throughout history accompanied by the equally meaningful persistence of a 'cosmological' symbolism" (4:8)? How could this symbolism survive the eclipse of the ordered cosmos as the paradigm of societal order? How could it survive into the modern age which turned the cosmos into a dedivinized astrophysical universe governed by the laws of dedivinized nature? And what could remain meaningful in this symbolism when reality came to be experienced in the new center of consciousness as world-transcending? If there is meaning and truth in the cosmological symbolism, how did those who participated in the theophanic events in the Ecumenic Age resolve the conflict between the newly revealed and the surviving old truth?

These questions move the issue from the *order* of the cosmos to its *lastingness*, for this is what creates the issue. The new center of consciousness experiences reality in the tension between existence and nonexistence. In the experience of transcendence the soul feels the pull of divine presence moving it from beyond the cosmos; the movement is directional, toward the Beyond. Why is it then that the differentiation of the truth does not affect "the experience of divine reality as the creative and ordering force of the cosmos"? Voegelin answers: because divine presence is experienced "not only in the soul but in the cosmos in its spatio-temporal existence" (4:9).

The serenity of this statement stands in stark contrast to the spiritual turbulence and agonies of the Ecumenic Age. The statement does not resolve the conflict between the experiences of the Beyond and the Beginning. In the Beginning the spatio-temporal existence of the cosmos emerged from nonexistence, and only myth—the cosmogonic myth of the creation—can symbolize the movement of divine presence into the space and time of the existent world. But the creator god of the myth now encounters "the Hidden or Unknown God who reveals himself in the movements of the soul" and draws the soul away from the Beginning toward the Beyond. And since the new experience "pertains directly only to man's consciousness of his existential tension," since it does not directly give him an image of reality as a whole, the truth of existence discovered by the prophets of Israel and the philosophers of Greece cannot simply replace the truth of the cosmos (4:8). Hence the early search for fundamental symbols expresses the structure of this issue. Drawing upon Israelite, Hellenic, and Christian sources, Voegelin sums up its results in a formula which, slightly simplified, reads as follows:[83]

The divine reality . . .
that moves man's consciousness from Beyond all cosmic contents . . .
also creates and sustains the cosmos from the beginning. . . .

"The Beyond and the Beginning, articulating the directions in which divine reality is experienced, have remained the unsurpassably exact expression of the issue to this day" (4:9).

Had Voegelin stopped at this formula, his philosophy of consciousness would hardly have become the philosophy of history it now is. For this is to pose the issue on the level of consciousness, not of history: the experience of the Beyond belongs to *differentiating consciousness*, while the symbolisms of the Beginning emerge from the *depth of the psyche*; consciousness must accept the primary experience of the cosmos as an undifferentiable given. Only in the vision of the *oneness* of the whole do the two directions in which divine reality is experienced come together. There is as yet no movement within the whole. Now "history" is experienced in consciousness as a mystery that moves toward transfiguration past all existent lastingness. This movement—and this is the truth of cosmogonic myth—begins with the cosmos entering from nonexistence into existence. What so begins is more than a lastingness and an order; it is existence itself. This beginning we can only call, in mythical lan-

83. The divine reality is the *theotes* of Col. 2:9; the "Beyond of all cosmic contents" from which man's consciousness is moved, the world-transcendent, is Plato's *epekeina* of the *Republic* 509b; and the Beginning is the *bereshit* of Genesis 1:1.

guage, the divine "creation" of the cosmos. It is also the beginning of the process of history in which "eternal being realizes itself in time,"[84] for this process is a movement in the cosmos. Voegelin can therefore say, in a sentence which is the apex of his philosophy of history, that "'history' is the area of reality where *the directional movement of the cosmos* achieves luminosity of consciousness" (4:242). But only a story of genesis, a cosmogonic tale, can express the divine-cosmic beginning of the process: "no more than the cosmos, I had to conclude therefore, will the cosmogonic myth disappear. Any attempt to overcome the myth or to dispose of it is suspect as a magic operation, motivated by an apocalyptic desire to destroy the cosmos itself" (4:10).

Gnosticism and the Balance of Consciousness. The discovery that the ultimate mystery of reality is the process in the divine cosmos marks Voegelin's decisive advance over his predecessors. He not only ascribes this insight to Plato; he finds it in Plato, giving chapter and verse (4:233–38). This is the characteristic mode of advance in the period of differentiating consciousness after the leaps in being. No spiritual outbursts, no theophanies have created a new epoch since, but the advance continues as the search renews and advances what had been given in antiquity. Voegelin describes this period as the philosophers' "exodus from reality," the exodus in which the movement within reality manifests itself. Plato called it the age of the Third God, the *Nous*; in this age, soul and man must be ordered in obedience to the *daimonion*, the voice of "what of immortality is within us." This "something" is the *nous* in man. The new age in the history of theophany has made the structure of reality, experienced in the Metaxy of differentiating consciousness, accessible to "noetic" exploration. Once again a contrast stands out: the contrast between the calm of exploration within the noetic field and the storms of spiritual outbursts that created the new consciousness and initiated the new age. In the turbulence of the theophanic events, the Beyond could be experienced with such power, consciousness could be so flooded with imaginations of reality transformed, that existence in the cosmos paled before it (2:234).

In the Ecumenic Age, contempt and even hatred of the world was indeed rife. Plato himself—according to Voegelin's analysis— had, with his identification of the Third Age of the *Nous*, come "as close to an apocalyptic symbolism as he could come without losing the balance of a consciousness that also comprehended the primary experience of the process in which the things come and go." With the separation between spirit and power, a paradoxical gap in consciousness opens between the world in which power is at home and a world "dynamically alive with theophanic events" pointing from all that passes away to the "ultimate transfiguration of reality" (4:227). Reality en-

---

84. This is the first sentence of "Eternal Being in Time." I am merely drawing out its implicit relevance to the problem of the Beginning and of history.

compasses both poles, both worlds, and only a consciousness that can participate without succumbing to the pull of the Beyond and without recoiling
from the threat of passingness can attain the balance in which the structure of
the whole becomes luminous. This precarious balance is firmly maintained
by the philosophers, dangerously maintained in Paul's overwhelming vision
of the Resurrected, and lost in the radical rejection of the existing world by
the fomenting spiritual movements of the Ecumenic Age, which reached
their clearest expression in the great Gnostic speculations of the second and
third century A.D.

The dynamics of theophany are unbalancing. They reveal reality moving
"toward a state undisturbed by forces of disorder," and imagination may be
carried away to symbolize this state as a new heaven, a new earth (4:240).[85]
Even the "noetic" theophany is experientially unstable; the revelation of the
God as the Nous in *both* cosmos and man may move consciousness toward
either pole, the Beyond or the Beginning (4:232–33). The philosophers
succeeded in maintaining balance, and so in the end did Paul, the prophet of
the third leap in being. But Paul experiences the vision of the Resurrected
with such force that, in the twinkling of an eye, he can move from participation in the whole to the anticipation of the imminent perfection, of transfiguration in his own and his listeners' lifetime. To Paul, his vision is "more
than a theophanic event in the Metaxy: it is the beginning of transfiguration
itself" (4:248). With the philosophers, the "noetic" stress fell on the structure of experienced reality; in the case of Paul's prophetic "pneumatic" experience it falls on "the exodus from structure." But the difference is no more
than one of accent; both conceptions "act out, in the luminosity of consciousness, the paradox of a reality that moves beyond its structure" (4:58). Paul's
vision, too, is an immediate response in the soul to divine presence: "the vision emerges as a symbol from the Metaxy, and the symbol is both divine and
human" (2:243). This is by no means the last word about the difference, as
we shall see, but this last word can only be spoken against the background of
the mightiest among the unbalancing spiritual movements in the Ecumenic
Age—ancient Gnosticism, which at its height produced speculative systems
that placed the Beyond *before* the Beginning.

These Gnostic speculations give voice to a total and radical alienation from
the cosmos and the human world.[86] For the radical Gnostic there is only one

85. Revelation in Voegelin's sense is not a handing down from on high of authoritative
knowledge and commandment; the "content" of revelation is the fact, the event of revelation itself. The pluralistic field of spiritual irruptions—theophanies and hierophanies—is not a field of
different enunciations. It is a field of differing responses to the same or different experiences.

86. Elsewhere I tried to spell out the logic of "radical Gnosticism" in detail. God, "the Un-
engendered One," is total reality, unrelatable to anything outside it. Of this divine reality one can
only say what it is *not*. This is the Beyond which, for the Gnostic, is not the beyond of future
transfiguration but the reality in which the fall into nonreality begins, to end with the restoration
of the wholeness of the Realm of the Light. The parallel with the Pauline vision, to be discussed

reality, "the depth," "the abyss," the Unknowable God. This reality is utter otherness, and no bridge leads from it to "this world" of existing nothingness. The Gnostic myth is a cosmogonic myth. It explains the creation of this existent nothingness as the consequence of a weakness, a downward movement originating in divine reality and ending in the creation of the cosmos by an ignorant, insolent, even evil creator god. The cosmos and all it contains is a realm of darkness and death: "Every soul of these ages has death assigned to it," as a Nag Hammadi text says, "but the *immortal* souls are not like these." These immortal souls are sparks of the divine Light which have fallen into the cosmic prison and are now in the power of its rulers. These are the elect, the Gnostics, the knowers, outwardly indistinguishable from the mortal souls yet unperishing and destined either to escape from the cosmic prison or to return to the Great Light when the cosmos and all it contains is destroyed and the unity of the One is restored. The radical Gnostic, we may say, is swept away by the Absolute, the Beyond: in Gnosticism "the balance is lost."

Voegelin's analysis of this "precreational psychodrama" (4:24–27) hinges on the spiritualist's experience of actual divine presence which so fills consciousness that the divine order contracts to the divine presence as a personal experience. The experience as such is "acosmic." Only in the response does the problem of the balance arise. Balance will be achieved if the order of reality as a whole is allowed to become luminous in the consciousness. When the overwhelming presence of the Beyond eclipses the primary experience of the cosmos, apocalyptic visions of the end of the world and the transfiguration of man will arise. The Gnostic spiritualist, by contrast, lets the movement toward the Beyond turn in the opposite direction. He expands "the acosmism of his experience into an anti-divine construction of reality as a whole": the cosmos is anti-divine, and the Beyond must therefore lie *before* any Beginning. Only the language of the old cosmogonic myth can cope with the meaningless "being there" of things, since the language of the search for truth cannot give expression to senseless existence. The ready symbol is the creator god who creates the cosmos in his own image—in this case the image of the anti-divine, unreal rebel against divine plenitude.

The modern Gnostic rejects the world as it is as radically as did his ancient forerunner. But he decisively reverses the speculation. For him it is the divine Beyond that is meaningless, indeed nonexistent: the only reality is that of

---

below, is obvious. The Gnostic's problem is of course that, no matter how radically he denies the cosmos and existence in time, cosmos and existence are experienced fact for him too. This experience he must deny by adopting the mode of radical nonparticipation in the world whose reality he cannot really deny. The lunatic fringe went even farther, trying to hasten the destruction of the cosmos by committing heinous crimes, in the belief that the world will end when its measure of iniquity is full. The purest form of nonparticipation is the ascetic "encratic" abstention from all sexual activity, so that the endless chain of births may be broken. (So also Schopenhauer in the nineteenth century.) Cf. my paper, *Festschrift Voegelin*, pp. 222–24.

passing existence. And since history does point to the Beyond, his "magic" wants to stop the movement toward transfiguration: the end of history is at hand, to be followed by a transfigured human world here and now, created not by a god but by man himself.[87]

Questions. In *The Ecumenic Age* the immense complexity and depth of the seemingly straightforward progression from compactness to differentiation comes to the fore. Yet one position is maintained with greater force than ever: "There is no history other than the history constituted in the Metaxy of differentiating consciousness" (4:243). The carrier of the advance of the truth is philosophy. This must have raised questions in the mind of many a reader, questions which have led more than one critic astray. Is philosophy really the one great carrier of the advancing truth? Is the new center of consciousness the only center in which divine-human reality rises to luminosity? How much does the continuing differentiation of symbolism add to the knowledge of the truth of being? And what of the third leap in being, Christianity? Did it merely complete the knowledge of the structure of reality by revealing divine being as reaching down to man? Voegelin's great chapter on "The Pauline Vision of the Resurrected" should be read in the light of these questions.

Paul was "a mythopoeic genius,"[88] a mythmaker "not controlled by the

---

87. Voegelin (4:260–66) discusses modern Gnosticism as "the egophanic revolt"—"revelation delivered speculatively." "Gnosticism, whether ancient or modern, is a dead end. This of course is its attraction. Magic pneumaticism gives its addicts a sense of superiority over the reality which does not conform." (4:27–28). But the problem lies deeper. For the ancient Gnostic the dissociation between power and spirit went so far that divine reality is totally powerless within the cosmos. Even the divine Messenger who comes to awaken the Gnostics to their true destiny must come secretly and in disguise; he has nothing to offer them, practically, except the "technical gnosis" of how, by the magic of passwords, they can escape from their prison. This powerlessness is the Gnostic's solution to the problem of the existence of evil in the world, a problem which the leap in being rendered irresolvable. It reappears in Voegelin's work as the question why the truth is rejected in the world (see pp. 64f. below). In his most recent paper on modern Gnosticism, "The Magic of the Extreme," he raises the question again by asking why the Gnostic wills the untruth although he knows the truth—did perhaps the gods will it so? His answer is Plato's "Regarding this matter we know nothing at all." We know only that the process of history will not cut itself off by attaining a truth that dissolves the discord between truth and untruth, a discord which motivates some men to ask "why existence should have a structure from which man must be saved." The ancient Gnostic answered with the myth of the fall into a wholly unreal world; the modern Gnostic makes the discord between truth and untruth a discord between men, where he represents the truth that will end the discord in reality. The title "The Magic of the Extreme" is taken from Nietzsche's *Der Wille zur Macht*, Aphorism 749: "The spell that . . . bewitches and blinds even our enemies is the magic of the extreme, the seductive power of all that is ultimate. . . ." For a full discussion of Voegelin's view of Gnosticism from *The New Science of Politics* to "The Magic of the Extreme," see the section on "Gnosticism and Modernity" in my contribution to *Festschrift Voegelin*, pp. 227–41. Cf. Voegelin, "Wisdom and the Magic of the Extreme: A Meditation," *Southern Review* n.s. 17 (1981):235–87.

88. In *The Ecumenic Age* the correct term *mythopoeic* unaccountably appears throughout as *mythopoetic*, which makes no sense. *Mythopoiesis*, to give it the correct etymological spelling, is the making of myth, not of mythical poems. The manuscript undoubtedly spelled *mythopoeic*.

critical consciousness of a Plato." He tells a tale of death and resurrection, a myth of Adam and Christ: "For as through one man came death, so in Christ all men shall come alive" (1 Cor. 15:22). In the third leap in being the appearance of Christ is followed by the vision of Paul, a decisive event in the Metaxy, constituting meaning in history: revelation taking the symbolic form of myth as "a symbolism engendered by the experience of divine presence in reality" (4:249). If Paul's tale of death and resurrection is myth, how is this type of myth related to compact intracosmic myth?

Compactness and differentiation are not separated by a chronological caesura. There is a process of differentiation at work in myth too. In its mytho-speculative types, compact myth is moving toward noetic consciousness. "When the breakthrough toward the luminosity of consciousness occurs, . . . the myth will lose its cosmological compactness," its symbolism will become luminous "as the exegesis of a theophanic event in the Metaxy," and the myth will become "an *alethinos logos*, a 'true story.'" The philosopher's myth "is carefully devised so as to make the tale of divine presence in reality compatible with the existential truth of man's tension toward the divine ground" (4:249). In contrast to the compact myth which rose from the depth of the psyche, the Platonic myth is indeed "carefully devised," and if it is not yet fully differentiated, that is because Plato, who was aware of the divine abyss beyond the Nous, deliberately surrounded with uncertainties the movement of the psyche toward this depth. The Pauline myth, however, is not restricted to the noetic structure of reality. It articulates "the *pneumatic* depth in divine reality beyond the Nous" (4:250). Paul does not carefully devise his tale, taking care not to suggest more than it can in truth say. Where the philosopher speaks of a movement *toward* transfiguration, Paul speaks of transfiguration as the *goal* of the movement—the state *beyond* man's involvement in the mystery of the timeless Beginning and of Time. That is why his myth *must* become the story of a fall and a return: "The movement, in order to have meaning, must come to an end. . . . In Paul's myth, God emerges victorious, because his protagonist is man," because "at one point, in man, the sonship of God is possible. The movement in reality, that has become luminous to itself in noetic consciousness, has indeed unfolded its full meaning in the Pauline vision and its exegesis through myth" (4:250–51).

This answers the question about Christianity, but it does not resolve the questions concerning philosophy. Paul's vision was a pneumatic, not a noetic event: it attained the full meaning which noesis had not attained. One cannot of course argue with theophanic events; it is an empirical fact that only the *sequence* of the three revelations opened up the full meaning; it is also a fact that only philosophy, differentiating noetic consciousness, drew from Paul's pneumatic insight the lessons concerning the structure of reality. But *could* noetic consciousness have attained the Pauline insight? Is it not in the very nature of the philosophizing consciousness that it "carefully devises" where the pneumatic seer *plunges* into the depth? "In the beginning was the Logos." Is John's Logos the Logos of the philosophers? If Plato's *Seventh Letter* is authentic, he himself experienced the irruption of divine presence far beyond what his philosophy expresses, what—according to this disputed text—philosophy *can* express in the differentiating mode. And if Voegelin's philosophy does what Plato's philosophy does not do, if it encompasses the Pauline vision, it does so at the price of reducing to the level of differentiating rational language what Paul could say only in the language of myth.

Unless I misunderstand Voegelin's thought, the *experiential* reach of philosophy is thus limited at both ends: at the Beginning and at the Beyond. Differentiating consciousness sets in after (or above) the primary experience of the cosmos; its center is the Metaxy, and it cannot *experientially* reach the abysmal Beyond. That is why this philosophy is surrounded by mysteries.

That within this experiential area *history* should be the central concern needs no explanation; it is history, not as the form of existence but as the experienced movement of reality, that marks the continuing advance of the truth of reality. Voegelin's philosophy therefore has to be a philosophy of history. And as a philosophy, it has to take the utmost care in exploring this truth in all the complexity that only the differentiating consciousness can reveal. For this truth is a truth of *order*, and the philosopher as a representative of this truth is responsible to himself and to his society for distinguishing order from disorder, for tracing the inner roots of disorder, and for setting forth firmly what is, and what is not, in order. The experiential limits of philosophizing are therefore its strength: only within these limits can the balance of consciousness be attained and preserved; any excess on either side becomes the source of disorder in the soul and of tragic and cruel disorder in society.

Nonetheless *The Ecumenic Age* must address itself to the ultimate question raised by the very success of the philosophy is renews, embodies, and advances—a question so decisive that Voegelin calls it *The Question* concerning the mystery of history:

1. Why is differentiating consciousness not given to all men at all times?

2. Why must the insights be discovered by such rare individuals as prophets, philosophers, and saints? Why is it not given to all?

3. "Why when the insights are gained, are they not generally accepted? Why must the epochal truth go through the historical torment of imperfect articulation, evasion, skepticism, disbelief, rejection, deformation, and of renaissances, renovations, rediscoveries, rearticulations, and further differentiations?" (4:316).

To these questions one might add yet another: what is so good about differentiation? Differentiation—classical philosophy—established the new truth before the so far highest leap in being, the epiphany of Christ; but then, the giant cycle went into its *decline* while differentiation continued to *advance* the knowledge of the truth. Was not the compact understanding of the truth easier on man?[89]

The disturbing questions concerning the fate of truth in history "are not meant to be answered; on the contrary, they symbolize the mystery of the structure of history by their unanswerability" (4:326). But they do help us to place Eric Voegelin's philosophy within the structure of history which it illuminates. If it speaks of the Beyond and the Beginning, it does so as a philosophy of process, and such a philosophy is clearly grounded in the philosopher's *present*. It cannot and does not make the claim to absoluteness that ideological systems make. And so Voegelin, looking ahead, asks: "What will be worth remembering about our present, and why?" This establishes the perspective in which not only this present but his own philosophy as a representative one must be placed: "Our present, like any present, is a phase in the flux of divine presence in which we, as all men before and after us, participate. The horizon of the Mystery in time that opens with the ecumenic expansion in space is still the Question that presents itself to the presently living; and what will be worth remembering about the present, will be the mode of consciousness in our response to the Question" (4:321). For Voegelin, philosophizing in the contemporary situation is an act of resistance "to the distortion and destruction of humanity" by those who want to "stop history" in the name of a second reality. This act of resistance is "an open act of participation in the process of both history and the Whole" (4:225).

---

89. This is the question Eliade raises. Life in this world was not easier before the leap in being, but it was easier to understand and to bear. With the leap in being, doubt assails even the knower of the truth which brought, not peace, but a sword: "I am inclined to recognize in the epiphany of Christ the great catalyst that made eschatological consciousness an historical force, both in forming and in deforming humanity" (4:20). More precisely, "Incarnation is the reality of divine presence in Jesus as experienced by the men who were his disciples and expressed their experience by the symbol 'Son of God' and its equivalents; while Resurrection refers to the Pauline vision of the Resurrected" as well as to other visions of this type (4:244). It is this vision which "has constituted meaning in history"; while Incarnation revealed the mutuality of divine-human participation. So much for the debate as to whether or not Voegelin is a Christian.

TOWARD THE PROCESS OF UNIVERSAL MANKIND: THE FORMATION OF VOEGELIN'S PHILOSOPHY OF HISTORY

Jürgen Gebhardt

> In a time of civilizational disintegration, intellectual history does not follow a straight course. . . . In a time of disintegration the field of problems is socially open: the questions dominating the public scene will be precisely those which reveal disorientation and confusion, while the successful attempts at spiritual and intellectual orientation are relegated to socially obscure corners.

These are Voegelin's introductory remarks, in 1945, to his analysis of the crisis after Hegel. This "Last Orientation," as he calls it, intends to isolate "a complex of ideas which we consider systematically central and, therefore, suitable for furnishing a stable point of orientation in the increasing confusion of the century of crisis."[1] In the course of his analysis the "spiritual realist" Eric Voegelin articulates his situation in "an intellectual and social environment that is no longer receptive to the rational, technically competent thought of the spiritually well-ordered personality":

> If the realist would throw himself into the general melee as one of the contestants, he would defeat his philosophical purpose. In order to be heard he would have to become a partisan himself, and in order to become a partisan he would have to surrender the standards of rationality. If on the other hand he has sufficient spiritual strength as well as philosophical consciousness to take his position beyond the disorder of the age, . . . he will remain socially ineffective to the point of not even being misunderstood. . . ."[2]

The insight of the spiritual realist and the dominant ideas of the age part company in the present civilizational crisis. The critical historian of ideas can no longer present ideas on their own terms in the face of his own experience of reality. The current symbols, in the context of a despiritualized existence,

1. Eric Voegelin, "Last Orientation," unpublished ms., p. 126.
2. Ibid., p. 160.

have become void of historical truth. Truth in history shifts to the paradigmatic humanity of the spiritual realist, who "is faced by the Platonic problem of creating an image of man and society that will serve, or is supposed to serve, as an ordering principle in the historical situation."[3]

However, in the course of his Platonic quest for the ordering principle in a despiritualized society, the spiritual realist Voegelin discovers that it is the work of Schelling that "establishes a new level of consciousness and critique; and by virtue of this achievement [Schelling's work] becomes of increasing importance in a time of crisis as the point of orientation for those who wish to gain a solid foothold in the surrounding mess of decadent traditions, conflicting eschatologies, phenomenal speculations and obsessions, ideologies and creeds, blind hatreds and orgiastic destructions."[4]

In Schelling Voegelin recognizes a kindred mind whose ideas "can be a point of orientation for the understanding of the crisis because they are not engulfed in the crisis themselves." Voegelin sees Schelling's system as "the last gigantic effort to bind into a balanced whole the tensions of the European late civilization before they break asunder in the crisis of our time."[5] But in Voegelin's view Schelling's philosophy "marks the end of a period, not a beginning."[6] Thus, Voegelin does not suggest a return to Schelling, whose "grandiose effort . . . to reestablish a philosophy of substance . . . failed to become the starting point for a civilizational restoration: . . . the destruction of the speculation on substance under the impact of the model of mathematized science went on."[7] What Schelling did establish was the new level of consciousness and critique that was necessitated by the advancement of science. This new level of consciousness was a critical awareness of the source of speculation, the soul, and of the knowledge that would enable us to construct the universal process, i.e., the course of natural and human events understood as a meaningful unfolding of the universe. The process of the universe can be made intelligible, i.e., becomes history, through an anamnestic dialogue that is going on in the soul, and this dialogue provides the means by which the meaning of the external process is extracted from the soul: "Anthropology is now systematically made the key to speculation; nothing must enter into the content of speculation that cannot be found in human nature, in its depth as well as in its heights, in the limitation of its existence as well as in its openness toward transcendent reality."[8] In Voegelin's mind, Schelling's philosophy of historical and political existence established the insight that philosophy is identical with history, and history with the science of the soul.[9] "History receives meaning from the soul, while the soul discovers the historical meanings

---

3. Voegelin, "Nietzsche, The Crisis and the War," *Journal of Politics* 6 (1944):195.
4. Voegelin, "Last Orientation," p. 235.
5. Ibid., pp. 234–35.   6. Ibid., p. 125.
7. Ibid., p. 128.   8. Ibid., pp. 179–80.
9. Ibid., p. 184.

as strata in its existence." [10] In the intellectual biography of Voegelin this "last orientation" elucidates his turn from the history of political ideas to a material philosophy of history—necessary in order to respond properly to the crisis of the age. "The existence of man in political society," Voegelin concludes in 1952, "is historical existence; and a theory of politics, if it penetrates to principles, must at the same time be a theory of history." [11]

I

At this point in our study it will have become clear that I have no intention of delivering a doxographic presentation of a set of ideas that supposedly comprises Voegelin's philosophy of history. This cannot be accomplished, not only because of the enormous amount of material in question but also because—strictly speaking—Voegelin does not *have* a philosophy of history. He is engaged in an inquiry in the classical sense of a *zetema*—the search for truth, cognitive as well as existential, the symbolic explication of which is not an object to be talked about but an invitation to reenact the engendering experiences by meditation. Voegelin alluded to this existential dimension of cognitive process as early as the Preface to the *Autoritäre Staat*, in which he said:

> The theoretical treatment of any political subject . . . is being carried by the faith in the myth of cognition; the theoretical mind who is reading it will trace the argument—which is animated by the myth and therefore dramatic—between the theoretician and reality; he will want to know whether the struggle for the transformation of reality into truth has either ended in victory or defeat. [12]

The reflexive analysis of the symbolism that Voegelin is still in the process of creating has to begin by reconstructing the experiential context—in order to understand correctly the ongoing process of symbolization.

The statement "the movement towards truth starts from man's awareness of his existence in untruth" [13] may be taken as a retrospective confession. It poses, however, the problem of how a social and historical scientist, well versed in the scientific methodologies and the schools of philosophies of our time—in short, a scholar of the Weberian timber—becomes aware of his existence in untruth. While pursuing empirical social science, which strictly dissociates the validity of a practical imperative as an ethical norm from the validity of true empirical judgments concerning facts of historical modes of

10. Ibid., p. 233.
11. Voegelin, *The New Science of Politics* (Chicago: University of Chicago Press, 1952), p. 1.
12. Voegelin, *Der autoritäre Staat* (Vienna: Springer Verlag, 1936), p. iv.
13. Voegelin, *Order and History*, Vol. 1, *Israel and Revelation* (Baton Rouge: Louisiana University Press, 1956), p. xiv.

human existence, he is, certainly, completely in tune with his social environment. However, a sensitive mind might be troubled by implications of Weber's empirical science of history and society, namely that any relevance of the cultural phenomena to be studied depends on the transcendental presupposition that we are cultural human beings, endowed with the capacity and the will to express our view about the world and to bestow meaning upon it. We are, therefore, able to order the empirical reality analytically in a valid way through the construction of concepts congruent with those respective values of the scholar that illuminate the significance of a given section of empirical reality. But the validity of any historical value that refers to the meaning of our existence is beyond the empirical evidence of social science. There remains for us only belief in a transempirical validity of highest values, upon which we fix the meaning of our existence.[14] In the practice of research, the contradiction of Weber's approach became obvious to the critical practitioner of empirical science when his ultimate purpose—namely "the service to the cognition of cultural relevance of concrete historical contexts"[15]—is defeated because, in the process of determining the relevant historical phenomena, his purpose is referred to values that distort and deform the very empirical reality to be cognitively apprehended. One might surmise how disturbed the critical practitioner, Voegelin, was by such disregard for the scholar's basic virtue of intellectual integrity (Weber's *intellektuelle Rechtschaffenheit*), especially when this disregard was encountered in so many eminent academicians who dealt with the structure of empirical reality in an allegedly scientific way. Voegelin's early writings are permeated by the recognition that intellectual dishonesty is not accidental but is the very structure of reality of a social world he had to live in. He experienced it as the dominant "climate of opinion," first of all in academia, but also in politics more generally. For Voegelin, this discovery that scientists ignored or repressed empirical material in order to safeguard their own intellectual position is intertwined with his experience that scientific incompetence in dealing with the major political and social forces of his time transformed the principle of reality-mongering into the basis of political action, which led to the spiritual, and, ultimately, the physical destruction of human beings. "The overt phenomenon of intellectual dishonesty . . . caused my opposition to any ideologies, Marxist, Fascist, National Socialist, what you will, because they were incompatible with science in the rational sense of critical analysis."[16] At that time (1925), rational science in the sense of critical analysis meant, for Voegelin, thinking through the Weberian paradigm, the concepts and judgments of which permitted one

---

14. Max Weber, "Die Objektivität der Erkenntnis," *Soziologie—Weltgeschichtliche Analysen-Politik*, ed. Johannes Winckelmann (Stuttgart: Alfred Kröner Verlag, 1968), p. 260.

15. Ibid., p. 261.

16. Voegelin, "Autobiographical Memoir," pp. 45–46. Transcription of taped interviews done by Ellis Sandoz in 1973. Quoted by permission. Copyright by Ellis Sandoz.

to "order the empirical reality analytically in a valid way," [17] i.e., in the light of "ultimate value-ideas" that elucidate a continuously changing and finite section of the chaotic stream of events moving through time, these "ultimate value-ideas" themselves evading empirical proof of their validity. To the 24-year-old Voegelin, the question that confronts the observer of Weber's encyclopedic *oeuvre* is this: What is the purpose of Weber's huge accumulation of material? "Max Weber has asked himself this question and he has answered it in terms of his metaphysics of history." [18] According to Voegelin, the "nucleus of Max Weber's philosophy of history" is the idea that the historical relevance of our culture consists in its "rationalism," negatively determined by "disenchantment" and "daily life" and positively understood in terms of experimental science and responsibility. [19]

There is no need to follow in detail Voegelin's elaborate explication of Weberian rationalism; a brief presentation of his findings will suffice. [20] He points out that only by grasping the values inherent in all the layers partaking in the construction of Weber's science—the European cultural community characterized as rational, the national community, and the personal demon—is one able to understand the nature of this encyclopedic history. The rationalism of European culture implies an evaluative orientation toward life, an orientation that cannot be proven to be objectively valid but appears in history as fact nonetheless. Within the scope of this European rationalism, the different national communities brought forth specific types of rational science, value-free science being typical for Germany, just as pragmatism is typical for English and American social science. The scientific activity of Weber, however, is a concrete action that has already opted for one specific type of rational science. To put it another way, the content of Weber's philosophy of history, the emergence of rationalism, is not only the content but also the form in which Weber's science materializes. It is the form of the German type of European rationalism: value-free science. Whether value-free or pragmatic, any rational science is bound up with a superior sphere of values which is specific with regard to the historical sciences: the selection of viewpoints guiding the order of historical material is an act of evaluation, and this methodological presupposition sets a limit to the *Wertfreiheit*. Weber assumes that the historian knows how to refer the events of reality to universal cultural values and, accordingly, how to point out the historical context that is relevant *for us*.

The criterion "for us" completely eliminates the possibility that these value ideas can be determined objectively; the value-ideas become the carrier of the *personal* element of any cultural scientific research. Without them there could

---

17. Weber, "Die Objektivität der Erkenntnis," p. 260.
18. Voegelin, "Über Max Weber," *Deutsche Vierteljahresschrift für Literaturwissenschaft und Geistesgeschichte* 3 (1925): 178.
19. Ibid., p. 188.   20. Ibid., pp. 180–93.

be no principles for selecting material. Weber's value-ideas—basically the ideas of Rationalism—first, impose a meaningful logical structure upon the historical material; and, second, they infuse into the objective interpretation this particular personal element of value-reference insofar as the value-ideas articulate the mode of the historical events mirrored in the mind of the scholar. On the one hand, the content and form of history are mutually interdependent; on the other hand, the content of this history—the development of culture toward rationalism—provides the perspective to understand the determinative reasons for choosing the science of history for a profession. The value-ideas form the history, and history in turn tells us why we form history the way we have formed it. The crucial point, however, is that—in truth—this is not told for *us*, but told for Max Weber: it is not *the* history but *his* history telling why *he* decided to become a scholar. Beyond its logical structure Weber's encyclopedic science is defined by the nexus between personality and subject matter: the historical material is the grand basis for the superstructure of his metaphysics of history, consisting of a speculative attempt to understand himself as well as his times.

Voegelin penetrates the existential core of Weber's science of society and history, this core being the desire to comprehend one's own existence and at the same time to legitimate it. At the roots of the objective rational structure of the historical world we find, as the source of the meaningfulness bestowed upon the historical world, the demon holding man's fibers of life. In the discourse with his demon Weber constructed his history so that he himself, passionately and in resignation, with his rationalism and with his demon of ultimate decision, attains a comprehensible position which exemplifies that the ultimate meaning of life does not consist in finding this meaning but in continuously creating it.

II

In this early analysis of Weber's science we see the central idea of Voegelin's later writings emerge: the scientific presentation of sociocultural phenomena of necessity involves an interpretation of history. However, in the course of his studies, which aimed at a broad empirical range of comparative civilizational knowledge, Voegelin parted company with the Weberian approach. The concepts "ordering empirical reality analytically in a valid way" do not, in the light of the dominant value-ideas of the age and at the discretion of the personal demon, explicate the full meaning of the historical-cultural world. To the contrary, any empirical reality unfolds its own meaning as a historical form of spirit, a form to be apprehended by the scholar on its own terms. The interpretation must go along with the meaning inherent in the material; it must abstain from adhering to transcendental value-systems. Weber's concepts, Voegelin argues, are derived from a metaphysics of rationalism which seeks to master and order reality rather than observe it with loving *skepsis*.[21] The presence of spirit is the ordering principle of historical material. Social bodies are the embodiment of spiritual forms constrained by finite properties. The analysis of those objectivations of the spirit, i.e., the field of study, drives at the meaningful center from which the structural order of the specific features of the spiritual form emanate.

In this respect relevant phenomena are "self-expressive" (*selbstsprechende Erscheinungen*), as Voegelin tells us in his first book, *On the Form of the American Spirit*, in 1928. The unifying structure of complexes of self-expressive phenomena materializes in the self-reflection (*Selbstbesinnung*) of the philosopher because the subject and the object share the medium of the process of cognition.[22] The concepts of theoretical language rationally order a field to make it intelligible by letting the phenomena speak for themselves in order to discover and evoke the underlying experiences of the spirit that shape the historical world. "These are still the principles of Voegelinian method," Gregor Sebba states,

> The restriction of the "material" to what is theoretically relevant, letting the interpretation emerge from it; the principle that the selection of the material must follow the selection which history itself has made: "*the historical line of meaning runs like a rope across an abyss into which everything plunges that cannot stay on the rope.*"

Rightly Sebba quotes Voegelin's statement "as a first intimation of the way 'meaning' in history was to become a growth center of his thought."[23] We touch here on the origins of the Voegelinian philosophy of history: history is a complex fabric of open-ended lines of meaning; meaning unfolds, grows, and dies off; we do not know where a particular line of meaning will lead us.

If, however, the meaningful structure of empirical reality evolves from a common historical world of spiritual experience of human beings, the experience of the personal spirituality of man has to become constitutive for any understanding of the historical modes of human self-interpretation. The roots of all political and social order are traced to the experience of persons in community. The historical varieties of interpretations of order represent the whole range of sociohistorical objectivations of the human spirit. They differ in structure and in respect to the embodiment of the empirical components of the whole constitution of human being, comprising inorganic, vegetative, animal, and spiritual being, the *differentia specifica* of humanity. Man, being an epitome of the constitution of being, realizes himself in the historical objectivations of the spirit.

The personal spirit of man is the ordering center of human existence: it is

21. Voegelin, *Über die Form des amerikanischen Geistes* (Tübingen: J.C.B. Mohr Verlag, 1928), p. 14.
22. Ibid., p. 5.   23. See the essay by Sebba, this volume, p. 9.

the center of action as well as the point of irruption for spiritual reality beyond the person. The ordering center of man's personal spirit reveals the ontological structure of human existence, the idea of the *menschliche Gesamt-
wesen*: the human being as a whole is the substratum of the varying historical
objectifications of the spirit. In the course of his analysis of the historical roots
of the contemporary world of ideas in *Rasse und Staat* (1933), Voegelin con-
ceives of the historical line of meaning as the meaningful pattern of the "historical unfolding of mankind."[24] The empirical phenomena of human existence in society and history are "self-evocative" because the philosopher shares
with other men the spiritual experience of the unity of the whole of human
being that is the ordering principle of the plurality of fundamental experiences of the spheres of being. The phenomena are self-evocative because the
nature of man is at the root of all social reality, and the theory of the essence of
man (*Wesenslehre vom Menschen*), or philosophical anthropology, is the appropriate scientific instrument for deciphering the meaning of cultural phenomena.[25] It is, at the same time, the critical standard of empirical science
with which to safeguard oneself against the deforming and eclipsing of reality
in the name of value-ideas common in the world of science as well as in the
world of political action.

Voegelin's work of reclaiming reality from its contemporary deformation
was, in my opinion, touched off by the experience of American empiricism,
and was strongly influenced by and carried on under the intellectual guidance of Max Scheler. The motivating force was a search for truth in the area
of cognition, a search that would fulfill the conventionally accepted standards
of empirical science. But, being a scientist in the fullest sense, Voegelin's cognitive search for truth forced upon him the problem of the existential dimension of truth. The existential habit of cognitive openness toward all the facets
of reality, attentive to the whole range of experience, develops an appercep-
tive dynamic of its own by illuminating domains of reality previously hidden.
In Voegelin's writings of the late '20s and early '30s, we find him groping for
an intellectual apparatus that would represent the structure of social reality in
full and disentangle the language symbols of analysis from those of the deformed language of the day. This reminds us that the experiential emergence
of reality in the mind is bound up with the conscious creation of an adequate
symbolism.

III

These different lines of reasoning meet in Voegelin's first major attempt to
come to grips with the dominant social and intellectual forces of the contemporary world—foremost among them National Socialism— in *Die politischen*

24. Voegelin, *Rasse und Staat* (Tübingen: J. C. B. Mohr Verlag, 1933), p. 125.
25. Ibid., pp. 18–35, 121, 125.

Religionen (1938). National Socialism is, in his words, to be recognized as not merely a political and moral phenomenon, as most of its conventional opponents think. The essence of it is to be found in its spiritual and religious roots. This radical view takes into account the whole reality of a cultural phenomenon; i.e., it includes the religious dimension. "The religious view of National Socialism must be permitted to proceed from the assumption that there is evil in the world" and that the evil is "an authentic substance and force operating in the world."[26] The strange wording here tells us something about the difficulties of symbolizing experiences appropriately. "The religious question is a taboo for secularized minds."[27] The politicastering intellectuals scruple to raise the question seriously and radically so as to penetrate into the core of National Socialism, but only so could one establish the true meaning of this historical phenomenon.

In the light of philosophical anthropology, the meaningful pattern of the historical unfolding of mankind is bound up with the dynamics of order and disorder of human life in society. Again the cognitive and the existential side of the problem are brought together in the analysis. The empiricist cannot reduce human life in political community to the profane sphere of law and power. The community is also a sphere of religious order, and the cognition of a political phenomenon is in a salient point incomplete if it neglects the religious forces of the community and their respective symbols. Political community draws upon all features of human being from the physical to the spiritual and religious ones. Hence, the political community is always a dimension of the comprehensive human experience of the world and the divine.[28] Religious experience, however, is any search for the utmost reality, the *realissimum*, that then becomes the sacred center of order. Every being within the order of being can be asserted to be the *realissimum*, the crystalizing nucleus for political community. "But it is not irrelevant how the realm of human-political organization is incorporated into the order of being." Experiencing a world-immanent collectivity like the state, the race, the people, or the class as the *realissimum* involves the deformation of the structure of reality: "In the sense of an undogmatic *vita contemplativa*, the vision of being in the richness of gradation from nature to God, the world-immanent religiousness and its symbolisms conceal the most essential parts of reality."[29] Voegelin's cognitive judgment is rooted in the existential experience of the philosopher who was on the point of reaching out for the Hellenic and Christian experience by means of Scheler's philosophical anthropology. Scheler's *Realontologie* provided the theoretical instruments for the attempt to rebuild a critical science of politics and history out of the historical situation of the age, taking into account the full amplitude of our empirical knowledge. Here the crisis of the

---

26. Voegelin, *Die politischen Religionen* (Stockholm: Bermann-Fischer Verlag, 1939), p. 8.
27. Ibid., p. 9.   28. Ibid., pp. 63–64.
29. Ibid., pp. 64–65.

Western world is understood in terms of the loss of reality, and this loss of reality extends from the dominant science of cultural phenomena based on neo-Kantianism and Positivism into the social reality of the ideological mass movements. Voegelin's critical analysis of the crisis discloses a meaningful pattern of the course of historical events.

> [T]he ideological systems themselves become historical phenomena in a process which reflects . . . the human tension between order and disorder of existence. There are periods of order followed by periods of disintegration, followed by the misconstruction of reality by disoriented human beings.[30]

Pursuing the themes of *Die politischen Religionen*, Voegelin started to theorize about the manifold symbols "by which political societies interpret themselves as representatives of a transcendent truth," as belonging to the "intelligible succession of phases in a historical process."[31] At first this was done by revising the conventional history of political ideas or political theory. By *history*, Voegelin understood "the unfolding of a pattern of meaning in time,"[32] and on this principle he intended the history of theory to be harmonized with political history. And, as he stated in the same essay, Voegelin also accepted in principle the revised pattern of general history developed in Toynbee's *A Study of History*. This pattern breaks with linear historical process, which has mankind move in continuity through the ancient, medieval, and modern phases, insofar as it incorporates the Near Eastern preclassic civilizations and the Hellenistic period and addresses the problem of parallel histories. The other revision of the history of political theory concerned the content. In this revision Voegelin's argument draws on the results of the earlier analysis of the historical objectivations of the human spirit: the adaptation of the history of political theory to the process of politics requires the break "with the widely accepted conception of political theory as a theory concerned with the explanation of governmental authority."[33] An elaborated theory of ideas would have to include "the so-called nonpolitical ideas" usually classified as religious.[34] This project of a history of political ideas was at the time still grounded in the Greek and Christian ontological conception of man's partaking in the comprehensive order of being and was mainly concerned with the unfolding of meaning within the civilizational process of the Western world, from its beginnings in the Near East to modernity.

We have already touched on Voegelin's change of mind in his "Last Orientation," which made him turn from the attempt at harmonizing the history of

30. Voegelin, "Autobiographical Memoir," p. 106.
31. Voegelin, *The New Science of Politics*, p. 1.
32. Voegelin, "Political Theory and the Pattern of General History," *The American Political Science Review* 38 (1944):748.
33. Ibid., p. 752.   34. Ibid., p. 753.

political theory with political history itself, to a philosophy of history which was to explicate the intelligible structure of history in terms of "a reality to be discerned retrospectively in a flow of events that extends, through the present of the observer, indefinitely into the future."[35] In order to understand properly the extent and claim of this philosophy of history, we have to analyze the complex of engendering experiences. First, we have to note that the earlier motifs and themes of Voegelin's work are still present: the state of science in the various disciplines demands a conception of man, society, and history congruent with "the reality that is within the range of our empirical knowledge."[36] The study itself should not be read "as an attempt to explore curiosities of a dead past, but as an inquiry into the structure of the order in which we live presently," with the remedial effect of leading the reader out of the disorders of our time.[37] But, second, we have not explained yet why the open-ended line of historical meaning, i.e., the unfolding of mankind in terms of varying modes of human being, discloses an authoritative structure whose symbolic form is by necessity the Western symbolism of the philosophy of history. In his "Autobiographical Memoir" Voegelin states:

> I had to give up the "ideas" as objects of a history and to establish the experiences as the reality to be explored historically. These experiences, however, one could explore only by exploring their articulation through symbols. The identification of the subject-matter, and, with the subject-matter, of the method to be used in its exploration led to the principle that lies at the basis of all my later work: the reality of experience is self-interpretative.[38]

In studying Schelling, Voegelin became increasingly aware of the inadequacies of the general pattern of a history of political ideas based upon the ontology of the hierarchical order of being. We notice that the inquiry is, as always, guided by the self-evocative character of the phenomena that permit a valid ordering of empirical reality analytically. In the course of seeking the ordering principles, the order emerges from empirical reality in the mind of the searching philosopher. In light of this insight the scientific concepts heretofore used are recognized as the misconstruction of reality by disoriented men. Cognitive endeavor implies, at the point where the structure of reality emerges in the observer's consciousness, an advancement toward existential truth. The cognitive and the existential dimension of the inquiry merge in this process of emancipation from the language of deformed existence, and the *logos* of the meditative encounter of existence and being becomes the language of the critical science of the philosopher.[39]

35. Voegelin, *Order and History*, 1:ix.
36. Ibid., p. xiii.   37. Ibid., p. xiv.
38. Voegelin, "Autobiographical Memoir," p. 81.
39. Cf. Wolfgang Schadelwald, *Die Anfänge der Philosophie bei den Griechen* (Frankfurt: Suhrkamp Verlag, 1978), p. 122.

At the core of this encounter we find the personal act of recapturing the reality of knowledge, the existential recollection, Plato's *anamnesis*. Anamnesis raises the comprehensive knowledge of human-social existence, attuned to the order of the cosmos and history, from unconsciousness into the presence of consciousness. Voegelin's philosophy claims to be a paradigmatic reenactment of the Platonic anamnesis within the horizon of the present age. But it is to Schelling that Voegelin owes the insight into the anamnestic constitution of knowledge of the soul—determining history as the science of the soul. Referring to the *Weltalter*, Voegelin summarizes Schelling's idea of history as "the immersion of the materials into the meaning that is welling up from the unconscious of the soul of the historian."[40] The source of "meaning" is now clearly circumscribed as the anamnestic dialogue that is going on in the soul. This anamnesis is neither completed nor will it be completed soon, and we do not know, therefore, the meaning of history as a whole; the future is still open. . . . The "dialectic" of this dialogue of the soul is "a striving for consciousness through anamnesis (*Wiederbewußtwerden*)."[41] "The truth of speculation is neither 'given' in vision nor does it result, as it were, 'automatically' from the dialectical movement of an idea; it is an elaborated, reflective truth that has to be verified permanently by recourse to the anamnestic dialogue."[42] The discovery of the anamnestic dialogue was, in my opinion, crucial to Voegelin's new attempt at the symbolic interpretation, in terms of a philosophy of history, of the historical unfolding of mankind. In the long run, however, not only the interpretative pattern of the historical process changed but also its original theoretical underpinnings, its metaphysics and ontology, were discarded in favor of a philosophy of consciousness and reality.

Voegelin's anamnesis moves in two ways: into the depth of reality experienced and symbolized by other human beings in the past; and, into the depth of his own life, making consciousness the unfolding of his own participation in reality. In his *Anamnesis* (1966) Voegelin published the documents of his own anamnestic dialogue. His personal anamnesis focused on the meditative quest for the experiences which formed man's consciousness. These meditative acts purport to illuminate the roots of philosophizing in the biography of the philosophizing consciousness. Twenty brief sketches, each giving an early decisive experience in childhood, are presented. "The phenomena described were definitely phenomena of consciousness because they described my consciousness of various areas of reality as a child." *Anamnesis* recollected the types of experience that constitute consciousness.

The experiences of participation in various areas of reality constitute the horizon of existence in the world. The stress lies on experiences of reality in the plural, being open to all of them and keeping them in balance. . . .

40. Voegelin, "Last Orientation," p. 216.
41. Ibid., p. 184.   42. Ibid., pp. 186–87.

To restore this openness to reality appeared to be the principal task of philosophy.[43]

This personal anamnesis happened, however, in the community of experience, in like-mindedness with concrete human beings of the past and the present. The order of the person as well as the order of the historical process emerges in the anamnestic act. The previously mentioned emancipation from the "demonic" historiography, that misuses historical materials for the purpose of making the historiographer the climax of all preceding history, must be supplanted by a "proper history of the spirit."[44] This was written in 1943 as a criticism of Husserl, but it holds true for many a "philosophy of history" of the 18th and 19th centuries as well. This history of the spirit is

to penetrate every historic spiritual position to the point at which it comes to rest in itself, i.e., where it is rooted in the experiences of transcendence of the respective thinker. Only if spiritual history is pursued for this methodical end can it accomplish its philosophical end, namely to understand the spirit in its historicity or (in other words) to understand the historical expression of the spirit as variations on the theme of experiences of transcendence. These variations succeed each other empirically and factually, not arbitrarily. They do not form an anarchic series. They let us discern lines of order, even though the order is somewhat more complicated than the metaphysicians of progress themselves desire. . . . A genuine historical reflection has . . . primarily to penetrate the historical-spiritual form of the other to the point of transcendence and to school and clarify one's own experience of transcendence in the course of the penetration. Understanding the historical form of the spirit is a catharsis, a purification in the mystical sense, for the personal end of illumination and the mystical union; objectively, this process carried on systematically upon extensive materials can lead to the elaboration of lines of order signifying the revelation of the spirit in history; thus objectively and finally, it is the way toward the creation of a philosophy of history.[45]

"The order of history emerges from the history of order" is the first sentence of the work that was intended to realize this program.[46]

IV

Our reconstruction of the formation of the Voegelinian philosophy of history has so far explored the complex of motivating experiences that engendered an interpretation of man in history and society. This interpretation was intended

43. Voegelin, "Autobiographical Memoir," pp. 71–72.
44. Voegelin, *Anamnesis* (Munich: Piper Verlag, 1966), p. 31.
45. Ibid., pp. 31–32.   46. Voegelin, *Order and History*, 1:ix.

to serve as an ordering principle in the contemporary situation of civilizational crisis and disintegration. However, at this point we shall not present the monumental implementation of the Voegelinian program in the four volumes of *Order and History*. We shall, rather, now put his inquiry into the context of modern thought, raise the methodological questions involved in the claim to the authoritative character of his enterprise, and, finally, consider the fundamental changes in the structure of his philosophy of history which result in the conception of an ongoing process of universal humanity whose meaning is expressed in an eschatology.

The collective singular *history* is a neologism of the 18th century. *The* history, history *per se*, history in general, denoting the whole sociopolitical fabric upon the globe over time, was unknown before the age of the French Revolution. The term became the central language symbol of the new modes of self-interpretation of Western civilization. Accordingly, the authoritative explication of the novel complex of experiences, newly symbolized as the philosophy of history, underwent formulation between 1750 and 1850.[47]

In the opening chapters of *From Enlightenment to Revolution*, Voegelin traced the genesis of the speculative systems of philosophy of history to the erosion of the spiritual substance of Christianity in the face of the dynamics of the Western civilizational process: "The bearers of Western civilization do not want to be a senseless appendix to the history of antiquity; they want to understand their civilizational existence as meaningful. . . . From the dissatisfaction of being engaged in a civilizational process without meaning there are engendered attempts, beginning with Voltaire, at a reconstruction of meaning through the evocation of a new 'sacred history,'" called the philosophy of history.[48] The Christian Church futilely opposed the civilizational process and thereby engendered "an increasing opposition among its bearers against the claim of the Church to be the institution that preserves authoritatively the Western spiritual tradition."[49] Part of the solution to this problem

> would have to be a new Christian philosophy of history and of mythical symbols that would make intelligible, firstly, the new dimension of meaning which has accrued to the historical existence of Christianity through the fact that the Church has survived two civilizations; and that would make intelligible, secondly, the myth as an objective language for the expression of a transcendental irruption. . . . Obviously it is a task that would require a new Thomas rather than a neo-Thomist.[50]

47. Cf. Reinhart Koselleck, "Die Herausbildung des modernen Geschichtsbegriffs," *Geschichtliche Grundbegriffe II*, ed. Otto Brunner et al. (Stuttgart: Ernst Klett Verlag, 1975), pp. 647–91.

48. Voegelin, *From Enlightenment to Revolution*, ed. John H. Hallowell (Durham, N.C.: Duke University Press, 1975), pp. 22–23.

49. Ibid., p. 21.   50. Ibid., p. 22.

Voegelin, however, has his doubts about the churches' capacity to open up themselves to the predogmatic reality of knowledge, since they have imprisoned themselves in their secondary ideologies of dogmatic traditions. It is the philosopher's empirical science of the order of man in history and society that has to undertake the quest for an adequate symbolic form of the modern age.

In spite of his radical critique of the great systems of philosophy of history from Voltaire to Hegel, Voegelin does not deny the adequacy of that symbolic form to express the consciousness of contemporary global society. The great systems construe the history of the human species as a closed world-immanent civilizational process charged with the meaning of progressive human self-redemption from the human condition. Consequently, the process of history is to culminate in the personal and social existence of the representative of the system. "[T]he philosopher of history must," Voegelin argues against the progressivist position,

> therefore, remain critically aware that the past and future of mankind is a horizon that surrounds every present, even though it becomes conscious only through the leap in being [as Voegelin calls the spiritual irruptions in history which bring about differentiating insight into the structure of reality]. Though we know, by virtue of our existence in historical form, that the truth about order differentiates in the course of history, we neither know why mankind has a past, nor do we know anything about its goal in the future. The millenniums in which the mystery of history has reached the level of consciousness have not diminished the distance from its eternity. The philosopher must beware of the fallacy of transforming the consciousness of an unfolding mystery into the gnosis of a progress in time.[51]

This fallacy destroys the ultimate mystery of human existence:

> [M]an . . . is an actor, playing a part in the drama of being and, through the brute fact of his existence, committed to play it without knowing what it is. . . . The role of existence must be played in uncertainty of its meaning, as an adventure of decision on the edge of freedom and necessity.[52]

The historical field of human self-actualization in the manifold modes of existence in historic form reflects the existential structure of the Platonic "In-Between" (*metaxy*) of human existence circumscribed by the tension between life and death, immortality and mortality, perfection and imperfection, time and timelessness, between order and disorder, truth and untruth, sense and senselessness of existence. Voegelin's philosophy of history presents neither an absolute truth nor dogmatic propositions about the meaning of *the* history. It sets forth rather the meaningful pattern of those constants of en-

---

51. Voegelin, *Order and History*, 2:5.   52. Ibid., 1:1.

gendering experiences of human beings which constitute whatever permanence there is in the history of mankind: man himself in search of his humanity and its order. The comparative study of the empirical material, "if it goes beyond registering the symbols as phenomena and penetrates to the constants of engendering experience, can be conducted only by means of symbols which in their turn are engendered by the constants that the comparative study is seeking. The study of symbols is a reflective inquiry concerning the search for the truth of existential order; it will become, if fully developed, what is conventionally called a philosophy of history."[53]

The ideological systems of history of the 18th and 19th centuries failed to embody the existential truth of man's participation in the comprehensive reality of god, man, society, history, and nature in a symbolic form which could serve mankind as a governing principle in its quest for sociopolitical order. This failure, however, and the advancement of the empirical sciences of man, induce the philosopher to engage in the ongoing work of creating the image of reality beyond the dogmatisms of deformed humanity. "Today we are at the beginning of great philosophical developments, through the development of a philosophy of history that can for the first time explore the phenomenal realm in its global breadth and its temporal depth."[54] Most commentators on Voegelin overlook the mutual interdependence of progressing empirical knowledge and experiential penetration of the material in his philosophical inquiry. Further, for all his critique of the contemporary climate of opinion, Voegelin does not give in to the cultural pessimism pervading the various conservativisms, nor is his critique of the age grounded in that mood of doom currently so fashionable. *Materialiter*, the philosophy of history as the appropriate mode of the self-interpretation of modern man, is legitimized by the "hard fact that philosophy of history has indeed arisen in the West and nowhere *but* in the West. . . . For a philosophy of history can arise only where mankind has become historical through existence in the present under God." Hellas, Israel, and Christianity are at the root of Western philosophy of history.

> While the phenomenal restriction of the historical horizon to the Near Eastern, Mediterranean, and Western societies must be abandoned in the face of increased historical knowledge, the Europocentrism of position and standards cannot be abandoned by the philosopher of history, because there is nothing he could put in its place. History is made wherever men live, but its philosophy is a Western symbolism.[55]

The problem of mankind and its history therefore does not come into view through an increase in the number of civilizations studied. Mankind is consti-

53. Voegelin, "Equivalences of Experience and Symbolisation of History," *Eternitá e Storia: I valori permanenti nel divinire storico* (Florence: Vallechi editore, 1970), pp. 215–16.
54. Voegelin, *Anamnesis*, p. 278.   55. Voegelin, *Order and History*, 2:22–23.

tuted as the subject of order in history in the "unfolding of an order that reveals mankind as something more than a species." In the advance from the truth of cosmic-divine order in the cosmological societies of the Near East to the differentiated experience of transcendent divine order in Hellas and Israel, the order of human existence in society acquires the consciousness of representative humanity—meaning that mankind has come into existence in historical form.[56]

Voegelin's philosophy of history reformulates Toynbee's conception in which the civilizational societies are held to be the intelligible fields of historical study. The intelligibility of the comparatively analyzed civilizational patterns of the historical process is, according to Voegelin, provided in the idea of the constancy of human nature, unfolding in the history of mankind from compact to differentiated order. "Such order as can be discerned in the process including digressions and regressions from the maximal levels of differentiation, would emerge, if the principal types of man's existence in society, as well as the corresponding symbolisms of order, were presented in their historical succession."[57] In the light of this understanding of the historical process, modern civilization, caught up in the dilemma of civilizational progress and spiritual regression due to a strictly innerworldly religiousness of self-redemption, has reached a crisis: under the impact of rapidly increasing empirical knowledge in all fields of science, the misconstructions of reality crumble; and man's ongoing search for his humanity and its order brings forth novel images of reality, which reflect more closely the differentiating experiences of the In-Between.

The dynamics of empirical research and the related theoretical reflection induced Voegelin to reformulate the problem of mankind's history in his more recent writings. The revisions stress more heavily the millennial continuity of the differentiated historical dimension of humanity and tie it more closely to the new modes of human self-interpretation of the empirical and philosophical sciences of today. The consciousness of representative humanity emerges in this analysis from a historical configuration called the Ecumenic Age. This historical configuration comprises the period from approximately the eighth century before Christ to the eighth century after Christ; and it is determined by the triadic unity of ecumenic empire, spiritual outbursts, and historiography. The concept of an epoch or "axis-time" in Jaspers' terms,

> marked by the great spiritual outbursts alone, is no longer tenable. Something "epochal" has occurred indeed; there is no reason why the adjective should be denied to the disintegration of the compact experience of the cosmos and the differentiation of the truth of existence [in Hellas and Israel as well as in China]. But the "epoch" involves, besides the spiritual outbursts,

56. Ibid., pp. 2–3.   57. Voegelin, *Order and History*, 4:1.

the ecumenic empires from the Atlantic to the Pacific and engenders the consciousness of history. . . ."[58]

From this critical period in the history of mankind, the Ecumenic Age, "there emerges a new type of ecumenic humanity, which, with all its complications of meaning, reaches as a millennial constant into the modern Western civilization."[59] The differentiating experiences of the Ecumenic Age brought forth the symbolic form of historiography, but the implications of the process of history could not yet unfold:

> It takes time, to be measured in centuries and millennia, to acquire the empirical knowledge that inevitably lies at the basis of an understanding of the historical process, and still more time to penetrate the accumulated materials analytically. . . . And today, . . . even though the ecumenic horizon has become global and the temporal horizon has expanded into unexpected depths, the empirical knowledge of the process is still so incomplete that every day brings surprises in the form of new archaeological discoveries, while the experiential penetration of the materials is badly lagging behind."[60]

The philosopher has to realize that he is still inconclusively grappling with the problems set by the differentiation of consciousness in the Ecumenic Age. But again the cognitive component of the inquiry, empirical knowledge, is bound up with the existential advance toward truth. The "events in history" are the "very process of differentiating consciousness that [constitute] history." Once human existence has become luminous for its historical dimension, then the empirical knowledge of the process has to be included in the philosopher's mode of response to the quest for truth in existence.[61]

V

At the core of the differentiated understanding of man's existential structure of the In-Between there is the empirical fact of man's quest of the mysterious ground of being. The realm of equivalent answers in time and space structures the field of historical orders and their symbolization. It is no longer possible (in light of modern knowledge) to align the empirical types of order in any time sequence, nor is there a single manifestation of truth in history. Rather, there is only "an open historical field of major and minor divine-human encounters, widely dispersed in time and space over the societies who together are mankind in history."[62] It is the emergence of the consciousness of representative humanity in the Ecumenic Age of the West which enables the

58. Ibid., p. 312.   59. Ibid., p. 58.
60. Ibid., pp. 330–31.   61. Ibid., p. 332.
62. Voegelin, "The Beginning and the Beyond," unpublished ms. (1975), p. 12.

philosopher to unravel this complex web of meaning within the historical field.

But the discovery of universal humanity in the Ecumenic Age implied more than Voegelin's original assumption that mankind emerged from the Judeo-Christian formation of the historical consciousness as the subject of history. It implied also the tension between the universality of meaning and the pragmatic limitations of the processes from which the consciousness of universal mankind emerged in a plurality of historical settings. "Were the societies not involved in the [Western] process—the non-Mediterranean Africa and Europe, the Far East, and the Americas—excluded from its universality?" How do we deal with the chronologically parallel second Ecumenic Age in China? "Are there several mankinds who go through the disintegration of cosmological consciousness, independent of one another? Obviously, the question of the subject of history, previously discussed within the context of the Western Ecumenic Age, now imposes itself on the level of a global mankind."[63] Under the impact of these lines of meaning the pluralistic historical field itself engendered by "the manifold of differentiating acts, occurring at various points in time and independently in concrete human beings and societies,"[64] constitutes the intelligibility of civilizational processes. Voegelin is forced to conclude, then, that universal mankind is not an existing entity but symbolizes the historical equivalence of the plural modes of man's participation in the *one* reality.

In the philosophy of history, the historical process is understood in terms of the spatio-temporal dimension of the In-Between of human existence drawn into the process of reality. The historical field, delineated by man's search for his humanity and its order, reflects the process of reality insofar as reality itself becomes luminous in the events of human experience and the corresponding imaginative symbolizations. At this point the cognitive and the existential moment of the *zetema* merge again. Wherever the process of reality becomes luminous, a line of meaning appears in history. In the search for existential truth, the philosopher is obliged to open himself to the whole of reality:

> The process cannot become luminous with meaning through a study of men who contract their humanity into a power-self and invent Second Realities for the purpose of obscuring the reality that has meaning. It will reveal its meaning only where men are open toward the mystery in which they participate by their existence and allow the reality of the process to become luminous in their consciousness.[65]

By following empirically the patterns of meaning as they reveal themselves in the self-interpretation of persons and societies in history, the philosopher re-

63. Voegelin, *Order and History*, 4:305.
64. Voegelin, "Autobiographical Memoir," p. 84.
65. Voegelin, *Order and History*, 4:184.

enacts the modes of questioning that constitute the historical field of mankind. This reenactment is the philosopher's response to man's desire to locate the truth of existence in history, and the philosophy of history is the symbolic form that results.

This symbolism explicates paradigmatically the universal humanity evolving from the breaking forth of comprehensive prepersonal reality into self-illuminating truth in pluralistic historical form. In this the philosopher acts as the representative of the whole of humanity, enabling modern man in search of his humanity and its order to discover the meaning of global civilizational process through his own participation in the mystery of the process of reality. This participation unveils neither an ultimate truth of existence nor a finite meaning of the process of universal humanity, but it brings forth a consciousness of the common humanity of mankind, grounded in the experience of the directional movement of reality, which reaches toward the beyond of any spatio-temporal dimension of human existence. This "movement that draws man into existential participation is a movement toward a more eminent degree of reality, not toward perdition; it is experienced as the *athanatizein* of the philosophers or the *aphtharsia* of Paul. The experience of reality . . . has a built-in bias toward more reality. . . ."[66]

In the last analysis universal humanity is an eschatological index. The nondoctrinal eschatology of Voegelin's philosophy of history involves the insight that ceremonial burial customs provide the first evidence for the dawn of self-consciousness in the developing hominids. And, as his philosophy of history also recognizes, self-consciousness is awakened through the philosopher's experience of immortalizing by way of living the life of the intellect. Appropriately, in its eschatological aspect Voegelin's philosophy of history does not formulate the *telos* of the historical process. Rather, it restores the *telos* of man in earthly existence: the search for his humanity and its order under the horizon of the global society of mankind.

66. Ibid., p. 271.

NOTES ON VOEGELIN'S CONTRIBUTIONS TO POLITICAL THEORY

William C. Havard, Jr.

I

From time to time one runs across or hears about a rank-ordered listing of outstanding American political scientists, usually consisting of about ten names. Rumor even has it that on one occasion two of the eminences who had been singled out for a distinction of this type were engaged in a dispute over some matter having to do with the state of the discipline, and one of them closed out the argument (without regard to the substance of the issue) by pointing out that his position should carry the day because he stood a place or two ahead of the other in the rankings. So far as I know Eric Voegelin's name has never appeared on such a list. Indeed, with some regularity he has been excluded by the implication or the outright assertion that he is not a political scientist at all.

The foregoing paragraph is not intended to be totally facetious. For a number of personal and professional reasons any adequate assessment of Voegelin as a political theorist, especially in present context, will also have to be—at least inferentially—an assessment or critique of the state of political science.

In the first place, Voegelin's professional self-identity has always been as a political scientist,[1] however puzzling this may seem to colleagues who, though not quite sure what political science is or what its practitioners should be doing, are sufficiently uncomfortable with Voegelin's language and conceptual concerns to want to label him as something else. But all of his teaching appointments have been in political science, and he has boldly affirmed the de-

A version of this essay first appeared in *Polity* 10 (1977):33–64, and is reprinted here, with some revisions, by permission.

1. In an unpublished "Autobiographical Memoir," taped by Ellis Sandoz, Voegelin explains his selection of a career in political science in preference to other possible choices as ". . . partly economic, partly . . . principle" (p. 3). Professor Sandoz has graciously permitted me to use the notes as "reinforcing" references in this paper. Relying on other sources, I have discussed some of the early influences on Professor Voegelin as a political scientist, as well as his "position" vis-à-vis neo-Kantian Positivism, in my essay, "The Changing Pattern of Voegelin's Conception of History and Consciousness," *Southern Review* n.s. 7 (1971):52.

pendence of any science on the existence of a collegial working relationship, for "science is not the singlehanded achievement of this or that individual scholar; it is a cooperative effort. Effective work is possible only within a tradition of intellectual culture."[2]

Despite the characteristics apparently identifying him as a member of the political science profession, Voegelin is rightly suspect in that role, not only by those who are somewhat uncertain about the possibility of a science of politics, but even more so by those who are positive that a science of politics based on the methods of the natural sciences is not only possible, but has been, or is about to be, achieved. For one thing, Voegelin persists in the use of a terminology that does not convey the immediate meaning that the orthodox political scientist ascribes to it. He talks for instance, about the "science" of man and society and its origins in the *episteme politike* of the classical philosophers, whereas they understand "science" in the reductionist sense which Voegelin identifies as a

> . . . scientistic creed . . . characterized by three principal dogmas: (1) the assumption that the mathematized science of natural phenomena is a model science to which all other sciences ought to conform; (2) that all realms of being are accessible to the methods of the sciences of phenomena; and (3) that all reality which is not accessible to sciences of phenomena is either irrelevant or, in the more radical form of the dogma, illusionary. The creed implies two great denials: it denies the dignity of science to the quest for substance in nature, in man and society, as well as in transcendental reality; and in the more radical form, it denies the reality of substance.[3]

Stranger still, Voegelin talks about the empirical basis of theory even when his references are to meanings in history, experiences of transcendence, symbolism, and such abstract "values" as order. Every "scientist," on the other hand, knows that scientists are supposed to do their work without resort to value-judgments, that values are subjective and are properly advanced as "preferences" which are outside the bounds of cognitive validation, and that science is based on "facts" apprehended by observation of external (objective) phenomena.[4]

It is a disturbing experience for those whose language symbols derive from the "climate of opinion" (which Voegelin frequently cites as Alfred North Whitehead's term) within contemporary culture to be confronted with a lan-

---

2. *The New Science of Politics* (Chicago: University of Chicago Press, 1952), p. 23.

3. "The Origins of Scientism," *Social Research* 15 (1948):462.

4. Voegelin often makes the distinction between a generic understanding of science as *episteme*, which is open to any question pertinent to human experience, and the appropriation of the term *science* by those who wish to consider as legitimate only those questions that can be responded to by the methods of the sciences of natural phenomena. Perhaps the earliest extended discussion in the strict context of the social sciences is in the Introduction to *The New Science of Politics*, esp. pp. 3–13.

guage that suggests they are operating from an epistemologically and methodologically closed "position," rather than from openness to the exploration of reality based on an abiding tradition of inquiry reaching at least to classical antiquity. It is not surprising, therefore, that most political scientists (and American ones, particularly) should react defensively in the face of this threat to the substantiality of their self-contained intellectual world. It is far easier to make dogmatic assertions about the meaning of science and to relegate Voegelin to the status of a "metaphysician," or "worse," than to come to grips with his work. During the roughly twenty years (ca. 1950–70) when the struggle within the discipline was between an aggressive behavioralist movement, solidly united under the Positivist creed, and an amalgam of groups (mostly rather passive and generally aphilosophical) commonly designated by behavioralists as "traditionalists," Voegelin tended to be assigned somewhat quizzically to the latter category by the behavioralists, although there is not much evidence of his having more than a *pro forma* acceptance by most of the diffuse elements of traditionalism. In their standard work on the profession, Somit and Tanenhaus have summed the matter up most appositely: "On the other side of the ideological fence, there was Eric Voegelin's impressive but less widely read *The New Science of Politics*." [5]

Voegelin's understanding of *theory* also tends to differentiate his activities as a political scientist from those who might be considered more representative of the state of the discipline in its current self-conception(s). In reading Voegelin it does not seem possible to me to abstract a firmly fixed concept of what theory is out of the totality of the inquiry in which he is engaged. He is wary of everything that approaches a definitional fixing of the experiences he examines. He uses the terms *theory*, theoretical, and *retheoretization* as familiar language symbols which connote neither a logically coherent explanation capable of being tested and used as a framework for directing experimental inquiry, nor a synthesized explanation of the results of empirical analysis, nor a union of these two cognitive functions to form a paradigm according to which a "science" might proceed. Even if theory has a guiding role with respect to science and is also, in a special sense, the sum of the state of affirmed knowledge at a given time, it is much more than this. Although the term is not altogether satisfactory, one might say that theory, for Voegelin, is more *process* than logical construct abstracted from the whole experiential activity

5. *The Development of Political Science: From Burgess to Behavioralism*, (Boston: Allyn and Bacon, Inc., 1967), p. 188. Although neither Voegelin nor the behavioralists would be likely to accept the designation of their work as "ideological," a good many of the more vigorous proponents of behavioralism have exhibited some of the behavioral characteristics of persons engaged in an ideological cause. Voegelin has had followers, to be sure, but he has continued his work (including some cogent discussions of the nature of ideology) without propagating doctrine by means of a claque organized as a "movement." Neither his mode of behavior nor his animadversions on ideology has prevented others from ascribing to him a wide range of ideological positions, and most of these ascriptions blatantly contradict one another.

that produced it. A scientist is involved with theoretical activity from the time he is confronted by the first stimulus to inquiry, through the framing of the questions he seeks to answer, into the selection of appropriate methods, and on to the framing of the symbols by which he interprets and communicates the experiences that both direct this process and are the objects of its investigation.

This implied union of subject and object, through which the theoretical process moves, however, pushes us beyond the limits of the present argument and into the more substantive problem which Voegelin delineates as man's awareness of being a participant in the embracing reality of which he is a part. For the moment it is sufficient to stipulate that the structure of reality is such that man's participation in it by way of the theoretical activity is never complete. Although the constant object of the search may be identified, knowledge is not accessible in final form to man as subject-participant because it lies outside the limits of man which result from his being part of the natural world as well as consubstantial with the divine ground of that world. The condition of man, then, is an essential source of his theoretical activity, as well as a limit on the results to be achieved by theory. Not only may the theoretical activity be misdirected, but because it takes place within the flux of history, its achievements may be misplaced or lost over time and have to be recovered by way of recollection and retheoretization, which involves recreating the experiences through which the theoretical attainments were realized rather than a mere recovery of the symbols by means of which they were expressed. Realization of the limit-end of the quest is as much a fact of the theoretical activity as any of the other logically analyzable, but practically inseparable, components of the whole of this activity.

Although the term *theory* has not been clearly or consistently delineated in the literature of American political science,[6] a cursory examination of the recent tendency to modify the noun (often with other noun-adjectives) provides some insights into the prevailing inclinations towards a scientific orthodoxy, an orthodoxy quite at odds with Voegelin's theoretical contribution. The separation of "empirical" theory from "normative" theory, for instance, further illustrates the point made earlier about the extent to which the dominant trend has been toward the acceptance of the natural sciences as the definitive model for the science of man and society and, beyond this, the extent to which method has come to displace theoretical relevance as the determinant of the choice of objects to be studied in the pursuit of a science of politics. I do not want to dwell too long on this subject, but it should be noted that the context in which "empirical theory" usually appears includes the assumption

6. For a reasonably succinct discussion of the confusing range of meaning ascribed to "political theory," see Neil A. McDonald and James N. Rosenau, "Political Theory as Academic Field of Intellectual Activity," *Journal of Politics* 30 (1968):311–44.

(more often implicit than explicit) that politics has an objectively ordered structure analogous to the order of nature which has been successfully penetrated by the mathematized natural sciences.

The further modification of "theory" into the stratified conceptions of "explanatory theory" (the lower order) and "causal theory" (the higher order) implies a progressive development, the culmination of which is a predictive science of politics. Although disappointment has been expressed about the slowness with which the massive enterprise that American political science has become in recent years is moving toward this perceived goal, little evidence can be adduced to show that the proponents have seriously addressed the question of what a definite knowledge of politics predicated on such foundations would imply. Would a technology of manipulative control over man and society emerge from the completion of such a theoretical pursuit? And would the results produce a utopia or a nightmare? Thus far, the failure of a science of politics modeled on the natural sciences to produce even an explanatory theory, let alone a causal one, has led (at least within the discipline) to little more than the suggestion that, in the period of waiting for the Godot of grand theory, the profession should concentrate on "middle-range" theory, apparently in the interest of insuring the continuation of the Positivist mode, as well as perpetuating the concern with problems that do not disturb the status of either the political "system" within which the theoretical activity takes place or the theory itself as it tries to cope with politics in the context of the full range of human experience.

From the appearance of *The New Science of Politics* (1952) Voegelin has been engaged in a theoretical effort at its highest level. That effort has involved two tightly interrelated activities. First, he has offered a devastating criticism of political science as it has virtually destroyed our grasp of political reality through the Positivist reduction. In the course of this criticism he has also demonstrated how Positivism opened the way for immanentist ideologies to replace a science of man and society based on ontology. Second, he has produced an increasingly complex and authoritative articulation of what is involved in the restoration of the theoretical content of a science of politics that explores the reality of politics from the perspective of the generality of human experience. In 1968 Gregor Sebba characterized Voegelin's participation in theoretical activity in these terms:

> The question: What is political science? is being answered anew out of a radical reconsideration of the question: What is political reality, and what cognitive avenues lead to its critical understanding?

Two factors have so far stood in the way of recognizing this extremely rapid development of new theory, quite apart from its newness. The first factor is that, in contrast to behavioral social science, it is not the result of many theoretical and technological research advances initiated by a number of social scientists and continued by a host of workers backed by enormous institutional support; it is the work of one independent thinker, Eric Voegelin, who published his first book four decades ago, launched his major enterprise a dozen years ago and is still forging ahead at a pace which leaves his best readers behind. . . .

The second factor is of course the enormous demand which the new development makes upon the newcomer to such studies. To gain an adequate understanding—not even a critical one—he must be able to follow some of the most abstract philosophical reasoning found today, he must have a thorough knowledge of the history of thought, philosophy, metaphysics, epistemology, religion and theology, of political theory, and of political history from the Sumerians to the present; he must know the present state of scholarship in fields like anthropology, biblical criticism, comparative literature, psychology—the list is by no means complete. All this is very far from the concerns of the practicing political scientist today.[7]

This summation provides more than a brief assessment of the extent of the separation between Voegelin's new science of politics and the new science of behavioralist politics which is still in the ascendency in the profession; it also suggests some of the difficulties of attempting even a simple exegesis of Voegelin's work, let alone trying to draw on his achievement to provide a sustaining core of theory around which an intellectual culture devoted to the *episteme politike* might be developed. Some of these problems of interpretation and potential extrapolation can be understood only in the light of the interplay between certain biographical events and the chronological development of topical concerns in Voegelin's work. Obviously an analysis of this type cannot be attempted here, but at least a cursory exposition of some of the features of his scholarship and writing may furnish a useful background against which the substance of his contribution to political theory may be made a little clearer.

II

The unity of Voegelin's work is not to be found in an emphasis on historical chronology, or in a particular object of study (whether it be a historical unit of social or political organization or an abstract concept in its historical manifestations), or in a focus on any one method for describing man's experience with politics. The most obvious feature of his *bios theoretikos* is the constancy of the search; the evocative pull of the literal *philosophia* is, one might say, the motive of his total dedication to scholarship, demonstrated both in his teach-

7. "The Present State of Political Theory," *Polity* 1 (1968):263–64.

ing and his voluminous and complex research. But this is a personal quality that does not necessarily produce theory of sufficient coherence to be designated a science. One can point to other scholars who worked tirelessly to produce reams of books and articles, some of which have become minor classics on special subjects, but whose cumulative results do not seem to be informed by any principles that would entitle these results to the name *science*.[8]

Throughout Voegelin's work, one can detect the persistence of the questions designed to establish theoretical relevance, the abiding nature of the general topics one must elucidate in the course of the inquiry, and the way in which methods emerge from and are applied to the problems thus identified. Because these constants do not always stand in the same relation to one another within the various parts of the work, and because the constants themselves are always being sharpened and extended in relation to their particular applications to the historical materials on which he works, Voegelin appears to some who have not read him carefully to range over an impossibly large source material which he interprets almost capriciously on the basis of abstract conceptions having little concrete meaning. On the contrary, the work is cumulative in a dual sense: each new subject addressed expands the scope of the empirical inquiry (usually in terms both of historical extension and the variety of symbolic forms examined) and simultaneously displays a refinement of the larger theoretical context within which the particular problem is set. Critical analysis is thus guided by the state of theory previously developed, even while the expanded range of criticism is extending, sharpening, and reinforcing the general theory on which a science of politics is predicated. As Dante Germino has noted: "To Voegelin political science and political theory are inseparately bound together."[9]

The point can be illustrated by a brief overview of the order in which the work has unfolded. In this context it is worth noting that the internal patterns of Voegelin's theoretical development closely parallel some of the preconditions and subsequent developments in his general interpretation of the way in which a science of order has emerged under various historical circum-

8. Walter Lippmann affords an example which is almost too easy and not, as some of academic political scientists would have it, because he was just a "journalist" (although the pressure of keeping abreast of, and writing about, public affairs on a day-to-day basis may have played a part in limiting his potential as a political theorist). Even when, by reason of his obvious analytical craftsmanship, Lippmann's books attracted the attention of serious students of international politics, public opinion, and political philosophy, he never reached the point of breaking through to the unifying reality behind his insights into particular problems. Not only did he move through several varieties of ideology (most of them within the general framework of liberalism) without going much beyond the treatment of each set of problems as sequential correctives of each other, even when his critical faculties were at their best, but he perceived that fundamental gaps existed in "the public philosophy"; he saw rather more the results of the deficiencies than what kind of theoretical inquiry would be needed to understand and correct them.

9. *Beyond Ideology: The Revival of Political Theory* (New York: Harper and Row, 1967), p. 163.

stances. In *The New Science of Politics*, where he first explains at some length the nature of his general quest, he points out that the expansion of political science to its full grandeur ". . . as the science of human existence in society and history, as well as the principles of order in general, has been typical for the great epochs of a revolutionary and critical nature."[10] At that point he identifies three great epochal crises in Western history, each marked by the production of a major theoretical development: the foundation of political science by Plato and Aristotle in the Hellenic crisis, St. Augustine's *Civitas Dei* in the crisis of Rome and Christianity, and Hegel's philosophy of law and history in ". . . the first major earthquake of the Western crisis."[11] In between, minor epochs occurred and secondary restorations took place, e.g., Bodin in the sixteenth century.

This conception of the stimulus to a theoretical science of order in man and society, or the restoration of the principles of such a science, out of a crisis in the existential order of man and society is a constant, but its application, so to speak, changes in the context of the unfolding analysis of a larger and larger field of empirical historical materials. Among other examples that might be cited, two seem to me to stand out. In his later treatment of Hegel,[12] Voegelin had moved so far away from the epochal theme (which implies historical regularity in the responsive relation of science to crisis) and had developed his own critical theory to such an extent (through further studies of pre-Socratic philosophy, Gnosticism, and the seventeenth century Neoplatonists, among others) that he was able to discern in Hegel's response to the crisis of Western modernity, as manifested in the French Revolution, a perversion of the ordering symbols of philosophy in the form of an egophanic revolt against reality, which was less a restoration of a science of order than a symptom of how deep the Western crisis of order had become. On the other hand, the conception is given new content and vigor when Voegelin applies it in his remarkably compact analysis of the classical experience of reason. Voegelin does not deal with ". . . the 'idea' or a nominalist 'definition' of reason but with the process in reality in which concrete human beings, the 'lovers of wisdom,' the philosophers as they styled themselves, were engaged in an act of resistance against the personal and social disorder of their age."[13] Here we see the concept in application in a fuller dimension than ever, following the intervening work on the *polis*, Plato, and Aristotle, and the elaboration of a philosophy of consciousness in *Anamnesis*. The originating influence of personal and societal disorder is closely related to the penetration through the symbols to the experience of reason as the substance and source of understanding of reality, and

10. Voegelin, *The New Science of Politics*, p. 2.
11. Ibid.
12. "On Hegel—A Study in Sorcery," *Studium Generale* 24 (1971):335–68.
13. Voegelin, "Reason: The Classic Experience," *Southern Review* n.s. 10, (1974):237.

the starting point for the philosophers' discovery of reason is boldly interpreted as their revolt against the disorder of their age.

Voegelin's awareness of these disorders, as they manifested themselves in
the ideologies of the twentieth century and the wars and revolutions into
which mass movements based on these ideologies debouched, was also the
point of departure for his search for a science that might explain not only how
such disorder came about, but also what sources one might draw on for a
restoration of order. As a student in Vienna in the early 1920s he was apparently fairly well adjusted to the "climate of opinion" of the time and place. For
a time the neo-Kantian Positivist circle influenced him, especially since he
was an assistant to Professor Hans Kelsen. But other experiences, too complex to go into here, pushed him in new directions which led eventually to
the study of order and history. The process was in close keeping with his
suggestion that political science starts from an assessment of the concrete political events in the immediate range of one's experience. The value neutrality
of the pure science of law (and of Max Weber) was no defense against the
insurgency of ideologies, so Voegelin increasingly became interested in political ideas as manifestations of ideology.

The books and monographs of the 1930s—on the race idea, the authoritarian state and political religions—were part of the effort to come to grips
with these problems. His subsequent assessment of these works follows his
pattern of retrospection at any given time on almost any of his earlier work:
they were all right as special studies, but were not sufficiently well-informed
by some theoretical principle or principles that later work revealed to be more
than tentative. The study of the authoritarian state, for example, which was
his first attempt to penetrate the role of contemporary ideologies, right and
left, was written before Voegelin had fully analyzed the distortion of language
characteristic of ideologies. The term "authoritarian" itself is too closely related to ideological ways of characterizing regimes to serve as an adequate
theoretical category for examining the effort of a state to assert its authority
against ideological movements bent on imposing themselves by using constitutional arrangements which they then destroy. Similarly, the study of political religions relied on a literature that treated ideologies as a secular variety of
religions, a usage that tended to distort the experiences by mixing them up
with problems of dogma and doctrine and by lumping together a number of
phenomena that should have been differentiated more fully for comparative
purposes.[14]

The interplay of the rising interest in the history of political ideas, the

14. "Autobiographical Memoir," pp. 41, 50–55. A slightly more extended discussion of the
relation of *The Authoritarian State* (1936) to both the 1921 Austrian Constitution (Kelsen was
the principal draftsman) and the Dollfuss corporative constitution of 1934 is to be found in my
"The Changing Pattern of Voegelin's Conception of History and Consciousness," pp. 56–57.

broadening of contacts with the intellectual world beyond Vienna (especially the time spent in the United States, England, and France under a Laura Spelman Rockefeller grant in the 1920s), and the course of political events in Austria in the early 1930s led Voegelin into the study of Christianity and classical antiquity. Shortly after his move to America in 1938 he started to work on a history of Western political ideas; at first the project was conceived as a textbook, but the scope of the materials soon outran that objective. The history was written in large part by the late 1940s, and it covered the typical period from the Hellenic origins until well into the nineteenth century. The theoretical focus that emerged in this work was the concentration on Christianity and classical philosophy as the experiential substance out of which Western civilization emerged, and which constituted the sources of order for Western man and society. The critical standards against which the ideas of major figures in Western thought were examined were supplied by Voegelin's exegesis of Plato and Aristotle and the major sources through which the Christian experience was interpreted. In his later work he was to differentiate more fully the symbols and concepts of Christianity and classical philosophy, yet the understanding that emerged in this later work was already present in compact form in the earlier "History of Political Ideas."

By the late 1940s Voegelin was uncertain about the future course of the history. He felt compelled to push his inquiries far beyond the boundaries set by the product as originally conceived, now altered from a textbook to a multivolume interpretation of the patterns in the history of Western civilization, patterns revealed by an examination of political ideas. The studies of both Christianity and the classics required further consideration of the deeper historical background of their origins, so the Hebraic studies and the exploration of the historical sources on the Ancient Near Eastern empires were begun. In the course of the work on Schelling, Voegelin also began to question the conception of a history of ideas as a means of elucidating political reality. He began to see the necessity for getting beyond "ideas" to the symbols through which societies expressed their meanings for existence in history, and then to penetrate the symbolizations in order to understand the experiences of reality that the symbols express. The problems of the relations of ideas to symbols and of symbols to experience is an extremely difficult one which cannot be discussed in detail here. For the moment it is sufficient to leave it that the perception of this problem, together with the expansion of the historical perspective to other civilizations, led to the abandonment of the history of political ideas as a method of grasping political reality.[15]

15. Although materials developed from the history have been worked into *The New Science of Politics; Wissenschaft, Politik, und Gnosis* (Munich: Koesel-Verlag, 1959); *Anamnesis: Zur Theorie der Geschichte und Politik* (Munich: R. Piper & Co., Verlag, 1966); and *Order and History*, 4 vols. to date (Baton Rouge: Louisiana State University Press, 1956–), Voegelin refused separate publication of the history of Western ideas, in whole or in part, until the appearance of

The invitation to give the Walgreen Lectures in Chicago in 1951 offered the opportunity to formulate some of the theoretical principles emerging from these historical studies that had caused him to place the history of ideas in abeyance. The lectures were published, of course, as *The New Science of Politics*, and the book is in many respects an attenuated version of the theory that has been unfolded in the subsequent twenty-five years. Having gone far beyond the origins of his search in the disorders of his own time, Voegelin was now expressing in cryptic form the ways in which Western society had symbolized its existence in history, how those symbols had differentiated over time, and how the symbols that most closely approximated reality had been deformed to the point of producing the present crisis of order. The major conceptions are all here in early stages of elucidation. Included (among a host of lesser themes) are the forms of representational symbols embodied in the cosmological myths of the earliest civilizations, the representational symbolization of transcendence through Greek philosophy, revelation in Israel, and the soteriological truth of Christianity. All of these subjects were to be explored in detail and under more completely worked out theoretical principles in *Order and History*.

Perhaps of most importance in *The New Science of Politics* was the examination of Gnosticism as the particular source of explanation for the conversion of the Christian symbols of transcendent reality into immanentist interpretations which are distortions of reality and sources of disorder. Voegelin discusses the way in which Gnosticism developed during the course of the struggles attending the decline of the ancient world and the emergence of the new multiethnic ecumenic empires, with Christianity emerging as dominant in the West. In view of Christianity's symbolization of existence as divided between the eternal, transcendent realm of God and the finite, mundane realm of man, with salvation for man possible only beyond the world, the Gnostic vision of the world as a place of total chaos which would itself be transformed into a world of perfected, durable order by divine or human in-

<hr>

From Enlightenment to Revolution, ed. John H. Hallowell (Durham, N.C.: Duke University Press, 1975), which selectively covers the period from Voltaire through Marx. I think that Professor Voegelin underestimates the importance of the history, not only as a major factor in leading him into more penetrating methods of theoretical inquiry, but also as a source for understanding his theories of man and society and his philosophy of history. The theories are embedded in the historical criticism: even if "ideas" are twice removed from experiences of reality, the language through which they are expressed is a symbolic form which Voegelin analyzes with great skill to demonstrate the distortion of reality or (in some instances) the effectiveness of the symbolization of reality embedded in the expressions of ideas. In the "Autobiographical Memoir," he indicates the variations in points of time at which various influences made their initial, if still unformed, impacts on his thinking; many of the fully developed theories are thus discernible in their incipient (and sometimes more than incipient) stages in the history, which itself has undergone many revisions. Elsewhere I have argued that the best approach to Voegelin by the neophyte is through *From Enlightenment to Revolution*. See my essay, "Voegelin's Diagnosis of the Western Crisis," *Denver Quarterly* 10 (1975):esp. 133–34.

tervention was, of course, in its manifestation within Christianity, heretical. As Voegelin indicates, Gnosticism persists in various forms through the entire course of the Western Christian era, but was generally contained until the erosion of meaning behind the Christian symbols permitted Gnostic symbols of reality to take over the representational function among the nation states of the Western world. The result is a steady acceleration in the intensity of the revolt against God and man in the attempt to realize one or another of the Gnostic dream worlds that have become the new versions of reality. The path has been from progressivism through utopianism to totalitarianism.

A problem of interpretation arises here that again illustrates the difficulty of entering into a serious discussion of Voegelin's theory with the general run of political scientists. Even some of his closest readers have had difficulty perceiving in the application of the concept "Gnosticism" to the analysis of the political disorders of modernity anything more than a useful analogical tool (and an exceptionally loose one at that) for characterizing and categorizing historical events.[16] It is difficult enough to comprehend that the Christian (and classical philosophical) symbolizations of reality have been sufficiently evocative of the experiences of reality to be able to touch the consciousness of so large a segment of mankind as to form the basis of reality for a civilizational order persisting through two millennia. But the notion that this entire history was acted upon by a persisting doctrinal conversion of those symbols (including especially the trinitarian symbols of sacred history and eschatological expectation, both of which were immanentized), and that these deformations of reality evoked mass movements that constantly threatened and eventually broke through the whole structure of society, has not been easy to assimilate, even for those not already living within the representational interpretation of one of the "second" realities. For the latter, Voegelin is apparently a sort of intellectual anachronism who is trying to apply the outmoded internecine arguments of the Christian Middle Ages to a modern secular ("scientific") world in which they have no place.[17]

In a manner that should now be familiar to all who have followed his intel-

16. In his essay, "Order and History: The Breaking of the Program," *Denver Quarterly* 10 (1975):122, John Corrington says that Professor Altizer once observed to him that "Professor Voegelin finds everything to be Gnostic." Corrington thought at the time that the remark was defensive (in light of Voegelin's comments on "death of God" philosophy and theology), but he admits that he sees some substance in it after having read *The Ecumenic Age*. The problems, in other words, tend to enlarge as Voegelin moves from historical studies toward the elucidation of "pure" theory.

17. In a review article, "The Science of Politics: New and Old," *World Politics* 7 (1955):486, Robert Dahl complains that "Voegelin reifies endlessly . . ." and says that he will follow suit. The statement was made as a criticism of Voegelin's reference to the fact that pre-Christian societies symbolized themselves as representatives of transcendent truth (an antecedent of the later analysis of the cosmological myth as a "compact" symbol of the undifferentiated conception of the quadripartite structure of man and society, God and the universe). The point is that Voegelin was not reifying anything; every society exists as part of reality by reason of its symbolic interpretation of what it is, and everybody who deems himself as member of that society participates

lectual odyssey, Voegelin chose the occasion of his inaugural lecture at the University of Munich (1958) to elaborate the meaning of Gnosticism in its recent context and to illustrate by an analysis of some major German thinkers (Hegel, Marx, Nietzsche, and Heidegger) how their Gnostic speculations differ from a philosophy of politics.[18] In the introduction Voegelin carefully explains that Gnosticism was not an arcane Christian heresy which he had chosen for analytical convenience. He points out that "the idea that one of the main currents of European, especially of German, thought is essentially Gnostic sounds strange today, but this is not a recent discovery. Until about a hundred years ago the facts of the matter were well known."[19] He goes on to cite the earlier literature, as well as the revival of interest in the subject in the 1930s as part of the general (if not widely recognized) revival of the historical sciences over the past several decades, which have contributed so much to his own work. He also further identifies the problem of the recovery of science when he notes that, in America, the Gnostic nature of ersatz religions was recognized by William James early in the twentieth century, and that James also knew that Hegel's speculation was the culmination of modern Gnosticism, but his critical opposition had little effect because today intellectual movements of the Gnostic type dominate the public science in both America and Europe. "The attempts to come to grips with the problems of personal and social order when it is disrupted by gnosticisms . . . has not been very successful because the philosophical knowledge that would be required for the purpose has itself been destroyed by the prevailing intellectual climate. The struggle against the consequences of gnosticism is being conducted in the very language of gnosticism."[20]

---

to a greater or lesser degree in the experiences behind the representative symbols of the society's truth of existence.

Dahl offers so many other arguments in the review that are characteristic of the difference between Voegelin's conceptions of science and theory and those of the orthodox political scientists that the entire discussion could be used as a foil for an analysis of the ways in which contemporary political science fails or refuses to come to grips with Voegelin's theory. One is tempted to digress into an analysis of this piece, but one or two self-evident examples should suffice: Dahl notes at one point that one of three parts of *The New Science of Politics* is ". . . a historical examination of the rise of *what Voegelin calls* 'Gnosticism' . . ." (*italics supplied*). And he concludes the review, without paying even passing regard to Voegelin's discussion of the post-Cartesian reduction of the meaning of science, by demonstrating how he participates in that reduction when he says that Voegelin ". . . has not only 'un-defined' science; he has un-scienced it" (p. 489). I do not mean to cap this note with an *ad hominem* argument when I say that the review is a good illustration of the appropriateness of Dahl's place (usually at the top) on lists of the type referred to at the beginning of this essay.

18. The lecture was published, with an introduction on the nature of Gnosis and an added section on "Der Gottesmord," under the title *Wissenschaft, Politik, und Gnosis*. A previously published essay on "Ersatz Religion" was included in the American edition: *Science, Politics, and Gnosticism*, trans. William J. Fitzpatrick (Chicago: Henry Regnery Co., Gateway Edition, 1968).

19. *Science, Politics, and Gnosticism*, p. 3.

20. Ibid., "Foreword to the American Edition," p. vi.

The treatment of Gnosticism is rich in meaning, not only in itself, but for its elucidation of the manner in which Voegelin's achievements as a theorist are realized. Several items deserve mention, if only in passing. First, it is obvious that the participants in the intellectual culture in which he works are historians, philosophers, theologians, anthropologists and others, and not "social scientists." His mastery of the literature, primary and secondary, is extraordinary, not only for its breadth but for his control of it. Second, his own objections to "positions"—as starting points for speculations that culminate in closed "systems" which resolve by exclusion all problems that do not fit into the internally self-sustaining "model" of reality—are amply borne out by his own example: he not only responds to questions raised about the lacunae in his presentations (including those recognized through his self-criticism), but he is constantly making the new departures necessitated by the openness of science.[21] Third, the question of Voegelin's language, much complained about by those who wish to depict him as an obscurantist, and a source of difficulty at times even for those who have scrupulously attempted to comprehend him,[22] is clarified both by implication and by direct reference. Here and in subsequent work it is made plain that he is not inventing a technical language of his own, but is seeking to recover the precise meanings of the language appropriate to philosophical discourse. The purpose is dual: to circumvent misinterpretation by not relying on a language that has been corrupted by the deculturation of our times, and to assure (through textual and contextual accuracy) that more of the nuances, let alone the broader expressions, of the philosophers are not lost in the interpretations. Again, the critical and reconstructive efforts go forward together. Increasingly, Voegelin has indulged those who have followed him open-mindedly, and implicitly answered those who have regarded his language as wholly contrived,[23] by carrying the Greek (or occasionally other language) terms in parentheses alongside the English equivalent.

The New Science of Politics was a prefiguration of the study of "The order of history [which] emerges from the history of order."[24] *Order and History*, in a manner similar to the history of ideas, has gone through a metamorphosis

21. See the penultimate paragraph in ibid., p. vii, in which he refers to the study of modern Gnosticism as ". . . inevitably work in progress . . . ," in the present state of science, and then goes on to point out his own extension of the study into the subject of alienation.

22. Much of the commentary on Voegelin that aims at broadening the general basis of understanding of what he is about tends to track his terminology (and sometimes even his syntax and idiomatic usage) so closely that its interpretative value is depreciated. This tendency is understandable, however, in light of his frequently repeated strictures on the debased uses to which "Language symbols" may be put, and the steadily enlarging vocabulary which his philological skill brings into his writings as he widens the scope of his inquiry.

23. See Dahl, "The Science of Politics: New and Old," p. 484, for a precise example of this mode of criticism.

24. This is the first sentence in the Preface with which Voegelin opens the initial volume of *Order and History*, Vol. 1, *Israel and Revelation* (1956), p. ix.

which is still in process. It was originally planned as a six-volume work ranging over the civilizations of the Ancient Near East through the Hellenic civilization, into the multicivilization empires since Alexander, the Christian empire in the West, the Protestant centuries, the emergence of the modern national states, and the development of Gnosis as the symbolic form of order. The first three volumes—*Israel and Revelation, The World of the Polis*, and *Plato and Aristotle*—appeared in 1956 and 1957. Pursuing the object of identifying from historical sources the ways in which the various societies symbolized the meanings of their existence, which included the quaternarian community of being (God and man, world and society), Voegelin found the earliest societies expressing their meanings through the cosmological myth in which the elements of the community of being were not differentiated. The major "leaps in being" through which consciousness of the experience of existence found symbolic expression were revelation in Israel, philosophy in Hellas, and the soteriological truth of Christianity.[25] The first three volumes of *Order and History* analyze, with the usual mastery of historical material combined with theoretical rigor, the varieties of mythic symbols, the crises that evoked the noetic experiences of the philosophers, the revelatory experiences of Moses and the prophets, and the ways in which the experiences of participation in the structure of being affected the order of the civilizations under consideration. It was anticipated that the course of Western civilization would be pursued down to the present in the final three volumes.

Seventeen years elapsed between the publication of Volumes 3 and 4 of *Order and History*. In the introduction to *The Ecumenic Age* Voegelin explains that a "break" occurred in the program he had originally laid out for the projected six-volume work. As the work proceeded ". . . the structures that emerged from the historical orders and their symbolization proved more complicated than . . . [he] had anticipated."[26] The principle of the study (that the order of history emerges from the history of order) was not wrong, but the expansiveness of the project carried it beyond the originally established boundaries. The mere quantity of empirical materials resulting from the continuing rapid advancement of the "historical sciences" would have necessitated that the three additional volumes be expanded to at least six, and the five types of order and symbolization set forth at the beginning (the Ancient Near East and the cosmological myth, Israel and the revelatory form of existence in history, Hellas and the development of philosophy, the multi-

25. This sentence is a synthesized statement based on prefatory comments in *Israel and Revelation* and sections of *The New Science of Politics*, esp. pp. 76–77. Although I think it is adequate for the stage of the work now being considered (ca. 1950–60), later published work, including *Order and History*, Vol. 4, *The Ecumenic Age* (1974) raises some questions about the relation between the noetic experience of philosophy and the pneumatic experiences of Christianity that are not completely resolved.

26. *Order and History*, 4:2.

civilizational empires and the emergence of Christianity, and the modern national state and Gnosticism) were "regrettably limited." That situation was "awkward enough," but

> what ultimately broke the project . . . was the impossibility of aligning the empirical types in any time sequence at all that would permit the structures actually found to emerge from a history conceived as a "course." The program as originally conceived, it is true, was not all wrong. There were indeed the epochal, differentiating events, the "leaps in being," which engendered the consciousness of a Before and After and, in their respective societies, motivated the symbolism of a historical "course" that was meaningfully structured by the event of the leap. The experiences of a new insight into the truth of existence, accompanied by the consciousness of an event as constituting an epoch in history, were real enough. . . . Still, the conception was untenable because it had not taken proper account of the important lines of meaning in history that did not run along lines of time.[27]

Without complicating the issues unnecessarily at this point, we might refer tersely to some of the consequences of this broadened perspective on the historic order. For one thing Voegelin discovers that, even in the cosmological civilizations, history is not conceived as simply cyclical, but the very genesis of the historical imagination involves the symbolization of the existence of the concrete society as originating in the infinity which preceded time, and as continuing indefinitely into future time and even beyond time. Second, the appearance of ecumenical civilizations not only in the West, but in the Far East, involves the consciousness, even within the confines of nonuniversal concrete (tribal and ethnic?) societies, of the universality of much of mankind's experience (though we have no *historical* experience of a world empire, only the apparently complex and repetitive aspirations for such an order). Finally (but not definitively), the complications of the relations between symbolizations of experiences of order and the ways in which those symbols are employed in the societies themselves seem to be much greater than in the earlier work. To take only one example, the movements to establish multiethnic (ecumenic) geographic empires by conquest may be described as arising out

27. Ibid. The comments about the epochal nature of the leap in being are intriguing in the light of some of the later interpretations. The Greek philosophers, for instance, not only developed philosophy as a symbolic form to express a differentiation of experience beyond the form of the myth, but they were conscious that this symbolization constituted a new epoch in history (the awareness of a break in linear time which would thenceforth establish a "Before and After" conceptualization of history). In light of some later suggestions about the "equivalences" of various symbolic forms without respect to temporal sequences, one wonders whether the engendering experiences are the same in the equivalences, and whether the effectiveness of the symbolizations is the critical element in constituting and sustaining the concrete existences of societies. If so, the "leap in being" is not so much a differentiation of experience as an advance in the communicative expression of the experience.

of the almost purely power considerations (*libido dominandi*) of the conquering imperators, with the ecumenical religions (and their symbolizations of spiritual order) conveniently at hand for use, not as the substantial foundations of order, but as palliatives for the disorders of the society. The contingencies in experience that follow from the nature and condition of man make even the most fully differentiated experiences of the noetic and pneumatic forms less than complete (any other construction of the problem would be Gnostic); the necessarily inadequate translation of the experiences into communicative symbols involves still further loss of immediacy in the experience of reality (*vide* St. Paul and the reception of the symbol of Christian eschatology, the expectation of Christ's return within the era of the living); and the historical circumstances attending the reception of the symbolizations make possible the immediate perversion of the symbols, not to speak of the process of deformation over time.

The shift in the structure and context of *Order and History* was also affected by Voegelin's intense concentration on the philosophy of consciousness in the interim between the first three volumes and the latest one (although this consideration was not as fully discussed in the Introduction to Volume 4 as were the historical factors). The shift in interest was manifested most clearly in the publication of *Anamnesis* in 1966. Although some of the discrete studies that make up this volume originated in earlier periods of Voegelin's career (he notes that he was interested in the subject as far back as the 1920s), the core pieces—some previously published—were written or substantially modified in the decade just prior to the appearance of the book.[28]

Perhaps the change that this new direction brought to *Order and History* is most succinctly summarized in the following statement: "History is not a stream of human beings and their actions in time, but the process of man's participation in a flux of divine presence that has eschatological direction. The enigmatic symbolism of a 'history of mankind,' thus, expresses man's understanding that these insights, though they arise from concrete events in the consciousness of concrete human beings are valid for all men."[29] The change seems to imply that while the search for the history of order continues as part

---

28. Although no complete English language edition of *Anamnesis* is available, two essays which concentrate on the book are among the better commentaries on Voegelin (the closing section of Germino's piece excepted). These are Dante Germino, "Eric Voegelin's Anamnesis," *Southern Review* n.s. 7 (1971):68–88; and Ellis Sandoz, "The Foundations of Voegelin's Political Theory," *Political Science Reviewer* 1 (1971):30–73. [An abridged American edition of *Anamnesis*, trans. and ed. Gerhart Niemeyer (Notre Dame, Ind.: University of Notre Dame Press, 1978) omits most of Part Two of the German original but includes the essay "Reason: The Classic Experience," reprinted from *Southern Review* n.s. 10 (1974):237–64, and a new Introduction by Voegelin. Of the omitted material, however, some has been published elsewhere in translation, such as the expanded recension of "Historiogenesis" in *Order and History*, 4:59–113.—Ed.]

29. Voegelin, *Order and History*, 4:6.

of man's ineluctable search for the meaning of existence, the order of history will not emerge from the welter of historical events. There may be concrete *orders* in history, but there is no overall order beyond the discernment of the orders and disorders in the souls of men. These recurrently manifest themselves in symbols through which the panoply of political orders are more or less fully represented in the flux of history.

The contents of Volume 4, as well as the suggested contents of the projected fifth and final volume of *Order and History*, reflect this changed emphasis. Like *Anamnesis* these volumes are a series of discrete examinations of a tremendous range of problems loosely unified by their origins in the experience of consciousness in man. The organizational principle has changed from one directed equally by the perception of a "course" of history and the constancy of the object of the quest for ontological meaning, to one guided by the urge to probe deeper into the experiencing psyche behind the symbols by which man has expressed his experiences of participation in the divine ground of being. Some of the pieces in Volume 4 and those projected for Volume 5 are explorations of broad conceptions of experience (e.g., historiogenesis, immortality, equivalences of experience and symbolizations, the classical experience of reason, etc.) while others explore the experiences and their symbolization by representative individuals (e.g., St. Paul, Hegel, Schelling, Henry James, etc.). Although extracted from history, and in some instances taking the experience of history itself as a theme, these studies are more nearly approaches to a pure theory of being than to a study of order and history as such.

III

Voegelin's contribution to political science cannot be understood, in my view, without some insight into the process out of which his theoretical attainments have emerged—hence the foregoing sketchy summary. But it is also obligatory, especially under the present circumstances, that some effort be made to formulate the content of his theory a little more coherently. One way of engaging in so risky a venture in so brief a compass is to take his own criteria of a theory of politics and assess the extent to which he has met them. Although I have expressed reservations about discovering in him any "fixed" meaning of the term *theory*, I have located three dispersed statements which seem to constitute the sum of Voegelin's expectations from theory. One of the requisites for political theory explicitly stated at numerous places in his works, and implied in others, is a fully articulated philosophical anthropology or concept of the nature of man.[30] A second criterion is established in the opening sentence of *The New Science of Politics*: "The existence of man in political society

30. Some of Voegelin's most cogent presentations are to be found in his lesser noted critical works. For that reason the following example of his often stated attachment to the principle of a

is historical existence; and a theory of politics, if it penetrates to principles, must at the same time be a theory of history."[31] Finally, Voegelin's foreword to *Anamnesis* begins as follows: "The problems of human order in society and history originate in the order of consciousness. The philosophy of the consciousness is therefore the core of a philosophy of politics."[32] A philosophical anthropology, a theory of history, and a philosophy of consciousness, then, are essential to a theory of politics.

An adumbration of Voegelin's philosophical anthropology is difficult for two reasons. The first is a problem of surface simplicity: I have no reason to doubt the possibility of extracting from a variorum treatment of Voegelin's comments on the subject a fairly clear set of propositional statements that summarize his conception of the nature of man. Such a summary starts with the most elemental distinctions and moves to more differentiated conceptions of an ontology. Robert Penn Warren stated what could be the opening proposition with devastating succinctness when he said that man is a machine with consciousness.[33] Although conscious of the finiteness of his existence within the world, man is also conscious of participation in the structure of being of which he is a part. Human existence is beset by the tension of living in an "In-Between" state (the Platonic Metaxy) in which the confinements of life in the world are all too present (mortality, disorder, alienation, meaninglessness), but in which there is also the pull toward transcendental reality (the divine ground) as the source of the intimations of immortality, order, and consubstantiality with being. The order of the individual soul is dependent on its orientation towards the ground of being, and the order of society depends on its analogy to the structure of order in the soul of the well-ordered man. The possibilities for man's orientation towards the ground of being as a source of order in his own soul (and thus of his awareness of the possibility of order in society and history) is not, however, something that can be made simply a matter of doctrinal prescription, or dogmatized. It takes place within the individual consciousness, and the process is one which has to be experienced by the individual. Nonetheless, the process of attunement to the divine order has been symbolized in widely differentiated ways: in classic philosophy through the concept of *nous* (i.e., reason as the differentiating attribute of mankind and the one through which man participates in divine being; the terms "noetic" and "noesis" derive from "nous"), in St. Augustine

---

philosophical anthropology is taken from a review of Hannah Arendt's *The Origins of Totalitarianism* in *Review of Politics* 15 (1953):68. "It is difficult to categorize political phenomena properly without a well-developed philosophical anthropology. . . ."

31. Voegelin, *The New Science of Politics*, p. 1.

32. Voegelin, *Anamnesis*, p. 7.

33. Cf. Warren's statement on the "'unmasking' of life as a mechanism cursed with consciousness," in "Homage to Theodore Dreiser on the Centenary of His Birth," *Southern Review* n.s. 7 (April 1971):399, with his remark, ". . . for that is what we are, machines capable of vision," in "Democracy and Poetry," *Southern Review* n.s. 11 (January 1975):28.

through the dichotomy of the *amor Dei* and the *amor sui*, and in Bergson through the contrast between the opening of the soul to transcendence and the closure of the soul against ultimate reality. Here the propositional statement must end because we are already beyond the point of surface simplicity and must penetrate the symbols if we are to reconstitute the experiences themselves.

The second difficulty in summarizing Voegelin's philosophical anthropology arises in making this penetration, in moving from a description more or less familiar to us from doctrinal sources in metaphysics and religion to a philosophical reconstruction of the experiences of consciousness, especially as these experiences were symbolized through the origins of philosophy in Plato and Aristotle. In two long essays, "Was Ist Politische Realität?"[34] and "Reason: The Classic Experience,"[35] Voegelin extends the content of philosophical anthropology to the point of making it virtually one with his philosophy of consciousness. Although the essays are long, they are so compact that they virtually defy summary exegesis. They must be read in their entirety to realize the full import of Voegelin's theoretical reconstruction. The problem is further compounded by the fact that, although they select from the entire corpus of classical philosophy, they are not simply recapitulations of key concepts in Plato and Artistotle, but are philosophical reconstructions of the experience of consciousness in its noetic manifestations.

Although these key essays cannot be summarized here, the range of their contents may be indicated without distortion: in the effort to separate philosophy (love of wisdom) from philodoxy (love of opinion), they cover the origins of philosophical inquiry; they explore the ways in which the dialectical argument proceeds; they reconstruct the process by which the noetic potential is explored to its depths and heights (with particular emphasis on the search for the divine ground and the ultimate luminosity which the noetic consciousness brings to its own oneness with being), and they then move into the experience of order in man's psyche and the articulation of that order through symbols that are representative of the noetic potential shared by mankind.

Some of the implications of these explorations for the science of politics will be considered later. For now it must be sufficient to mention three. First, not every human being will live the noetic life, nor be the full ordered or mature man characterized by the Aristotelian concept of the *spoudaios*. But the noetic order is open to all men, at least to the extent of their capacity to be drawn to it when they perceive it in others; and the philosopher, in particular, will represent in his person the attainment of the order of reality open to all men. The possibilities for the order of society arise out of these ordering potentials in man. Second, an extension of the noetic potential at the pragmatic

34. In *Anamnesis*, pp. 283–354. [Translated edition, pp. 143–213.—Ed.]
35. "Reason: The Classic Experience," pp. 237–64. [See note 28, *supra*.—Ed.]

level is to be found in the capacity of every man for the exercise of common sense in relation to most aspects of both private and public life.[36] Third, the ordering potential of the noetic consciousness also provides the means of critically understanding the nature of disorder even when it is carried to the point of psychopathology. The essay on reason analyzes the way foundations are provided for criticism of the disorder in society through the grasp of the closure against the noetic meaning of reason in man. Since existence in tension is not abolished by its discovery, noesis has educational, diagnostic, and therapeutic functions.

Because of what seems to me a change in focus from a philosophy of history as such in the earlier works to a philosophy of consciousness in relation to critical historical events in the later ones, not much need be said here about the theory of history as part of Voegelin's overall commitment. At a minimum it may be noted that history is the field in which the drama of humanity, involving the quest for order in man and society, takes place. The science of man and society, then, is necessarily involved with the historical sciences. The materials of empirical history are the sources from which societies may be seen to emerge out of the symbolizations of order that constitute their self-interpretations, as well as the sources through which the disorders of man and society are perceived. Furthermore, the leaps in being through which man has differentiated his consciousness of reality are events in history which are epochal in the sense that they change the order of history and are recognized as doing so by those who symbolize them.

A theory of history is necessary also because the conception of history is part of man's interpretation of his order of being; in the very apprehension of history man makes it a part of the self-interpretation of man and society in their existential reality. But history, or at least the symbols which include history as part of the representative order, can also become part of the disordering escape into unreality. Gnosticism, for instance, is characterized in part by its projection of an apocalyptic end of history. All attempts to make history a closed conception are stigmatized as derailments from reality into "second" realities. The *episteme politike*, then, is a science of man, society, and history.

IV

I have indicated that an assessment of Voegelin's contributions as a political theorist would necessarily involve an assessment of the political science profession. That judgment was made largely on the basis of Voegelin's virtually single-handed effort (at least among contemporary political scientists) to develop a science of politics grounded in theory which is both epistemologically

36. The part played by the apprehension of the philosophy of common sense of the Scottish School (especially Thomas Reid) in Voegelin's theory is an interesting problem which cannot be pursued here. [See Voegelin, *Anamnesis*, pp. 351–54.—Ed.]

and methodologically at odds with the Positivist orientation now dominant in the discipline.[37] The question, then, is whether or not Voegelin has produced a sufficiently comprehensive and cohesive theoretical foundation on which those who aspire to be part of an "intellectual culture" could build cooperatively to extend and perpetuate a science of politics. If so, what has he provided in this theory that makes it the more effective way of understanding political reality, and how does one work from it as a "paradigm?" These questions can be addressed by an appraisal of four aspects of Voegelin's work: (1) the generality of his theory, i.e., the coherence of his conception of politics as a constant in human existence and the relation of the political experience to experience as a whole; (2) the effectiveness of his criticism of other concepts of political reality as the means of opening the way to understanding politics through his reconstruction of the *episteme politike*; (3) the suitability of his formulation of theoretical principles as a guide to what we seek in a science of politics; and (4) the issues in Voegelin's theoretical conclusions that require further clarification if the theoretical foundations themselves are to be extended. Once again, only the briefest excursions into these vast areas of inquiry are possible within the limits of this essay.

1. On the issue of the generality of his theory, the central point to be emphasized once again is that Voegelin has not attempted to explain politics as a special or limited form (in Michael Oakeshott's terms, a "mode") of experience. A theory of man and society that is not solidly related to an ontological theory cannot explain anything more than the ephemera of politics because politics arises out of man's special place in the chain of being, and that place involves man's participation in the structure of which he is a part. The source of the structure of society, like the origin of man's own structure, is not a given which one can comprehend solely from an external perspective. The ontological understanding of man can take place only from within; its appropriate method of inquiry involves examination of the experience of consciousness, and the results are expressed through philosophical symbols. Since politics is a part of man's temporal existence, man himself is the creative source of his political experience. To use Oakeshott's terminology again, politics is a self-moved manner of activity.[38] But the nature of that self-moved activity de-

37. This is not meant to imply that all practicing political scientists are Positivists. It is rather to say that most of those who have self-consciously engaged in, or looked forward to the possibility of, the formulation of a comprehensive theory of politics have had Positivist orientations. Others have worked on political problems in eclectic ways without displaying much interest in theoretical issues. Germino has identified the principal figures who have made recent contributions to the revival of political theory on a non-Positivist basis—particularly Oakeshott, Arendt, Jouvenal, and Strauss, in addition to Voegelin—but he seems to me to have placed Voegelin in a unique position in his book, not only in terms of space devoted to him in comparison with the others, but also in the greater emphasis placed on the critical work of Oakeshott et al., as contrasted with the focus on Voegelin's theoretical constructiveness. *Beyond Ideology*, esp. chaps. 7 and 8.

38. See "Political Education," in his *Rationalism in Politics* (New York: Basic Books, 1962), p. 115.

pends on what man is—not just as a participant of politics, but as a participant in the totality of existence. The order of society that man seeks to structure through politics depends on the experience of order he is capable of realizing as part of the order of being. And that order, of course, while not infinitely open to man's comprehension because its source is the ground of being of which man is only a part (although a consubstantial part through participation in the noetic consciousness), is sufficiently open to enable him to structure the order of his being through reason (*noesis*) as he explores the order of consciousness through the tension toward the ground. The order of society, then, depends on the symbolization of the order of being as an analogue of the man whose soul is in order. Although awareness of participation in the order of being takes place only in individuals, and in various levels in different persons at that, reason is the universal substance that differentiates man in the structure of reality. The capacity to symbolize the experience of participation in the order of reality through philosophy affords a measure which makes a universal science of politics possible. At the same time the limits of man's existence in the world as expressed by the Platonic Metaxy mean that the states of order in man and society are in historical flux, and the theoretical activity which seeks to comprehend that order is never complete.

2. That we are not accustomed to thinking of an ontological foundation of politics is part of the problem that gives rise to Voegelin's critical achievement. Most of the debate over a science of politics takes place at the level of "political ideas" and not at the level of the meaning of politics in the structure of noetic reality. Even the relatively undistorted symbols of political reality, which are the means of expressing the existence of a particular society in history, tend to become doctrinalized and dogmatized in a way that does not evoke the experiences that constitute the order of reality the society represents. And where those symbols have been deformed in the service of an ideology, the loss of reality is so complete as to constitute a crisis of order.

Voegelin's criticism started, as indicated, from the crisis of our times, with its activist movements generated through ideologies (which in his most extended characterization Voegelin refers to as revolutions against man and God). His criticism then moved back through the history of ideas to the forms of symbolization, and from there to the effort to reconstitute the experiences that produced the symbolizations. The vast body of criticism which was produced in the course of these explorations is a most valuable source for approaching his theoretical principles; even for those who do not have the philosophical urge to penetrate to theoretical principles, it constitutes a body of regulative ideas which may prevent more pragmatically oriented political scientists from making some of the grosser theoretical errors common to the profession. The clarity and comprehensiveness of the criticism are impressive in their own right; furthermore, some of the best of it can be found in reviews and journal articles not reprinted as part of the larger studies.

One of the best examples (especially because it does not have the coruscating effect of some of the attacks on the Gnostic depredations) is the essay on "The Oxford Political Philosophers."[39] It will be remembered by his readers that Voegelin indicated in the closing paragraph of *The New Science of Politics* that the American and English democracies, through their institutions, most solidly represented the truth of the soul and were at the same time the strongest powers, thus providing some hope for ". . . repressing Gnostic corruption and restoring the forces of civilization."[40] But in the essay under consideration he was concerned to point out how the prevailing tradition of political philosophy in Oxford fell short of meeting the tests of theoretical relevance. By taking British institutions as the model for a valid general theory of politics, the various philosophers—with the single exception of G. R. G. Mure—(1) narrowed the object of theory from a civilizational whole to a particular national state, (2) tended to treat the various political movements within the contemporary national state as movements on the level of secular power politics (which they are not), and (3) failed to penetrate to principles because they engaged in debates about the rights of man and what institutions are best, instead of elucidating the larger problems of a philosophical anthropology. In appraising the specifics of the "theory" of several leading figures, Voegelin shows how each tended in his own way to turn the secularized institutions of Britain into a civil theology (without analyzing the symbols they lauded for establishing political order in British history), and then turned the principles on which this special set of political institutions were based into the principles of politics as a whole. Here, as in all of Voegelin's criticism, the concrete presentation of the materials under scrutiny is informed by the ". . . aim, however dimly seen, of developing a [more embracing] theory. . . ."[41]

The criticism of the Oxford philosophers, though pointed, is mild because it represents the examination of a stage in political science in which some of the symbolic manifestations of the public order in Britain are protected against erosion or deformation by elevation into doctrine or dogma, and this protection is in some ways commendable. But it is still a digressive defense as well as an inadequate one; what is needed in the face of the revolutionary ideological threats to the ordering institutions on which the Oxford philosophers concentrate is a penetration to their sources in reality.

In more extended criticism Voegelin analyzes the way the secular creeds advance their destructive work, moving from the milder forms of progressivism and liberalism to utopias based ever more demonically on closed systems of thought, and on into the revolutionary movements of Nihilism, National

39. *Philosophical Quarterly* 3, no. 11 (April 1953):97–114.
40. *The New Science of Politics* p. 189.
41. "The Oxford Political Philosophers," p. 99.

Socialism, and Communism—all of which have as their eventual purpose the transformation of man and society in the name of an immanentist reality, rather than the preservation of an environment in which man will have the opportunity to live a life attuned to the order of reality.

The standards of Voegelin's criticism are sufficiently supple to be used at almost any level of analysis from simple institutional description to the more complex abstractions embodied in ideas and symbols. We have already noted how these standards apply to political science as practiced by both the Positivists and the Oxford philosophers, and we have emphasized the respective ways in which both limit the objects of inquiry and dogmatize certain symbols and ideas. We can now extrapolate by noting how Voegelin's critical analysis might be extended to the movement within American political science that has lately challenged behavioralism's claim to be the "new" political science. I refer, of course, to the activist movement that is generally identified with the Caucus for a New Political Science. Many of the criticisms of the discipline (especially as it has tended towards behavioralism) by the leading spokesmen for the Caucus are shared with Voegelin: the argument, for instance, against a slavish imitation of the natural sciences on the grounds that the human experiences most pertinent to politics are excluded by such a commitment, and the view that the value neutrality of behavioralism covers a role that is strongly supportive of the status quo. Voegelin might also find the consciousness of the crisis of liberalism among some members of the Caucus a potential stimulus to inquiry into the loss of meaning in some of the symbols of the existing political order. But he would also discern in a number of the tendencies among those who claim to be the proponents of the newest insurgency in political science little more than a profusion of leftist ideology and a plea for activism as a surrogate for the restoration of theory. In many ways the latest wave of the future within the discipline is even more symptomatic of the crisis in both politics and political science than the rather innocuous addiction of behavioralists to scientism.

3. The body of theoretical principles that Voegelin has been articulating over the past quarter century or more includes some of the subjects which have already been touched upon briefly. Among these, as main objectives of inquiry, are a philosophical anthropology that differentiates man as a participant in the structure of existence in history, and the search for the experiences of order in man out of which those symbols were produced. This body of principles also includes the application of methods directed by the content of the philosophical anthropology and the objects of inquiry (these being mainly an empirical examination of order in history and a philosophical probe into the order of consciousness).

At this point, however, it seems useful to stress once again the *limits* imposed on the efforts to restore a science of politics grounded in such theoretical principles. These limits, too, should be considered with the principles themselves. The first is the limit of knowledge that is open to man by reason of his "In-Between" place in the structure of being. The consciousness of having to live with the tensions of existence, rather than being able completely to overcome them by an act of egophanic revolt, is the main defense against the ideological and activist inclinations towards the destruction of the existential order. The second is the limit on the extent and duration of order in concrete society. Societies are nonnoetic, even though their respective orders depend on the noetic symbolization of their existence. The noetic life can be lived only by individual human beings, and this means that a noetic response to disorder is the only possibility for evoking a restoration of the *episteme politike* out of a crisis of social order. Since the order of society is not a self-correcting "system," but is the result of the infusion of order through a symbolization involving the noetically ordered man writ large, the principles of a science of order in man and society will not be fixed for all time, but must be constantly in process of restoration and extension. Finally, and in a sense closely related to the constancy of the theoretical activity, the noetic life itself imposes limits on the pragmatic political activism of the theorist. It is the philosopher's obligation to engage in the theoretical activity and to seek to bring the results of that activity to bear on the order of society by expressing them in open debate on principles. But the philosopher's symbols of order cannot be imposed by actions that effectively reduce them to doctrines to be exploited in the struggles for existential power. Noetic persuasion, not the will to power, is the only effective way of the philosopher as seeker after truth. (Socrates is still the symbolic model for the obligations attaching to the person engaged in the *bios theoretikos*).

4. In his own body of general theory and the criticism which led into it, Voegelin has also set a virtually limitless set of problems on which to work. Not least of these is the problem of analyzing his own theoretical achievement. In large part this chapter has concentrated on the process that has taken him to the current state of his theoretical generalizations about politics. Since the perpetual openness of the inquiry has been stressed so heavily, it is time to provide a sample of the type of questions growing out of his theoretical principles that still need to be addressed by Voegelin or someone else working within the paradigm he has established. Leaving aside the omnipresent questions of internal consistency, three problems seem to me to require further exploration or further explanation from Voegelin or from some person who may have a clearer reading of him than I have. These are: (1) the possibility that the introspective method of apprehending noesis in the fullest sense may result in something that is very near solipsism; (2) the opaqueness of the relations between the differentiation of the experience of order and the effective symbolization of that experience as the representation of the meaning of the concrete society's existence in history; and (3) the problem of the

relation between philosophy and Christianity as sources for the symbols of order by which Western civilization has represented its truth of existence in history.

Regarding the first of these problems: as Voegelin moves his theoretical inquest from symbols to experience as expressed through a philosophy of consciousness, it seems to me that the inquiry from within becomes so nearly totally subjective that it virtually defies expression, let alone expression in symbols clear enough to permit the noetic order of the philosopher to appeal to the noetic potential in nonphilosophers and thereby be effective in bringing order to society. This point is not raised because I find Voegelin's exegesis of the experience of reason in the classical philosophers inadequate. Indeed it is a *tour de force*, although the penetration to the divine ground through noetic consciousness is described in terms reminiscent of the ineffableness of mysticism. All of us are aware of the inadequacies of language and other symbols for expressing our deepest experiences in an evocative way, even if we have not had the temerity to inform our instructors in creative writing (as one student is reported to have done) that we had lived a poem so intensely that we could not write it. What really bothers me is that in his latest work Voegelin seems to find so many possibilities for distortions of the symbols through which the experiences of order in the noetic consciousness are expressed that the prospects for societal order on anything other than the most precarious basis are very dim indeed.

The second problem, which should be capable of clarification by empirical study of the emergence or restoration of social order in concrete societies, is closely related to the first one. That is, if the order of society is nonnoetic, but dependent on the noetic order in man for its realization, what is the relation between the noetic experience of order and the symbolizations that express the order of the society? If the self-interpretations that constitute society are not noetic, yet the *episteme politike* is properly based on a noetic interpretation of man and society, political science should still be able to tell us how the nonnoetic interpretations represent an order that is at least a doctrinalized or dogmatized version of noetic order. In particular, are religious symbols invariably involved in the symbolic self-interpretations of any society as the nonnoetic expression of the society's relation to the divine ground?

Posing the question in this way leads immediately to the third sample issue. In the earlier works Voegelin regularly stressed that the main constitutive symbols in the order of Western civilization were Christianity and classical philosophy. Even in parts of *The Ecumenic Age* he seems to treat the differentiation of consciousness through the noetic and pneumatic experiences as being on essentially the same level.[42] But some of his closest readers have been puzzled by the way in which the concentration on the philosophy of consciousness has been accompanied by an apparent shift of emphasis to

42. Cf. *Order and History*; Vol. 4, esp. chap. 7 at 327.

philosophical symbolization as the unique form for expressing the order of reality.[43] The criticism also contains some rather disturbing comments that suggest that doctrinal and dogmatic concerns have dominated the pneumatic symbolizations from their beginnings, and even St. Thomas Aquinas is given a few sharp raps as a nonnoetic propositional metaphysician. Has noesis, through its experience of the divine ground, superseded the pneumatic experience of Christianity entirely? In this instance, at least, one might wish that Voegelin had pursued his originally expressed intention of examining "The Christian Centuries" as part of his study of order and history. The study of "The Pauline Vision of the Resurrected" in *The Ecumenic Age* is hardly a theoretical counterpart of the philosophical analysis of consciousness in *Anamnesis* and the essay on reason in classical philosophy. Most of the shifts in the focus of Voegelin's theoretical interests over time can be explained in the total context of his work; as yet this one does not seem to be accounted for.

Despite these and other lingering desiderata, it seems that he has opened questions neglected or even precluded from examination in recent political science, questions critical for the development of an adequate theoretical basis for the discipline. Whether this foundation will be built upon by enough political scientists to make an impact on the orientation of the discipline is, to say the least, problematic.

43. See, e.g., Gerhart Niemeyer, "Eric Voegelin's Philosophy and the Drama of Mankind," *Modern Age* 20 (1976):28–39. The problem has been addressed as a matter of intellectual control in Bruce Douglass, "The Gospel and Political Order: Eric Voegelin on the Political Role of Christianity," *Journal of Politics* 38 (1976):25–45.

ERIC VOEGELIN'S FRAMEWORK FOR POLITICAL EVALUATION IN HIS RECENTLY PUBLISHED WORK

Dante Germino

I

If pressed to provide a one-word reply to the question, What serves as Eric Voegelin's framework for political evaluation?—we could offer only one valid answer: Reality. Indeed, what other standard could possibly serve a political science worthy of the name? And yet, here, by raising *the* basic philosophic problem of the nature of reality,[1] we unlock a Pandora's box of difficulties.

True enough, most of us most of the time think we know what "reality" is. We pride ourselves in being toughminded and "empirical." Reality in politics, we have heard, is concerned with "who gets what, when, and how," with the struggle to attain prestige, power, and wealth, and with the corruption that so often attends this struggle. But most of us, at least some of the time, are uneasy about accepting this particular "reality" as normative. We think that both individually and as a nation we can do better than this, and part of our objective in describing what is going on is to awaken people to the need to do better. We become restless in the Cave, as we experience the pull of a reality beyond its confines.

At this point it would be possible, of course, to call a halt to such questioning by repressing, or ignoring, or denying the pull of a reality beyond that of the immediate political struggle. Such questioning appears unproductive and impossible to "operationalize." And so, too often we put aside the concerns of political philosophy as "irrelevant." Political science is assumed to deal with the "facts"; as for "values," we can derive them from our political culture.

The procedure of "separating" fact and value appears to work reasonably well as long as we can assume that our political culture supplies us with norms whose validity is "self-evident," to recall Thomas Jefferson. For some time now, however, it has been increasingly apparent that the moral consen-

This essay first appeared in *American Political Science Review* 72 (1978): 110–21, and is reprinted here by permission.
    1. Eric Voegelin, *From Enlightenment to Revolution*, ed. John H. Hallowell (Durham, N.C.: Duke University Press, 1975), p. 257.

sus we thought we could assume to pervade our political discourse has been increasingly challenged by the various movements and groups, domestic and international, that, for lack of a better term, we label "extremist." With the shaking of the moral foundation of our surrounding world, we can no longer feel as comfortable about dismissing philosophers and their sustained investigation into the structure and process of reality. At this point, we may even become attentive to what an Eric Voegelin has to say to us.

As I have observed elsewhere,[2] Eric Voegelin did not begin his career as a philosopher; rather, as a teacher of jurisprudence at the University of Vienna, he was led to philosophical speculation by his experience of the fragility of constitutional democracy in countless European states after World War I. He perceived that institutions rest on ideas, or symbols, of self-interpretation shared by a people and that if such interpretations go to pieces, the institutions do so as well.

And so Voegelin embarked on his life-long quest of the contours of political reality, a quest which led him from the immediate context of the political struggle in concrete societies to the ideas that animated this struggle in a particular national society, to the ideas that bound together a particular civilization and, further, to the comparative study of the structure of political ideas in the various civilizations that have emerged in world history. As his search expanded in scope and time, it also expanded in depth; for the leading or directing ideas of civilizations had to emerge from somewhere, and that "somewhere" turned out to be the depth of the consciousness of concrete, representative human beings. So the domain of "empirical" political reality expanded from constitutions to the ideas that undergird them and, further, from these ideas to the experiences of participation in political and social reality of which the ideas were expressions and, finally, to the comparative study of experiences of order and disorder in the psyche of representative human types: the philosophers, sages, and prophets who have done the most to illumine the drama of humanity. Philosophy, then, Voegelin teaches us, is not something optional for a political science worthy of the name; it is the *core* of that science. Political philosophy has to do with the exploration of the contours of political reality: a nonphilosophical political science is a contradiction in terms.

In 1974 and 1975 two publications appeared by Voegelin which provide rich documentation for his theory of man, society, and history. One of these works is the long-awaited fourth volume of *Order and History*, which although specifically about developments in the "Ecumenic Age," from the rise of the Persian to the fall of the Roman Empire, contains many passages, espe-

2. Dante Germino, "Eric Voegelin: The In-Between of Human Life," in *Contemporary Political Philosophers*, ed. K. R. Minogue and A. de Crespigny (New York: Dodd, Mead & Co., 1975), p. 111.

cially in the introduction that refine and develop Voegelin's overall philosophy. Another volume, edited by John H. Hallowell of Duke University, *From Enlightenment to Revolution*, is a portion of an earlier, unpublished study by Voegelin on the history of political ideas. Although written a quarter of a century before *The Ecumenic Age*, it logically constitutes a sequel to Voegelin's recent work, showing in detail the implications of his philosophy of consciousness, society, and history for modern political thought and life. *From Enlightenment to Revolution* also demonstrates the impressive continuity of Voegelin's intellectual development. In the analysis that follows, I shall concentrate principally upon these two recently published works.

In some respects, to be sure, my title distorts the character of Voegelin's teaching. Voegelin would resolutely oppose the view that he is presenting his own, merely personal or "subjective," framework for political "evaluation," both because he deplores idiosyncrasy in philosophy and because he considers the "language of 'values' to be the *caput mortuum* [worthless residue] of a bygone era of methodology." Nonetheless, he would also concede that we must use that language "if we want to make ourselves understood," and he is aware that, following several centuries of "deformation," any attempt to recover the "perennial philosophy" in our time must itself initially appear idiosyncratic.[3]

Voegelin evalutes political ideas and regimes on the basis of an understanding of the human condition gained from a comparative study of symbols concerning spiritual order and disorder which have appeared over time. Indeed, history may be characterized as a "trail of equivalent symbols in time and space" left by the "process" or "moving presence" of reality.[4]

If the meaning of a symbol is to be grasped, great care must be taken not to interpret it literally. To interpret literally the language of Plato or Aristotle, or of the *Iliad*, or of the Bible is to dogmatize and deform it, for symbols are indices of motivating experiences in the souls of the people who articulate them. We must constantly seek to relate symbols meant to illumine political reality to the experiences that gave rise to them. If the symbols are detached from their experiential context, then we witness the degeneration of philosophy into the dogmatic formalism of the various "schools," whether Neoplatonic, Stoic, or Scholastic, with their desiccated disquisitions on essences,

3. Eric Voegelin, "Equivalences of Experience and Symbolization in History," in *Eternità e storia* (Florence: a cura dell'Istituto Accademico de Roma, Vallechi editore, 1970), p. 215. Voegelin discusses the problem of so-called "value relativism" in an earlier work, where he said in part: "In order to degrade the politics of Plato, Aristotle, or St. Thomas to the rank of 'values' among others, a conscientious scholar would first have to show that their claim to be science was unfounded. And that attempt is self-defeating. By the time the would-be critic has penetrated the meaning of metaphysics with sufficient thoroughness to make his criticism weighty, he will have become a metaphysician himself." Eric Voegelin, *The New Science of Politics: An Introduction* (Chicago: University of Chicago Press, 1952), p. 20.

4. Voegelin, "Equivalences of Experience and Symbolization in History," p. 233.

substances, accidents, etc. From there it is but a short step to the rejection of philosophy itself by those modern intellectuals disenchanted with the detached symbols, which they see in their "literal" opaqueness "from the outside" and therefore regard as "irrational."[5]

As previously noted, Voegelin long ago discovered that "the most basic philosophical problem [is] the nature of reality."[6] Unfortunately, this is precisely the problem that leading modern "philosophers" tend to neglect, or to assume to have been resolved in some "common sense" fashion, or to be "senseless" and "unverifiable." If, however, one attempts, as Marx did, to abolish the "problem of reality," one also abolishes philosophy.

A philosophy worthy of the name—i.e., one whose symbols are recognizably equivalent to other symbols which have noetically illumined the nature of reality—will acknowledge that reality is not a "disorderly flux of events" but an intelligible process flowing through human beings. Inasmuch as philosophers are situated within the process rather than at some Archimedian point outside of it, they cannot—in any massive "Gnostic" sense—discern its meaning as a whole. The answers to the basic questions of human existence remain shrouded in mystery. Nonetheless, philosophers are also aware that they possess the faculty of *nous* through which the mystery of reality as process becomes luminous to itself *qua* mystery. Philosophy is a knowing and a not-knowing, a knowledge of ignorance and a *cognitio fidei*, or knowledge based on faith, in the sense of Hebrews 11:1–3. Faith is the existential virtue of the soul open to the nonmetric, invisible ground; it is the "evidence of things unseen." It is fallacious to apply to unseen nonmetric reality the same tests of validity one applies in the investigation of the phenomenal world.

II

Fundamental to Voegelin's political philosophy is a symbol derived from Plato: the "Between" (*metaxy*) of human life. The "human realm of being" is a part, not the whole, of reality. To employ a spatial metaphor, the Metaxy is a field lying between the "poles" of the "noetic height" and "apeirontic (boundless) depth." These poles establish the "limits set to the philosopher's exploration of reality," and the philosopher "cannot transcend these limits but has to move in the In-Between. . . ."[7] Voegelin writes that Plato "was so acutely aware of man's consubstantiality but nonidentity with divine reality that he developed a special symbol for man's experience of his intermediate status 'between' the human and divine: He called the consciousness of this status the

5. Voegelin, *From Enlightenment to Revolution*, p. 21.
6. Ibid., p. 257.
7. Eric Voegelin, *Order and History*, 4 vols. to date (Baton Rouge: Louisiana State University Press, 1956–), 4:11.

metaxy, the In-Between of existence." Voegelin goes on to observe that the "In-Between of existence is not an empty space between two static entities, but the meeting-ground of the human and the divine in a consciousness of their distinction and interpenetration."[8] He concludes that "[t]he philosopher is not allowed to settle down on the positive pole of the existential tension; only the tension in its polarity of real and non-real is the full truth of reality."[9]

In a discussion of Anaximander's symbolization of reality, Voegelin speaks of the Metaxy in connection with two modes of reality: (1) "reality in existence," comprising the realm of all created things, including human beings in their mortality, and (2) "reality in nonexistence," or noncreated reality out of which all existing things emerge, which Anaximander designated by the term *apeiron*—the Infinite, or the Boundless, or the Limitless, or the "timeless *arche* of things." "Reality was experienced by Anaximander . . . as a cosmic process in which things emerge from, and disappear into, the non-existence of the Apeiron." Reality in the mode of existence, therefore, is experienced as "immersed in reality in the mode of non-existence and, inversely, non-existence reaches into existence. The process has the character of an In-Between reality, governed by the tension of life and death."[10]

Human consciousness of existence as occurring in the Metaxy is engendered by theophanic events, and as such is in historical flux, as we can perceive by following the trail of symbols from the compactness of the old myth to the noetic and pneumatic differentiations of consciousness in Greek philosophy and Israelite-Christian revelation, which differentiations require a new mythical language about the experiences of coming into and passing out of existence.

Theophanic events, such as the vision of the *Agathon* by Platonic Socrates, of the Burning Bush by Moses, and of the Resurrected Christ by Paul, allow human beings to become fully conscious of the range of their humanity and of their intermediate status between mortality and immortality. The *daimonios aner*, or spiritually mature man, is conscious of participating in a process which, in a manner that must remain a mystery, will result in his immortalization (*athanatizein*); as the mortal-immortal, he will strive to attune himself to the highest that is within him, the divine spark. But he will not lose his spiritual "balance" and will be aware that here and now he continues to exist in the cosmos and cannot bestow grace upon himself or achieve immortality within time.

8. Voegelin, "On Hegel—A Study in Sorcery," *Studium Generale*, 24 (1971):351. This has also appeared in *The Study of Time*, ed. J. Fraser et al. (New York: Springer-Verlag, 1972), 1:434. It will also appear in *Order and History*, Vol. 5.

9. Voegelin, "On Hegel—A Study in Sorcery," *Studium Generale*, p. 360; *The Study of Time*, 1:443.

10. *Order and History*, 4:174–75.

The reader will doubtless be aware of a seeming ambiguity in Voegelin's language: the Metaxy is portrayed both *as* reality in flux and as the *consciousness* of reality in flux. The "ambiguity" is not attributable to sloppiness of language, however, but is inherent in reality itself. For human beings experience reality only through consciousness; at the same time they are aware of participating in a reality that is greater than consciousness. Consciousness is not the whole, but a process within the whole. There is, then, a truth *of* reality as a process in the Between moving beyond itself which is emphatically to be distinguished from a truth *about* "reality" conceived of as an object "external" to a (self-contained) consciousness.

The reality of human existence (or political reality in the full sense) is *metaleptic*: it can be experienced only through participation from within. It is not a "something," apart from the consciously participating human being, about which propositions can be advanced. Adequate symbols in political philosophy portray the participatory or metaleptic character of reality and are supple and fluid, moving with the flux of reality itself both as to range and depth; inadequate or deformed language about political reality expresses itself in doctrines and propositions and is based upon the eclipse of part of the experiential field. The "clarity" of deformed political language is bought at the terrible price of the simplification, reduction, and reification of human experience. It is, of course, possible to offer the objection that closed existence on the basis of reduction and simplification of experience is preferable to open existence in response to the pull of the divine ground as manifested in the theophanic event. Voegelin's answer to that kind of objection is on principle the same as Plato's in *Philebus* 16–17, or the prophet Jeremiah's in Jeremiah 45. For life is not a given, and the psyche is a battleground between life and death. The basis for the "preference" for the divine pull of openness over the demonic pull of closure—for theophany over egophany—is the love of life. If, of course, one prefers death in the secure, closed prison of world-immanent existence to potential immortality through faith and trust in the divine presence in the Metaxy, then there is not much that a philosopher can do about it.

Another obvious objection to Voegelin's teaching is that not everybody experiences the theophanic event and/or recognizes its authority, and that therefore it may be only a private, subjective opinion, or simply "one man's idea about reality."[11] Voegelin's answer is that, while the "structure of reality is not there to be seen by everybody under all personal, social, and historical circumstances," and indeed the "face of reality" becomes visible only to the psyche that is open to the divine ground, nonetheless, the differentiated, noetic experience of reality by the open-souled philosopher is representative for human beings. The experience is universally representative because human beings possess a "something" that can "respond to a theophany and engage in

11. Ibid., p. 186.

the quest of the ground." This "something" was called the *daimon* (or spiritual element) by Plato and the *theion* (divine particle) by Aristotle.[12] Every human being is in principle capable of "seeing" the "face" of cognitively structured reality if he or she will open the psyche and meditatively reenact the experience of the transcendent ground of Being, which is the intelligible source of order and structure in the world. *Without the noetic theophany of the philosophers*—which, although a discovery of the few, was for everybody, and everybody is capable of seeing why this is so—*there could be no cognitively structured reality at all*, for no "systematic exploration of structure in reality is possible unless the world is intelligible," and the world is intelligible only in relation to the one divine ground experienced in the theophanic event that is the divine *nous*.[13]

But why, a critic might continue, should one be bound by the language of past theophanic events, and, above all, by the "parochial" vocabulary of the Greek, Judaic, and Christian philosophers, even if one accepts the proposition that not to experience the one divine ground is not to possess a cognitively structured, intelligible reality? Why not leave us completely free to invent our own novel vocabulary? Voegelin's answer is that *there is no abstract language of political evaluation*; there is only the "concrete language created in the articulation of the event."[14] Consciousness itself is "not an abstract entity facing an abstract reality . . . rather it is the consciousness of a concrete man, living in a concrete society, and moving within its historically concrete modes of experience and symbolization."[15] It is fallacious to attempt to abolish "the historical process of consciousness"; the attempt can lead and has led only to deforming both our symbols and our humanity. Human existence has a time dimension. It is ultimately a mystery as to why in only two tiny corners of the world—Israel and Hellas—at a given epoch the fully differentiated noetic and pneumatic theophanies occurred. ("How odd of God/To choose the Jews." How odd, indeed, by any rationalistic secularizing account.) But it is *only* with these *concrete* events (of revelation and philosophy) that the one transcendent-divine ground, which is the basis of any cognitively intelligible structure of reality, came into view. Ineluctably, we remain heirs to this classical and Judeo-Christian discovery and symbolic articulation of the world-transcendent divine ground, and today we must seek to move

12. Ibid., p. 237.
13. Ibid. Voegelin is here restating the arguments against an "infinite regress" in Thomas Aquinas (*Summa Theologica*, I, Q. 2, A. 3). Without a "first cause," motion could not be explained, without a Beginning or Source (*Arche*), creaturely existence could not be explained, without an independent Being, dependent beings could not be explained, and without a final Cause, efficient causes could not be explained. The intractability of mythical speculation for scientific explanation is due precisely to the inability of mythical speculation to differentiate the transcendent Ground from intracosmic existence.
14. Ibid., p. 39.
15. Ibid., p. 75.

within the orbit of that discovery and articulation if we wish to make sense instead of nonsense out of the political world.

Although human beings exist in the Between, in openness of consciousness, they can experience the presence of the divine both as mediated through the "experience of the existence and intelligible structure of things in the cosmos" (which Voegelin calls the Beginning) and as immediately experienced in the "movements of the soul" (which he designates as the Beyond). These two modes of the divine presence in the Between require two different types of language. The Beginning, or the presence of divine reality "mediated by the existence and order of things in the cosmos" requires the language of myth, above all that of the myth of creation; while the Beyond, or the "immediate presence" of the divine in the soul, requires the "revelatory" language of consciousness. "This is the language of seeking, searching, and questioning, of ignorance and knowledge concerning the divine ground, of futility, absurdity, anxiety, and alienation of existence, of being moved to seek and question, of being drawn toward the ground, of turning around, of return, illumination, and rebirth." [16]

Voegelin's study of the trail of symbols that is history reveals man to be the creature capable of asking the Question (with a capital "Q"): "Why should a cosmos exist at all, if man can do no better than live in it as if he were not of it, in order to make his escape from the prison through death?" "This," he continues, "is the critical question that brings the mystery of reality into full view: There is a cosmos in which man participates by his existence; man is endowed with cognitive consciousness of the reality in which he is a partner; consciousness differentiates in a process called history; and in the process of history man discovers reality to be moving toward the Beyond of its present structure." [17]

Because of the ineradicable uncertainty and ambiguity permeating their existence, and because of the fragility and vulnerability of that condition, human beings are tempted to deform themselves and construct a closed system in whose prison they might find the security lacking in a life open to the tension characteristic of existence in the Between. Particularly since the differentiations of consciousness brought on by Greek philosophy and the Judaic-Christian revelation—both of which dissolved the compactness of the cosmological myth—the temptation to engage in Gnostic system-building has been extremely powerful. The differentiation of consciousness through philosophy and revelation—or what Henri Bergson called the "opening of the soul"—has decisively increased the range of human possibilities both for good and for evil. For human beings are left with the freedom to use their

16. Ibid., pp. 17–18.
17. Ibid., p. 19; cf. ibid., p. 320; "The Question is not just any question but the quest concerning the mysterious ground of all being."

new-found openness to the pull of the eschatological Beyond, either in "forming" or in "deforming" their humanity. Specifically, in thinking that inclines to Gnosticism, there is the danger that man may lose his existential "balance" because of his exclusive concentration on the pull of the eschatological Beyond to the neglect of his anchorage in the cosmological Beginning. "For a Gnostic thinker must be able to forget that the cosmos does not emerge from consciousness, but that a man's consciousness emerges from the cosmos." Particularly after the ascendency of Christianity with its strong eschatological emphasis, Voegelin has found the danger of derailment a serious one.[18] His interpretation of Christianity, especially since the publication of Volume 4 of *Order and History*, has become the subject of considerable controversy. We shall briefly return to this subject in the conclusion of this essay.

Human existence, then, for Voegelin is part of reality, and human beings who live in the Between of finite consciousness have the duty of "noetically exploring the structure of reality as far as it is intelligible" and of "spiritually coping with the insight into its movement from the divine Beginning to the divine Beyond of its structure."[19]

III

Mention of the "structure" of reality brings us close to the heart of Voegelin's framework for political evaluation. However, his position is stated with great philosophical precision, and not attending carefully to what he says may cause us to mistake him for the propagator of yet another "ism" or dogmatic system promising Gnostic redemption from the perils of mortal life.

Nowhere is it more clear than in his essay "Equivalences of Experience and Symbolization in History" his intention to walk the tightrope over the twin abysses of fanatical certitude and dogmatic skepticism in order to recapture the zetetic spirit of the *philosophia perennis*. Although reality has a "structure" with whose divine ground the open-souled person *seeks* attunement, human existence itself is a condition of flux and tension between truth and the "deformation" of reality. Therefore, "ultimate doctrines, systems, and values" are delusions "engendered by deformed existence." The "constants" that we discover to emerge in the time dimension of existence are not dogmas or a catalogue of disembodied propositions but tensional symbols which illumine the character of existence as occurring between imperfection and perfection, mortality and immortality, order and disorder, attunement and revolt, sense and senselessness, truth and untruth. "If we split these pairs of symbols," ob-

18. Ibid., p. 20. Voegelin himself has said, however, in response to the question whether he would call himself a Christian, "I try to be, and also to be a philosopher." (Conversation with the author, April 1975.)
19. Ibid., p. 28.

serves Voegelin, "and hypostatize the poles of the tension as independent entities, we destroy the reality of existence as it has been experienced by the creators of the tensional symbols." We then fall prey either to hedonistic apoliticism or to the "murderous" possession of ideological "truth."[20] Dream life then replaces wake life, in the language of Heraclitus and Plato.

To recapitulate, Voegelin teaches—and when I say "teaches," I mean much more than mere advocacy, for he offers voluminous documentation for his teaching, drawing on numerous disciplines and his enormous interpretive and linguistic gifts—that the language of politics may be evaluated in terms of its "correspondence" with "reality," provided that reality be conceived not as an "object" external to the consciousness of the investigator, but rather as a process within which man is situated and which he seeks to illumine from within. Political reality, or the "human realm of being" (*Seinsbereich Mensch*) is not the whole but a process within the whole. The human realm of being may best be characterized by Plato's term, the Metaxy. In the Between of human life, man experiences himself in tension between the poles of openness and closure, attunement and revolt, the divine height and the demonic depth. As the process of the reality moves through man and he through it, man questions the origin and the end of the structure which "contains" the process. The Question regarding the Beginning of the reality in which man participates is "answered" initially by the myth of the cosmos as sacred—i.e., as a creation of the gods and later by the great construction of Genesis 1—while the Question regarding the Beyond is addressed by the "saving tale" of the philosopher's myth of the soul's immortality and the promise of resurrection and redemption proclaimed in the Gospels and the letters of St. Paul. There is always the danger that the tension may collapse and a deformed "second"-reality construct may be substituted for symbols illumining the complexities of the only reality that is. (There can no more be two realities than there can be two universes, save in science fiction.) When the symbols are deformed, so are human beings because, although they do not live by symbols alone, they cannot orient themselves to the process of reality without having recourse to adequate symbols.

In Voegelin's teaching, then, there is the perpetual danger that we will yield to the temptation to collapse the tension of metaleptic (participatory) reality in the Between of human life and substitute for it a fallacious second reality reflecting our own compulsions and "egophanic" imaginings. Indeed, the contrast between "theophanic" and "egophanic" modes of existence is a leading theme of *The Ecumenic Age*. Theophanic existence affirms God as the measure of human conduct, while egophanic existence proclaims "man" in revolt against God as the measure. By *egophany* Voegelin means the attempt to expand the closed self, or ego, to the point where it usurps the place of God

20. Voegelin, "Equivalences of Experience and Symbolization in History," p. 220.

and opens up false standards or norms for action in the world. (Literally, *egophany*—a word coined by Voegelin—means "manifestation of the ego," while *theophany* means "manifestation of the divine.") The person who is conscious of his existence in the Metaxy, which is the "site" for the encounter between man and God in the concrete consciousness of individual men, responds and seeks to attune his life by the "theophanic events of differentiating consciousness." Thus, the symbols engendered by a Plato, a Jeremiah, or a Paul reflect the tension of existence in the Metaxy where there occurs the encounter with the divine, although such an encounter does not abolish the character of existence as a tension between contrary poles. Rather, the theophanic event reveals reality as a process moving beyond itself in a manner, which, while it remains a mystery, inspires, through the very act of participation itself, trust that the process will have a good end. For the "experience of reality has a built-in bias toward more reality."[21]

IV

Before proceeding to discuss Voegelin's application of his principles of political evaluation to modern developments, let me attempt to summarize those principles as they are expressed in his extremely important work, *The Ecumenic Age*. The reader should bear in mind that no summary can conceivably do justice to the richness of the argument in a major philosophical undertaking, and he or she is, accordingly, urged to read the volume in its entirety.

1. There is only one reality, whose structure as it appears to human beings is that of the Metaxy, or the tensional field of forces.[22]

2. The divine-human encounter occurs in the Metaxy in the form of the theophanic event, such as the manifestation of the divine *nous* in Plato's dialogues, or the revelation of the hidden God to Moses in the Burning Bush (Exodus 3), and the revelation of God in Christ to the disciples and St. Paul. These are "noetic" and "pneumatic" theophanies respectively.[23]

3. The theophanic events mark a differentiation in the consciousness of the structure of reality in that new symbols are engendered which are more adequate than those of the myth for expressing the truth of the "paradox of reality," i.e., reality exhibits a structure which is moving beyond itself. Thus, while the divine reality is one, its presence is expressed in the two modes of the Beyond (philosophy and revelation) and the Beginning (the myth of the visible cosmos as sacred in origin).[24]

4. The symbol "man" indicates the being within Being capable of consciously participating in reality as process and of articulating its structure.[25]

21. Voegelin, *Order and History*, 4:271.
22. Ibid., pp. 255 and *passim*.
23. Ibid., pp. 9–16, 242–44, 258–59.
24. Ibid., pp. 17, 253, 314–16.
25. Ibid., pp. 56, 202, 234–38.

5. As he acts in the world, man has the duty of self-critically exploring the structure of reality and of maintaining his intellectual and spiritual "balance" in the realm of the Between; in particular, he must not fallaciously attempt to substitute a second reality based on the delusion that he can abolish the structure and its tension. The source of the duty is the encounter with the divine presence in the theophanic event.[26]

6. Through a complicated process, proceeding through various stages, the order of existence has been inverted in the language and practice of modern political thought. Instead of the sequence man-society-history, found in the classical and Judeo-Christian symbolization of existence, we have the inversion history-society-"man" in the various ideological constructions. Specifically, the process proceeds from: (a) the "deformation" of noetic and pneumatic (or philosophical and revelatory) symbols, in the misguided attempt to protect them from compromise or corruption, by wrenching them from their experiential contexts and reifying them into dogmas or propositions, instead of treating the philosophical or scriptural text as a unit along with the theophanic motivating experience that produced it, to (b) the "egophanic revolt," which attacked not only the "deformed" symbols but also the theophanic experiences that engendered them, thereby enabling the ideological perpetrators of the revolt to pretend that they had abolished the reality of the Metaxy, substituting for it a tensionless, purely immanent, "reality" governed by some alchemic law of development manipulable by "man" and his expanded innerworldly consciousness.[27]

7. If, as contemporary students of man, society, and history, we are to have any hope of extricating ourselves from the "grotesque intellectual mess," which after two millennia of deformation of symbols (and, in the modern period, of the egophanic revolt) continues to obscure and eclipse the structure of reality, we must throw off the intellectual and spiritual encumbrances that weigh heavily upon us and reorient ourselves to reality as an "open field of theophany." Voegelin's own work is conceived of as a (preparatory and inevitably incomplete) attempt at "open participation in the process of both history and the Whole." We cannot begin to accomplish such a *metanoia*, however, until we reject the various "stop-history" systems put forward in the modern period by ideologists who are closed to the insights of myth, philosophy, and revelation. Only a recovery of the experiential basis of theophanic experience through a renewed philosophy of the consciousness, as distinguished from a mere reassertion of past symbols as "doctrines," can succeed in reversing the centuries-old trend toward egophany. Without such a philosophy of consciousness, the egophanic ideologues will have no difficulty in retaining their power and influence. With it, there is a chance, over many decades, of our regaining the full measure of our humanity.[28]

26. Ibid., pp. 11–16, 237–38.
27. Ibid., pp. 20–57, 260–71. 28. Ibid., pp. 313–16, 330–35.

V

While *Order and History* is Voegelin's *magnum opus*, the implications of his political philosophy for the evaluation of modern politics are nowhere so clearly spelled out as in *From Enlightenment to Revolution*, a volume which another distinguished political theorist, John Hallowell, only recently persuaded Voegelin to publish. As Hallowell explains in his Introduction, *From Enlightenment to Revolution* "consists of a portion of an unpublished history of political ideas which Eric Voegelin wrote in the nineteen forties and early fifties." Voegelin's "reluctance" to publish the work at the time was caused by his growing conviction that one cannot study the history of political ideas as if it were an "ongoing argument about commonly perceived problems of social order." For the ideas themselves are rooted in the experiences of participation in reality. If the motivating experiences are themselves distorted by passions—above all the *libido dominandi*—which deflect the psyche from the awareness of its anchorage in the reality of the Metaxy, then the "reason," cut loose from its moorings in reality, no matter how technically brilliant or logically airtight, can only articulate symbols that destroy the order of man in society and history. Voegelin, then, came to reject the widely held view that the history of political ideas is a "conversation" or rational debate about common themes, because such an interpretation "assumes a continuity of argument and a universal community of discourse which in fact does not exist."[29]

Voegelin's willingness to release his study of modern political ideas from the Enlightenment to Marx may be attributed in part to the fact that in the intervening years he has worked out a philosophy of the consciousness and a philosophy of history that form the basis of his interpretation of modern political ideas. However, a careful reading of this work will show that his basic philosophical orientation was already present in this earlier period, although not in fully elaborated form.

29. John H. Hallowell, in his introduction to Eric Voegelin, *From Enlightenment to Revolution*, p. vi. I have myself expressed the view that the history of political thought is a "conversation of many voices," most recently in my chapter in Nelson Polsby and Fred Greenstein, *Handbook of Political Science* (Reading, Mass.: Addison-Wesley, 1975), 1:229 ff. One problem is to distinguish between "error and the person who errs," as John XXIII expressed it. Voegelin frequently seems to suggest that not only the ideas of Hegel, Marx, and the rest of the "Gnostics" are erroneous, but that the thinkers themselves are spiritually diseased as persons. I must confess that I still find it difficult to accept this latter judgment and wonder if it is necessary to condemn these thinkers as whole persons in the way, again, that Voegelin *appears* to argue. Hannah Arendt's remark that there is an "abyss" between facile ideas and brutal ideas needs to be recalled here. And yet, there is an obviously powerful, if unintended, effect of Gnostic or messianic ideas on the climate in which a Hitler or a Stalin lives and works. Voegelin's point is that they do not emerge in an intellectual vacuum. Thinkers presumably have an obligation to weigh the probable consequences of their words on future generations of some not so philosophical human beings. However, we today can say all of this about Condorcet, Helvétius, Hegel, Marx, and the rest from the advantage of hindsight, of having witnessed the horrors of twentieth-century totalitarianism.

The most that I can say at present is that in *From Enlightenment to Revolution* Voegelin has opened up an enormously difficult and important problem of historical interpretation which

Without vainly attempting to recapitulate the entire account of *From Enlightenment to Revolution*, let me give some examples of the way in which Voegelin has applied the principles of evaluation articulated in his philosophy to the politics of the modern period.

While Voegelin is no apologist for the medieval ecclesiastical polity, and while he sharply castigates the Church for its resistance to free inquiry and to the autonomous development of modern science, he has concluded that what has come to be called the "secularization" process took place in the modern West in a manner which has been exceedingly unfortunate for the life of the spirit. The relegation of the Church, which in the medieval order had undertaken to represent the spiritual concerns of Christians, to the private sphere and the consequent assignment to the newly sovereign "secular" political institutions of a monopoly of society's public concerns, "left the field open for a respiritualization of the public sphere from other sources," such as the various ideologies, including nationalism, liberal and socialist versions of "economism," various biological and psychological reductionist doctrines, and a closed collectivist form of "humanitarian tribalism."[30] In the course of this process of "de-divinization" of the world and its reductionist "respiritualization," the classical and Christian understanding of man was destroyed and replaced by an enormously constricted image of "man." Man is no longer interpreted as the Aristotelian *spoudaios* or the Judaic-Christian creature bearing the *imago Dei*. He becomes "man" in quotation marks, an inventive, featherless biped who can get along perfectly well without bothersome experiences of transcendence and the pull of the divine Beyond.

During the long and complicated secularization process, the symbolic language of Christianity, drawn from both Hebrew and Hellenistic sources, loses its "transparency for transcendental reality." The Christian symbols of the Fall, Redemption, Resurrection, and the rest are taken as dogmas and are viewed "in a 'literal,' disenchanted opaqueness from the outside." When interpreted in this way—as if they were propositions referring to the world, to immanent reality, rather than mythopoeic symbols indicating the character of human participation in the Metaxy—they are judged to be "superstitious," irrational, and in conflict with logic, biology, etc.[31]

Thus, Voegelin argues, the secularization process, instead of deserving to be hailed as a forward step in the history of humankind, should be seen as a tragic story of experiential contraction, symbolic impoverishment, and the diminution of our shared consciousness of what had been known to be man.

---

should concern political scientists in general and all of us who write about the history of political thought in particular much more than it has.

30. Voegelin, *From Enlightenment to Revolution*, pp. 20–28.
31. Ibid., p. 21.

Voegelin's perception of modernity as a waste land thus approximates that of T. S. Eliot, whose poetry he quotes frequently.

The "progressive" thinkers of the French Enlightenment, such as Voltaire, Diderot, and Turgot, are particular targets of Voegelin's criticism, because of—among other reasons—their rejection of the Aristotelian primacy of the *bios theoretikos* over banausic activity and for their efforts to confine the meaning of virtue to conduct that is "useful" to society.[32] (Diderot, for example, had a pronounced aversion for the "useless contemplator.")

The implications of the contracted image of man in the writings of the *philosophes* were stated in more radically reductionist form by Helvétius in the eighteenth century and by Saint-Simon and Auguste Comte in the nineteenth. These thinkers and others, whom Voegelin analyzes in detail and with the most scrupulous regard for the sources, "have mutilated the idea of man beyond recognition. . . . This reduction of man and his life to the level of utilitarian existence is the symptom of the critical breakdown of Western civilization through the atrophy of the intellectual and spiritual substance of man. In the progressive, Positivist movement since the middle of the eighteenth century . . . the term man no longer designates the mature man of the humanist and Christian tradition, but only the crippled, utilitarian fragment."[33]

Throughout this explosive work, Voegelin is concerned to show that the entire vocabulary of modern Western politics—insofar as it does not continue to be influenced by residues of the classical and Judeo-Christian modes of thought—has been corrupted. Symbols such as "reality," "man," "reason," and "history" no longer mean what they meant prior to their having been "deformed." Thus, after several centuries of symbolic degradation and inversion, Marx is able to reject out of hand the fundamental philosophical question regarding the nature of reality by simply referring to what has by then "in common parlance" come to be called reality.[34] And in the "fragmentary anthropologies" of the moderns, the "normal man" is taken to be the imma-

---

32. Ibid., pp. 27–28.   33. Ibid., p. 95.

34. Ibid., p. 258. Voegelin here quotes the judgment of S. Landshut and J. P. Mayer, Introduction to *Marx: Der historische Materialismus* (Leipzig, 1932), 1:xxii. Voegelin points out that if Marx had been open to the question regarding the ground of human existence, he would not have produced an ideology which denies that man is situated in an order of being and a cosmic order to which he is subordinated. Had they raised the question, Marx and Engels would have correctly recognized themselves as "predicates" of a divine subject instead of indulging in the illusion that they were Promethean creators of a new reality. Had Marx raised the question of the nature of reality, he would have been led to recognize the "total context" of which he was only a minute part. Instead, Voegelin contends Marx engaged in "pseudo-logical speculation," and "grandiose ranting," with the result that he and his followers produced a "general intellectual mess" on the basis of illusory second-reality constructions. "And these," Voegelin wryly concludes in his section on Marx, "are the ideas that shake the world!" (ibid., p. 272). Voegelin's critique of Marx provides philosophical underpinning for Solzhenitsyn's judgment, in his 1974

nentist power-seeker of Hobbes or the pleasure-pain mechanism of the utilitarians, or the "megalomaniac intellectual" of Condorcet and Comte, or Marx's "socialistic man" who asks no metaphysical questions, or Nietzsche's *Übermensch* who extends grace to himself—in fact anyone except the whole person of the classical and Judeo-Christian teaching. The "spiritually mature" human being of the classical and biblical teaching comes to be regarded as a freak or relic from the past, someone to be psychoanalyzed or otherwise dissected or explained but certainly not someone to be taken as a model for emulation and a standard for evaluation.[35]

Just as the symbols "reality" and "man" acquired radically changed meanings during the modern process of deculturation, so in like manner did symbols such as "reason," "history," and the "science of politics." Reason, understood in the Platonic-Aristotelian sense as the faculty for self-critically illuminating the "total context" in which humanity's personal existence is situated, is degraded to the level of a faculty of cleverness and technical expertise, as an instrument through which human beings maximize their desires. It becomes the servant of the passions, inverting the Platonic psychology. The closed self, in its inverted existence, builds a prison where it finds a garden. Ultimately, the modern egophanic speculator seeks to freeze history itself, and we witness the rise of what Voegelin calls the "stop-history movements." The stop-history movements regard the latest phase of human evolution as the culminating one, and they reject on principle the possibility that future developments in political life and thought may be dramatically different from the present ones. The modern "progressive," trend-riding intellectuals are closed to the time-dimension of existence and to history as an open field of theophany.[36] They are, in fact, anything but "progressive."

VI

From his study of the widest possible range of evidence—e.g., the comparative study of symbols engendered over the millennia by those who have raised the basic questions about the Why of existence and the nature of reality as a process experienced in the Between of human life—Voegelin concludes that the modern world is now and may be for another century in the throes of a

---

Stockholm Nobel Prize interview, "Solzhenitsyn Speaks out" (reprinted in *National Review*, 6 June 1975, 606), that it is wishful thinking to draw a dramatic distinction between the "humanism" of Marx and the antihumanism of Lenin and Stalin.

As mentioned in note 29, the difficult problem as I see it is to reconcile the demands for intellectual perspicacity with those of human charity (to employ a distinction of the late Leo Strauss). Without indulging in sentimentality, we are obliged to be charitable to our fellow human beings in the Between. I cannot imagine that Voegelin would disagree with my last statement.

35. Voegelin, *From Enlightenment to Revolution*, pp. 69, 97, 132, 178, 258.

36. Ibid., pp. 27–73.

spiritual crisis of unprecedented proportions. The key symbols of our political discourse have become distorted and corrupted with "second reality" connotations. Our political science, under the impact of positivization which has done so much to restrict the range and depth of political inquiry and, indeed, of the concept of the political itself, has largely lost the capacity thoughtfully to raise the "great questions" of political philosophy. It accordingly has been a negligible force in combatting the fallacy of the two realities which lies at the root of extremist ideological thinking and in exposing the inversion of the proper sequence of man-society-history in so much of our contemporary political and social analysis, both within and without the academy.

Alfred North Whitehead once observed that "the world never recovers from the shock of a great philosopher." Whether this observation is valid for our time is certainly debatable. We appear largely to have lost the capacity to recognize a philosopher when we see one. That this is so is evident in part from the slight attention (relative to its importance) which Voegelin's work has thus far received in political science circles.

Of course, it is painful to recognize that a drastic revision of one's language, priorities, and evaluations may well be required if what Voegelin says is true. Whether his teaching is valid in general—and which aspects are in need of refinement or revision—is a matter which can be established only after a thoroughgoing debate *at the philosophical level*. It would be counter to the entire spirit of openness of inquiry in philosophy per se and of Voegelin's work in particular to accept his teaching automatically and uncritically. But it would also be counter to that spirit to reject it automatically and uncritically, and, given the climate of the times, the latter response is far more likely to be encountered than the former. In fact, to accept Voegelin's teaching as a *doctrine* would violate his fundamental premise of the priority of motivating experience over the "dead" letter.

A frequent form of the ritualistic rejection of a philosophical teaching is what Voegelin himself calls "positionism." That is, if one can label a thinker something different from one's own "position," then one is dispensed from the burden of having to think seriously about what that person has to say. Because of his openness to experiences of transcendence, for example, one not infrequently hears Voegelin dismissed as a "confessional" or "sectarian" thinker. And yet, Voegelin's chapter on "The Pauline Vision of the Resurrected" has prompted great concern from many Christians because of his treatment of the problem of the physical Resurrection and the general question of "historical Jesus."[37] It would be impossible here to deal with all the

37. Voegelin, *Order and History*, 4:239–71 (chap. 5). See the vehement review by Frederick D. Wilhelmsen in *Triumph* (January 1975), pp. 32–35, for an admittedly rather sensationalist manifestation of this concern. [Cf. Eugene Webb's extensive analysis of the issues referred to here, in this volume, *infra*.—Ed.]

complexities of the issue, but Voegelin's emphasis upon the Resurrection of Christ as a "vision" which takes place in the consciousness of the disciples and of Paul should not be understood as implying a merely "subjective" or allegorizing interpretation of the event. As with all theophanic events, the Resurrection for Voegelin occurs in and, indeed, engenders the reality of the Between of differentiating consciousness. It is therefore inappropriate to split the event, which is a unity, into an objective "something" and a subjective awareness of that "something." As Voegelin expressed the matter in principle:

> If the metaleptic [participatory] symbol which is the word of both god and man is hypostatized into a doctrinal Word of God . . . [it] can impair the sensitivity for the source of truth in the flux of divine presence in time which constitutes history. Unless precautions of meditative practice are taken, the doctrinization of symbols is liable to interrupt the process of experiential reactivation and linguistic renewal. When the symbol separates from its source in the experiential Metaxy, the Word of God can degenerate into a word of man that one can believe or not.[38]

Voegelin's intention throughout his work is not to advocate a "position," but "to follow empirically the patterns of meaning as they revealed themselves in the self-interpretation of persons and societies in history."[39] He is poles apart from the ideological doctrinaire, who imposes an a priori pattern upon events. Thus, in *From Enlightenment to Revolution*, after two chapters of relentless criticism of the epistemology and "ontology" of Marx, Voegelin credits Marx with having "laid his finger on the sore spot of modern industrial society," viz., "the growth of economic institutions into a power of . . . overwhelming influence on the life of every single man. . . ." Thus, he argues, Marx treated under the heading of "alienation" the problem that "in an industrialized society man is not the master of his economic existence." Voegelin also castigates economics as a science for its failure to follow Marx's path-breaking analysis of the relationship between man and nature to the point where it would have developed a philosophy of labor.[40]

Eric Voegelin has in many works, but principally in his *magnum opus, Order and History*, presented us with a philosophically profound analysis of the structure of reality in the Metaxy which is highly relevant to the concrete problem of political evaluation in our time. Although much of his analysis of modern developments is negative, his teaching is by no means unhopeful, and he recognizes that there are encouraging signs of intellectual and spiritual resistance to the symbolic impoverishment and degradation which have been dominant in modern politics, and beyond that, signs of the possibility of experiential and linguistic reactivation and renewal. But although he is

38. Voegelin, *Order and History*, 4:56.   39. Ibid., p. 57.
40. Voegelin, *From Enlightenment to Revolution*, pp. 299–300.

scarcely without hope, he is modest in his expectations about the impact of his own work on the crisis of our time: "Nobody can heal the spiritual disorder of an 'age.' A philosopher can do no more than work himself free from the rubble of idols which, under the name of an 'age,' threatens to cripple and bury him; and he can hope that the example of his effort will be of help to others who find themselves in the same situation and experience the same desire to gain their humanity under God."[41]

41. Voegelin, "On Hegel—A Study in Sorcery," p. 349; *The Study of Time*, 1:432.

PHILOSOPHY IN VOEGELIN'S WORK

David J. Walsh

Philosophy forms the analytic core for Eric Voegelin's study of order and history. This essay explores the meaning of the symbolism of Voegelin's work and attempts to show why this symbolism is one of the principal reasons for the success of his investigation. He has been able to understand the meaning of order and disorder in men and societies, as well as the problems which are raised for the order of history, because his inquiry proceeds from the symbolism analyzing the presence of order and structure within reality. This is in the manner of classic philosophy. It is the discovery of the divine *Nous* or Reason as the source of order in man's psyche, a source which extends to society and history and makes transparent the order of reality as a whole.

I

Philosophy in Voegelin's work is not simply one topic of reflection among others; it is the experiential and symbolic horizon within which the whole inquiry is conducted. This means that our investigation will not be satisfied by a review of his analyses of the works of various philosophers and their spurious imitators. Rather we must examine his own articulation of reality, which has taken over philosophical insights that belong to the history of order and has added his own developments to them. The very nature of a study such as *Order and History* is more than a report on the materials of history; it is itself an exploration and unfolding of reality in the historical struggle for order and its symbolization. The study of order and its history is, of necessity, an articulation of order, and the study of philosophic order is itself a work of philosophy.

Voegelin's conception of philosophy is found, therefore, in the whole of *Order and History* and not just in the sections that are explicitly devoted to that symbolic form. This situation requires an analysis of the viewpoint from which the entire study is conducted and not simply the isolation of his interpretations of conventionally "philosophic" thinkers. Voegelin himself is highly conscious of his work as an exercise in philosophy and has been increasingly concerned with developing the philosophical instruments by which the phenomena of man's search for order can be analyzed. He has spoken of the need for a philosophical anthropology and more recently of a philosophy of consciousness in order to restore political science, the science of man's order in society and history, to an openness to the reality in which all men live. This experiential core, which radiates its light over the dimensions of man's existence, is the object of inquiry for this essay.

The ordering center of experience, however, is not a given prior to the empirical study that is unfolded in *Order and History*. Its presence on a continuum with the major symbolisms of order means that its theoretical viewpoint cannot be completed before the empirical inquiry has successfully recovered the symbolisms of order. This symbiotic relationship between the instruments of analysis and the historical materials of the study has characterized Voegelin's development since he abandoned the "History of Political Ideas" for an investigation of experiences and symbols. In the foreword to *Anamnesis*, where he discusses the need for a philosophy of consciousness to form the center for a philosophy of politics and history, he makes this situation abundantly clear: "The particular studies should make us attentive to the empirical connection between the analysis of consciousness and the phenomena of order: just as consciousness is the center from which the concrete order of human existence in society and history radiates, so the empirical data (*Empirie*) of social and historical phenomena of order reach into the empirical data of consciousness and its experience of participation." [1]

Thus, a sympathetic consideration of the meaning of *philosophy* in Voegelin's work will have to take this configuration of relationships into account. It suggests that we might begin with the most general principles he explicates; then, examine their application to the interpretation of classic philosophy and the recovery of the noetic core of existence; and finally, turn to the developments that this philosophic viewpoint has undergone in its extension to include the experiences of existence that are furnished by the other major symbolisms of order. In this way, it seems we can best appreciate the meaning of Professor Voegelin's philosophy and some of the problems it entails.

II

"The order of history emerges from the history of order." [2] This is the opening sentence of *Order and History* and the most generic statement of its guiding principle. Making it more specific and filling it with concrete meaning

1. Eric Voegelin, *Anamnesis: Zur Theorie der Geschichte und Politik*, (Munich: R. Piper & Co., Verlag, 1966), pp. 8–9.
2. Voegelin, *Order and History*, 4 vols. to date (Baton Rouge: Louisiana State University Press, 1956–), 1:ix.

absorbs the four volumes published, so that all that is possible here is an indication of its basic implications. Voegelin himself acknowledges it as the general principle of the study in expressing his agreement with Polybius' historiographic method, "that the object of the study has to emerge as self-apparent from the events themselves."[3] This means that the events and their configurations must be identified by the self-interpretations which are included in the events themselves; in particular, the self-interpretation of a society must be studied as an essential part of its order. In the case of the "Ecumenic Age" for example, there would be no such unit of meaning unless it had been the self-designation that the contemporaries gave to the events in which they were involved. This approach is masterfully demonstrated in Volume 4 of Professor Voegelin's study, where the meaning of the Ecumenic Age is elucidated through an examination of the whole range of self-interpretation by the participants in the events concerned.

On the most fundamental level, thus, the principle means that the substance for a study of history consists in the self-interpretations by concrete men and societies of the reality in which they participate. In every period there are men who are capable of articulating their participation in the process of reality and of illuminating the order of their existence. This self-understanding is the inner order of their existence and constitutes the reality of their actions and symbolizations; the materials and events of history do not exist apart from their transparence for the existential order of the men and societies who produce them. This principle, that the reality of social and historical phenomena is constituted by their relation to the order within the souls of the men who have engendered them, is also the basic principle of philosophy: that the psyche is the experiential center of order which radiates its meaning over society and history. Plato has formulated it that society is "man written in larger letters," and Voegelin extends this to conceive history also, as man written in larger form.[4]

The symbols that have been created to express the order of man's existence in society and history have their origin in the experiences of participation in the order of being. They do not refer to any independent entities which are given outside of this experience, but articulate only the inner dimensions of the experience itself. This means, as Voegelin repeatedly emphasizes, that the symbols expressing the ultimate horizon of existential order are utterly different from language concerning objects in the external world. Unlike objects of sense perception, the reality of order exists only to the extent that a particular human consciousness opens to the source of order in experience and realizes this order by his growth into it. Through the actualization of order

3. Voegelin, *Order and History*, 4:122.
4. Voegelin, "Immortality: Experience and Symbol," *Harvard Theological Review* 60 (1967): 249.

within man, the order of existence becomes luminous and spreads its light over the process of reality as a whole. In this unfolding and pursuit of order by responsive individuals, the symbols that express it are an essential part of the search and its existential resolution, and must be interpreted in terms of their creation within these experiences.[5]

The reality of the historical symbols of order as articulations of the inner constitution of order in concrete human beings, is also relevant for Voegelin's own project. The "order of history" is itself a symbolism which emerges when the experience of order has become sufficiently luminous to penetrate to the time dimension of existence and to extrapolate the order that radiates from its center in consciousness. It is a symbolism created in the concrete attempt to unfold the order of existence by exploring the dimensions of the reality in which man participates. Thus, the symbolization of the order of history cannot take place before history as a dimension of existence has been differentiated—as it is in the Judeo-Christian tradition—nor before the order of the psyche has been identified as the source of order within history—as it has been in classic philosophy.[6] For this reason Voegelin must recover the experiences of order in which the symbolism of order and history were created— before the meaning of these experiences can be used to illuminate the order of history. And a principal event in this recovery is his restoration of the experience of noetic philosophy.

III

Professor Voegelin describes *Order and History* as a "philosophy of history" and as "a philosophical inquiry concerning the order of human existence in society and history."[7] The study, although it moves in continuity with the other symbolizations of man's existence, particularly the Judeo-Christian, receives its central orientation from the philosophic exploration of the structure of existence in man, society, and history. This is the symbolism in which the divine Nous or Reason has been revealed as the source of order in man, with his personal, social, and historical dimensions, and in the process of reality as a whole. Therefore, an inquiry that seeks to uncover the order of history as it emerges through man's search for order, must refer to the symbolism that has articulated the experience of structure in reality and particularly as it is in man's existence. The only symbolism where this has been achieved is noetic philosophy, and all attempts to articulate the experience of structure in man, society, and history must return to the experiences in which the symbolization of structure was engendered.

5. Voegelin, "Equivalences of Experience and Symbolization in History," *Eternità e Storia: I valori permanenti nel divenire storico*, (Florence: Vallechi editore, 1970), pp. 214–34, esp. pp. 220–23.
6. Voegelin, *Order and History*, 2:7.   7. Ibid., 1:xiv.

The instruments that enabled Voegelin to recover these experiences were the principles of experience and symbolization outlined above. Conversely, the principles that guided his investigation were themselves confirmed and expanded through the discovery of the classic symbolization of order by philosophy. This reciprocal recovery of the past and the present has been made possible, as Voegelin acknowledges, through the enormous expansion of the historical sciences in this century. In the classical area, this expansion has involved the labors of Greek scholars over the last forty years, which have produced an amazing restoration of the world of meaning that had been lost under a morass of conventional misunderstandings. However, Voegelin has played a special part in this achievement insofar as he has not by interest or training been exclusively preoccupied by Greek problems, and has thereby been able to grasp and exploit the theoretical implications of their discoveries. He has recognized the inner finality of noetic philosophy and has developed it, by placing it in an expanded context, as the guiding center for a contemporary study of order and history. By this means Voegelin has truly recovered the spirit of the Platonic philosophy and has certainly illuminated its meaning more fully, through the wider range of comparison with other experiences of order which now becomes possible.

The recovery of noetic philosophy has been achieved principally by a restoration of the experiential context from which it was derived. The relation between experiential foundations and symbolic expression has been one of the central themes of Professor Voegelin's study, and it was his commitment to these guiding principles that led him to recover the core of the philosophic experience. He perceived it as the only adequate approach in the present context, where the symbols of philosophy had become detached from the concrete experiences of existential order and had been misinterpreted as doctrines or pieces of information concerning external objects, which had then to be designated as either real or imaginary. The pervasive doctrinization of symbols is the situation that gave rise to Voegelin's notorious remark that "the history of philosophy is in the largest part the history of its derailment."[8]

In his response to this state of misunderstanding, he has carefully excavated the underlying experiences that gave rise to philosophy and that can once again infuse its symbols with meaning and reality. The means to this end have been the restoration of the context of concrete questions to which the articulations of Plato and Aristotle were a response. This was the context of the struggle and resistance by independent thinkers to the corruption of order *within* the poleis, and the massive disorientation produced *without* by the ecumenic empires.

The context that was consciously present as the background for the classic philosophers, Plato and Aristotle, was stratified by the historical traditions

8. Voegelin, *Order and History*, 3:277.

going back in depth. There is first the primary experience of the cosmos as an embracing whole in which man experiences himself as a consubstantial partner in the community of being that contains God and man, world and society. Voegelin considers that the "togetherness and one-in-anotherness" is the characteristic feature of this experience, which he explains is derived from the experience of the cosmos itself. "The cosmos is not a thing among others; it is the background of reality against which all existent things exist; it has reality in the mode of non-existence."[9] It is the experience of this underlying, intangible, embracingness of all that exists which is expressed in the cosmological symbolism whereby the intracosmic areas of reality provide one another with analogies of being. For example, the king's claim to rule over the four quarters of the world is derived by analogy with the celestial revolutions over the four quarters of the earth. It is essentially the experience of the tension of existence out of nonexistence, although the symbolism is unstable because the construction of mutual analogies between intracosmic realities does not adequately articulate the tension.

The problem is resolved only by the differentiation of the nonexistent reality of the divine ground through its self-revelation in a man's soul. This is the process that took place in the Hellenic poleis, which because of the absence of an imperial structure, permitted individual thinkers to more freely explore the rise and fall of the universally human reality or order, without restriction to its mediation by an empire. Voegelin traces the emergence of philosophy from this context in *The World of the Polis*, where he shows that even in the earlier mythic symbolizations, of Homer and Hesiod, this freedom was evident; their speculations on political catastrophes were concerned, not with an empire but with the fundamentally human problem of spiritual and moral decay of existence.

When the process of differentiation had gone far enough to dispense with the language of the myth, the core of the primary experience of the cosmos was formulated by Anaximander in his celebrated fragment. "The origin (*arche*) of things is the *apeiron* (Boundless). . . . It is necessary for things to perish into that from which they were born; for they pay one another penalty for their injustice (*adikia*) according to the ordinance of Time."[10] Voegelin draws a good deal of illumination from this pronouncement, expressing, as it does, the essence of the embracing order of the cosmos which remained the conscious background for the differentiations of the later thinkers. "Reality

9. Ibid., 4:72, 67–78, and ibid., 1, Introduction and chaps. 1–3.
10. Quoted from ibid., 4:174. [See Hermann Diels, *Die Fragmente der Vorsokratiker*, ed. Walther Kranz (7th ed.; Berlin-Charlottenburg: Weldmannsche Verlagsbuchhandlung, 1954), Anaximander A 9, B 1; also G. S. Kirk and J. E. Raven, *The Presocratic Philosophers: A Critical History with a Selection of Texts* (Cambridge: At the University Press, 1960), pp. 99–142. For Voegelin's earlier consideration of Anaximander, see *Order and History*, 2:181–83, 232–34.—Ed.]

was perceived by Anaximander (*fl.* 560 B.C.) as a cosmic process in which things emerge from, and disappear into, the non-existence of the Apeiron."[11] That is, to exist means to participate both in the Apeiron and in the stream of things that manifest the apeiron in time; reality, which is penetrated by the modes of existence and nonexistence, has the character of an In-Between process.

The later differentiations concern the nature of the insight itself in which the structure of the process is revealed. Parmenides discovered the Nous of man as the instrument by which he experienced the highest reality, the Is!, but he did not elaborate the relation between the *realissimum* and the rest of reality.[12] Complementary to the Parmenidean discovery is Heraclitus' articulation of the meaning of human wisdom as a process which remains in erotic tension toward the mysterious ground of existence.[13] These tentative differentiations of the process of reality and the source of man's experience of it, despite their brief development to the publicly representative status by the tragedians, were not sustained in Hellas, but fell victim to the distortions imposed by the social decline of order. Athens became the center of an empire and degenerated under the corrupting influences of its position, so that the socially representative individual became the new style of sophistic intellectual who reduced the earlier exploration of order to the utilitarian level.[14] In addition, the events outside of Hellas, in the formation of multicivilization empires, were already threatening its very survival. The historians Herodotus and Thucydides, in their responses to the situation, could not envisage an alternative to the senseless succession of empires which even extended its unintelligibility to the reality as a whole.[15]

IV

The recovery of the experience of reality as a mysterious process in which man participates had to take the form of a more consistent unfolding of the tentative differentiation that had already been made. This is the task Plato and Aristotle assumed; to the disorder of the surrounding social reality they opposed the order of true reality and thereby created the symbolism of philosophy. They brought together all the previous differentiations and elaborated their central discovery of the soul of man by identifying it as the *sensorium,* or instrument by which man experiences divine being, and also as the site of its formative manifestation within the cosmos. In order to avoid any impression of taking these insights as objective results, Voegelin carefully traces the infrastructure of the noetic experience in which the symbolism of

---

11. Voegelin, *Order and History*, 4:174.
13. Ibid., chap. 9.
15. Ibid., chap. 12, and ibid., 4:178–83.

12. Ibid., 2:chap. 8.
14. Ibid., chaps. 10–11.

philosophy was produced; he reconstructs it from the series of suggestions that can be pieced together from expressions scattered through the works of Plato and Aristotle.

There is, first, the experience of a state of unrest in which the realization that man is not a self-created being gives rise to the question of the ground of his own and all other existence. This is expressed in a group of symbols referring to restless wondering—wondering (*thaumazein*), seeking (*zetein*), searching (*zetesis*), questioning (*aporein, diaporein*). A second level of unfolding is the experience of being moved or pulled to ask the question—being moved (*kinein*), being drawn (*helkein*). Third, a man can become conscious of his questioning unrest as caused by the state of ignorance from which he wants to arrive at true knowledge—ignorance (*agnoia, amathia*), flight from ignorance (*pheugein ten agnoian*), turning round (*periagoge*), knowledge (*eidenai, episteme*). This infrastructure of experience, Voegelin considers to be the catalyst that brought the pre-Socratic occupation with noetic problems into focus as "a concern with the ordering of the psyche through its tension toward the divine ground." [16]

The wondering and questioning is the beginning of a theophanic event which can fully unfold only if the man who experiences it responds by articulating its dimensions in appropriate language-symbols. "The consciousness of questioning unrest in a state of ignorance becomes luminous to itself as a movement in the psyche toward the ground that is present in the psyche as its mover." [17] It is a revelatory event in which the noetic structure of the psyche becomes transparent to itself. The precognitive unrest becomes a cognitive consciousness, *noesis*, intending the ground as its *noema* or *noeton*; the desire to know becomes the consciousness of the object of desire; the ground can be reached through the *via negativa* which points to what is Beyond/*epekeina* (*Republic* 509b) all limited reality and purposes within the world; it is the One (*to hen*) who is present in all things as their ground and can be identified with wisdom and understanding (*sophia kai nos, Philebus* 30c–e).

The illumination of the truth of man's existence as the tension of the human nous toward the divine Nous made it possible to articulate again the process of reality as a whole. The In-Between which had become luminous as the structure of man's existence could now be seen to be the structure of all things that exist in the In-Between of the One and the Apeiron. The noetic structure implied in the earlier symbolism had been differentiated with the discovery of the divine ground as Nous and of man's consciousness as the site where the In-Between process of reality becomes luminous to itself. Plato develops the

16. Voegelin, "Reason: The Classic Experience," *Southern Review* 10 (Spring 1974):243. Reprinted in *Anamnesis*, trans. Gerhart Niemayer, (Notre Dame: Notre Dame University Press, 1978), chap. 6.
17. Ibid., p. 244.

Anaximandrian truth in the *Philebus* (16c–17a), "That all things that are ever said to exist have their being from One and Many, and conjoin in themselves Limited (*peras*) and Unlimited (*apeiron*)." Voegelin explains that for Anaximander the Apeiron had been the creative ground with Time as the limiting pole, but with the differentiation of the ground as the One who is present in all things, and is wisdom and mind, the Apeiron or Unlimited becomes a *materia prima* in which the One diversifies itself. Under another aspect these are the poles of the Limited and the Many, between which arises the number and form of things. This is the In-Between of all existence, which is unfolded in the *Symposium* as the erotic tension between knowledge and ignorance.

The differentiation of Nous as the source of order in man and the cosmos reveals the presence of structure not only in the personal psyche but in all the other areas of reality as well. Since it was in the area of social existence that the problems which led to the differentiation first arose, it was natural that the new insights should be articulated in terms of the order of society. Plato discovered that the structure of society was constituted by the order or disorder in the souls of its members and particularly of the ruling group. The consequences he unfolds in the assertion that political authority should be given to the man who has the true science of ruling, *logos basileia*—he who knows the true good of man through his own erotic tension toward the divine Good. Voegelin follows Plato's exploration of these implications, beginning with its interpretation as the transfer of authority, in *Gorgias*, and proceeding to the comprehensive formulation of the issue in the *Republic*. In this magnificent dialogue, Plato develops the true polis "according to nature," which has its foundation in the transcendent order in the souls of its rulers. The center of the exposition is the impressive elaboration of the theophanic experience by which a man undergoes the ascent to the vision of the divine Good, *Agathon*, and sees the true paradigm of order in his penetration by the transcendent order of God. The *Republic* exists, as Voegelin points out, in the suspense of an appeal to the corrupt Athens, and is characterized by the Socratic declaration of the condition under which it can be made actual: "Unless either the philosophers became kings in the poleis, or those who are now called kings and rulers become philosophers . . ." (*Republic* 473c–d).

The appeal went unheard and the condition was not met, but this did not impair the truth of Plato's experience; it simply meant that the existence of the disordered poleis had to be characterized as a fall from reality. The social field became a manifold of different types among whom the philosopher was only one, as Plato observes in the *Phaedrus*. In the *Statesman* Plato expresses it in the image he creates of the philosopher as the royal ruler who possesses the true means of restoring order. The final stage in unfolding these implications for social reality is reached by Plato in the *Laws*, where the Athenian

Stranger injects into the laws of the polis only as much of the philosophic substance as the inferior human material will bear, while himself withdrawing behind the veil of the myth.

These two aspects of philosophic substance and the means of incarnating it which had begun to separate, become even more distinct in Aristotle's creation of a science of ethics and a separate science of nomothetics or the art of the lawgiver. However, Voegelin observes that the inherent tendency was never fully unfolded into the discovery of a universal community of the spirit and the manifold of concrete political entities which may be more or less suitable for the ordering guidance of the philosopher. The actualization of the *bios theoretikos* with the ethical and dianoetic virtues remained tied to existence in the polis, probably because in the philosophic experience the eschatological movement of history still had not been differentiated. However, the failure to identify the movement of history toward its transfigurative goal does not diminish the philosophic discovery of the meaning of existence as a movement toward noetic consciousness, in which the dimension of history was concomitantly uncovered as the area where the tension toward the divine ground is unfolded. Plato and Aristotle recognized history as structured by the same process toward the ground as reality as a whole. Voegelin explains in his essay on "Eternal Being in Time" that philosophy constitutes history by bringing to luminosity the Logos of the penetration of eternal being in time: it makes history transparent as a field of tensions in being.[18]

The discovery of the process of history as the tension of man's attunement to the divine ground is the meaning that had been lost when the viewpoint of the imperial entrepreneurs dominated the historical reflections. It is restored when the mystery of the mutual participation of divine and human reality again becomes the center of experience, as it does with the Platonic conception of history. Voegelin distinguishes three components in Plato's philosophical constitution of history: (1) the In-Between, the Metaxy, as the area in which the cosmic process becomes luminous for its meaning; (2) the progression of consciousness to noetic heights as the historical dimension of meaning; (3) the structures that emerge from this progression of consciousness in the Metaxy as lines of meaning in history.[19] Voegelin comments that here the foundations for a philosophy of history were available, but it did not unfold into a philosophical investigation of the phenomena of history. The beginnings of such an attempt were made by Aristotle with his identification of the search for the ground as the reality that is equivalently symbolized in the Hesiodic theogony and in philosophy, and that allows him to conclude: "The *philomythos* is in a sense a *philosophos*" (*Metaphysics* 982b 18ss). These

18. Voegelin, *Anamnesis*, "Ewiges Sein in der Zeit," p. 262. Trans. G. Niemayer, *Anamnesis*, p. 124.

19. Voegelin, *Order and History*, 4:187–88.

directions were not pursued, even by the classic philosophers themselves, and Voegelin considers the reason to lie in the restriction of the philosophical articulation to the concrete situation of opposition—the disorder of the poleis—from which it had arisen.[20]

However, Plato had differentiated the structure of history as a movement toward the ground and laid the basis for a philosophical investigation of the empirical phenomena of history. Voegelin demonstrates this through his analyses of Plato's reflections on the historical course. The phenomena Plato proposed to articulate by means of his conception of history were the events that characterized and perplexed the Ecumenic Age as a whole. They were the expansive conquests of the ecumenic empires in which the distinct social and ethnic units became submerged through the formation of an ecumenic mankind, and the spiritual outbursts of philosophers and prophets that pointed toward the discovery of a universal mankind in immediacy under God. The problem for a philosopher of history was to understand the convergence of these lines of meaning without falsely constructing a "meaning of history." Plato was able to keep a balance through his reverence for reality as a process of the whole, which did not permit the treatment of its parts as independent entities. He realized that "Conquest and exodus, thus, are movements within reality."[21]

Plato had to handle this issue, as Voegelin points out, in the problem of symbolizing a movement which transcends reality while also remaining within it. In his differentiation of noetic consciousness, the etiological and directional structure of reality was illuminated as the movement toward the divine reality which is beyond existence in the tension. The balance of the tension toward the ground could be preserved only by recognizing that it is reality as a whole which is engaged in the movement toward eminent reality, and that conquest and exodus are not autonomous actions outside of that context. This is illustrated by Plato's description of the historical course in *Laws* III: the particular historical course is only as long as the memory of the last catastrophe in which civilization was destroyed and had to begin anew; it starts with the groups of mountaineers under a patriarchal rule, then the larger units with an aristocratic order, followed by the cities of the plains, and finally, the federated *ethnos*, or people. Plato shows that each society has its integral balance of good and evil irrespective of its stage in the civilizational advance, and he could accept the destruction of meaning itself by the process of reality, as well as the inevitable decline of the good polis.

Voegelin is impressed by the empirical openness and historiographic validity of this view of history, and he attributes it to Plato's preservation of the primary experience of the cosmos as his conscious background. It is man-

20. Voegelin, *Anamnesis*, "Ewiges Sein in der Zeit," pp. 276–80.
21. Voegelin, *Order and History*, 4:215.

ifested in the recognition that not even the noetic outburst is independent of the whole; neither its emergence nor its consequences are under the control of man. Voegelin explains, "Plato knew the ultimate mystery of reality to be the process of the divine cosmos itself; he did not impose an index of apocalyptic finality on the meanings which, at this or that point of its course, flare up in man's consciousness."[22] Hence, Plato was able to link noetic consciousness back to the process of reality in which it has mysteriously emerged, and the means he employed were the intracosmic myth that had absorbed the philosopher's truth.

Voegelin later clarified his analysis of the different symbolisms of philosophy and myth by distinguishing the two modes in which man experiences divine reality, the *theotes* of Colossians 2:9.[23] There is the immediate experience of the divine in the opening of the soul to transcendent being; this can only be expressed in the language of revelation, of which the representative symbol is Plato's Beyond, *epekeina* (*Republic*, 509b). There is also the mediated experience of the divine presence as the source of order within the cosmos; this can only be expressed by a cosmogonic myth, describing the creation and maintenance of the cosmos from the Beginning, as in Genesis 1:1. The two directions in which divine reality is experienced are a constant, and they must both attain adequate symbolization. Voegelin especially emphasizes that the revelatory experience affects only man's consciousness of his existence in tension toward the divine ground; it does not relate to any reality outside of that restricted area. Differentiation does not change the truth that man continues to live in the cosmos and that he needs to symbolize its order from the source in divine being. Plato recognized this necessity and created a cosmogonic myth which had accommodated the noetic revelation of divine reality in the philosopher's psyche. This was his creation of the philosophic myth.[24]

Plato's openness to the primary experience of the cosmos and its symbolization in myth is shown by his recognition that even the theophanic experience itself only has reality if it is related to the order of the cosmos from which it had emerged.[25] He knew that all that takes place, including man's experience of revelation, is within the play of the divine cosmos; the revelatory outburst itself is not an independent event but is part of the process of reality as a whole. This can be symbolized only by means of the cosmogonic myth, which, following Voegelin's previous interpretation, consists of mutual analogies between the different areas of reality; the tension of existence out of nonexistence cannot be known; it can only be symbolized by analogies within the realm of existent things. Consequently, in the words of Plato, man can only

22. Ibid., p. 223.   23. Ibid., pp. 7–11.
24. Ibid., 3:chap. 5, "*Timaeus* and *Critias*."
25. Ibid., 4:224.

know the truth of God's that is in the cosmos according to what is likely. In the *Timaeus*, Plato shows the way in which the cosmos is ordered by the same divine reality which is experienced in the noetic revelation and concludes that the cosmos is a living being possessing psyche and nous, *zoon empsychon enoun* (*Timaeus* 30b-c). He describes how this came about according to what is likely: the Demiurge overcame the necessity (*Ananke*) of formless matter and incarnated the order of Nous through his power of Persuasion (*Peitho*). All that man can know about the process of reality is its tension toward the divine ground. The mystery of the why and the how of this process can be known only through the "likely myth."

The preservation of this balance of reality was one of the principal achievements of Plato and there is an additional aspect to it which Voegelin later analysed.[26] In his investigation of the Thornbush symbolism of the Mosaic revelation, Voegelin uncovered the stratification of the symbols which expresses the different experiences of divine reality, until the divine depth beyond all revelation is reached, the symbolization of the "I am." Following this indication, in the parallel noetic revelation Voegelin discovers a similar stratification in Plato's works, leading from the intracosmic Gods, to the revelation of Nous, and finally to the suggestion of a divine depth beyond manifestation. However, the difference from the Mosaic revelation was Plato's reluctance to pursue the differentiation of the divine depth. He surrounded his awareness with a series of hesitations and uncertainties obscuring the divine reality beyond the cosmos which he declared could not be reached or adequately praised by man (*Phaedrus* 247). Voegelin explains that Plato wanted to protect the core of his experience which was the revelation of the Nous as the divine source of order in man and the cosmos. Plato knew that the revelation was unstable, because the experience of divine manifestation pointed to a divine reality beyond all manifestation, and the flooding of consciousness with this Beyond could destroy the insight into the tensional structure of reality and replace it by the attempt to bring reality under the control of man. The revelation of Nous as the source of order in man and the cosmos could be protected only by preserving the balance of man's participation in the process of the whole.

V

The symbolism of philosophy which expresses the structure of order within reality, both of man and the cosmos, was developed by Plato and Aristotle in opposition to a concrete situation of social disorder. Their achievement was to have articulated a universal order which was not tied to this original situa-

26. Ibid., pp. 227–28.

tion, so that when the historical context changed the further implications of the symbolism could be unfolded. This is precisely what Voegelin has done by recovering the philosophical symbolization of structure and making it the formative core of a contemporary study of order and history. The results are the uncovering of new insights not only into the materials of history but into the meaning of philosophy as well. In the present section we shall examine some of the developments the philosophical understanding of order has undergone through its application by Voegelin to the new context in man's search for order.

The principal event that has changed the context is the outburst of a more differentiated experience of order in the Judeo-Christian revelation.[27] Voegelin regards this as both a source of new insights and new errors, with a potentiality for deformation as well as formation, because it has differentiated the unbalancing depth of the Beyond which Plato preferred to leave in obscurity. The Christian revelation is parallel to the philosophic, and Voegelin begins his analysis of it by noting the similarities. Drawing on Paul's articulation of the Christian experience, he shows that the Pauline conception of history shares the Platonic understanding of it as the area of reality where the directional movement of the cosmos becomes luminous to itself. The theophany in both symbolisms has its center in the communication of the divine *pneuma* (spirit) with man's *pneuma* and extends to a periphery in the nous which has been ordered by the experience. The specific difference is that Paul prefers to emphasize the divine irruption, the pneumatic center, and to look from this center "toward transfigured reality rather than toward existence in the cosmos."[28] Paul's theophany was the vision of the Resurrected, which convinced him that man is destined to rise to immortality if he opens to the same divine *pneuma* that was in Jesus. However, he regarded it as more than a theophany—it was the beginning of the transfiguration itself. To express this he constructed a pneumatic myth in which the movement of reality, presently characterized by becoming and perishing, toward the divine depth, is revealed as an event in the history of the divine Beyond.

This represents a consistent differentiation of the directions that were already implicit in the philosopher's experience. Thus, the symbolisms are not exclusive but complementary. Voegelin explains the difference as arising out of the nature of theophany as a turbulence in its experiential depth whose form will depend both on the interaction of divine presence and human response, and on the perception of its significance for the problems of the social context. Philosophy emphasizes the structure of the man who undergoes the experience, and unfolds into a symbolization of structure in reality; Christianity stresses the change which the man undergoes in the experience and is

27. Ibid., chap. 5, "The Pauline Vision of the Resurrected."
28. Ibid., p. 246.

elaborated in terms of the ultimate transfiguration of history and reality. Neither experience excludes the other because the Platonic emphasis on structure does not eliminate the unrest which exists behind the uncertainties and hesitations; nor does the Pauline preference for the transfiguring exodus abolish the cosmos and its structure, with the ethical and political problems which arise in living within it.

Still, Voegelin considers that Paul's overemphasis on the transfiguring tale, by which he expected the second coming to occur within his own lifetime, is in need of exploration. The phenomenon is of special significance because the responses to the nonoccurrence of the Parousia have been constitutive of the self-understanding of Western civilization up to the present. Voegelin explains that it has its source in the "Paradox of Reality" or "Exodus within Reality" in which reality is experienced as moving beyond its present structure toward a state of transfiguration. But the truth is that reality as existing in tension toward its transfiguration in the divine ground is experienced as the structure of reality both before and after the differentiation, and the revelation of its structure does not change it. Therefore, Voegelin concludes, the imbalance in Paul's interpretation "can now be more exactly determined as an inclination to abolish the tension between the eschatological *telos* of reality and the mystery of the transfiguration that is actually going on within historical reality." [29] This is the first source of new problems for the philosopher, who, now that the dimension of history has been fully differentiated, must attempt to symbolize its structure as part of the process of the Whole.

The situation becomes more complicated, however, in that the philosopher not only has to grapple with the problems in experience but also with their deformation through secondary symbolisms or doctrines. Voegelin attributes the origin of this phenomenon to the Ecumenic Age, in which men were confronted with the break, which the spiritual outbursts in Israel and Hellas constituted with the older symbolisms of the societies, and with the shock of the pragmatic disappearance of the individual societies themselves in the ecumenic empires.[30] This induced the attempt to preserve the cultural insights of both the historical tradition and the new spiritual experiences in a form which would be suitable to the new type of society that was emerging. The task was taken over by men who did not have the spiritual depth to reactivate and pursue the meaning of the original experiences into their consequences as the order of universal humanity. Instead, the Stoics deformed the symbols of myth and philosophy, and the Jewish leaders operated similarly on the prophetic word of God, by misinterpreting the symbols as doctrines or scripture and, also, as referring to objects in the external world.[31] It was a compromise

29. Ibid., p. 270.   30. Ibid., Introduction.

31. Voegelin, "Immortality: Experience and Symbol," pp. 235–37, for a discussion of the process of doctrinization.

by which the "objective" propositions absorbed the pneumatic or spiritual component of the intracosmic gods and, thus, preserved the essential contents of the original experiences. Its protective and preservative function was not without merit; but it involved the creation of an imaginary medium in which the critical differences between myth and philosophy were dissolved. In the same way, Christianity also took on the doctrinal form that had become part of the conditions of social success in the environment of the late Roman Empire.

Voegelin traces to this context the transformation of philosophy into an occupation with topical problems concerning independent entities as if they were separate from the context of the Whole.[32] We have already mentioned his pejorative characterization of the history of philosophy as a derailment, and he retains the same viewpoint in his more recent work. "A new intellectual game with imaginary realities in an imaginary realm of thought, the game of propositional metaphysics, has been opened with world historic consequences that reach into our own present."[33] However, this situation need not be completely worthless if there is preserved an awareness of the experiential origin of the truths expressed by the derivative propositions. It only becomes socially disruptive, as it has in modern Western civilization, when that awareness is lost and "the deforming doctrinalization has become socially stronger than the experiential insights it was originally meant to protect."[34] Voegelin regards the problem of a return to the originating truth of experience as the overriding problem which guides the activity of a philosopher in the present.

It is unfortunate that returning to the originating truth of experience is also the task undertaken by many nonphilosophers, whose efforts at recovering experiential truth result in an even more serious destruction of reality. This phenomenon constitutes a further layer of problems for the philosopher's contemporary exploration of reality. The philosopher now must oppose the distortions caused by this new type of thinker of whom Voegelin regards Hegel as the most knowledgeable and articulate representative. The modern ideologist takes up the questions of the philosophic-Christian horizon but finds their doctrinal form of expression meaningless. He attempts to recover the original reality of experience but is deflected into the creation of a second reality in order to satisfy his own libidinous desire to control existence. Voegelin coins the term "egophany" to refer analytically to this state of alienation and libidinous obsession in a thinker. In this situation the "turbulence of theophany gives way to the revolution of egophany,"[35] and history must be re-

32. Voegelin, *Order and History*, 3:chap. 7, "Aristotle and Plato," where he finds the beginning of this tendency in Aristotle.
33. Ibid., 4:43.   34. Ibid., p. 58.
35. Ibid., p. 260.

constructed, including the symbolizations of theophany, to culminate in an imaginary, apocalyptic, self-realization of the thinker.

Voegelin identifies this phenomenon, a variant of the Pauline problem, with the attempt to achieve the transfiguration in "history" that was denied to Paul and everyone since. He demonstrates this by referring to Hegel's awareness of the derivation of his project from the Pauline vision of the Resurrected. In Hegel's absolute religion Christ is "the divine becoming man," but it is only in his own system of absolute knowledge that the divine achieves its conceptual realization: he declares the Pauline "depth" is abolished by the transfiguration achieved.[36] Moreover, he could reject the charge that he had identified God and man by maintaining that he had simply identified both their natures as self-consciousness. But such a sleight-of-hand could succeed only in an environment where the symbols have become so emptied of meaning as to be no more than pieces to be moved at will in a speculative game. As Voegelin explains, "By rejecting the dogma he could throw out the theophanic event it was meant to protect; by retaining its language, he could use it as a cover for his far-reaching egophanic enterprise."[37] This is the essential core of the modern ideological symbolism. However, it does play a part in the history of order, as Voegelin observes, inasmuch as the ideological constructions of "history" bear witness to the dimensions of the problem of transfiguration, related as they are to the Pauline experience through such processes as scotosis by secondary symbols and deformation by egophany.

The contemporary context of man's search for order, complicated as it is by the unbalancing components of revelatory experiences with their deformation by secondary symbolisms and the destruction of reality by the egophanic outbursts, as well as the difficulties created by the vast expansion of empirical knowledge, confronts the philosopher with problems that are certainly different from the comparatively simpler environment of Plato's reflections. Yet the task of the philosopher remains the same: to unfold his experience of Nous as the source of order in man, society, and history, as well as in the process of reality as a whole. The emphasis must change, however, and Voegelin has recognized this in his insistence on recovering the experiential origins of the symbolization of order in existence. Nothing can be gained by engaging in argument with ideologues because there is no common experience which could provide a set of common premises; all that can be done is to clarify the experiences that have been deformed by egophany. In response to the phenomena of the deformation of symbols and the destruction of reality, the philosopher has to recover the reality experienced and to insist on it as the only source of meaning for the original symbols. The difference from the Pla-

36. Ibid., pp. 260–66; also Voegelin, "On Hegel—A Study in Sorcery," *Studium Generale*, 24 (1971):335–68.
37. Voegelin, *Order and History*, 4:263.

tonic context can be seen in the greater self-consciousness in Voegelin's articulation of the intimate and essential relationship between experiences and
symbols, which he struggles to express in terms of the "non-objective" character of the experiences for which the symbols are no more than "linguistic
indices."[38] In response to the other problem of the expansion of empirical
knowledge, the philosopher can turn to the full range of historical materials
which science makes available as the field for his noetic investigation of reality—and embark on the creation of an *Order and History*.

There remains the problems in experiences themselves, arising from the
struggle for a balanced symbolization of reality. This is essentially the problem of symbolizing history as a process of transfiguration which points toward a transfiguration beyond all existence in process.[39] The issue first
became articulate in the Ecumenic Age when the two experiences of the
senselessness of concupiscential conquest and the luminosity of the divine
presence in theophany tended to dissociate into two apocalyptic or Gnostic
realities. The solution was found, as Voegelin explains, in the experience of
history as the mystery of the transfiguring process which is already going on
within time. Man experiences the presence of structure in reality as the movement of reality beyond its own structure, and he discovers that the structure
was present before and will continue after the differentiation, so that his insight is itself an event within the transfigurative process of reality. "History,
thus, reveals itself as the horizon of divine mystery when the process of differentiation is discovered to be the process of transfiguration."[40]

Voegelin emphasizes the origin of these insights in the experiential unity of
ecumenic empire, spiritual outburst, and historiography. He considers their
combination to be equivalent to the more compact *oikoumene-okeanos* symbolism which represented man's habitat and the surrounding horizon of divine mystery. The new triad constitutes a similar unity of experience because
there can be no recognition of history as the horizon of divine mystery unless
the ecumene has been opened by concupiscential expansion and the events
have been made meaningful in relation to the truth of existence in the spiritual outbursts. It is only at this point that history is revealed as the transfiguring process of universal mankind and interest begins to focus on the various modes of participation and their configuration in space and time. The
exploration of the equivalences of experiences and symbolizations which can
be arranged on a line of degrees of compactness and differentiation makes the
process of history transparent as the universal process of transfiguration.

The problem for the philosopher becomes the clarification of the question

---

38. Voegelin, *Anamnesis*, "Was ist Politische Realität," pp. 315–23. *Anamnesis*, trans. Niemayer, pp. 175–82.
39. Voegelin, *Order and History*, 4:chap. 7, "Universal Humanity."
40. Ibid., p. 314.

of the meaning of the process in order to preserve the balance of its mystery as the process of the Whole. He must articulate the question as part of the In-Between reality, which means that there is no answer apart from the mystery as it is made conscious through the questions themselves: the Question remains the same while all that changes are the modes of asking it. "What happens 'in' history is the very process of differentiating consciousness that constitutes history."[41] That is, history illuminates the mystery as a transfiguring process, in that, once it is differentiated, the response to the Question must include the empirical knowledge of the process. But it continues to be the process of the Whole and the trail of equivalent symbols in history which have all arisen from the depth of the Whole. Voegelin has explained, in his highly significant essay on equivalences in history, that there is a depth of the psyche beyond consciousness from which a stream of equivalent experiences and symbolizations emerge into history.[42] This depth is the cosmos, the *anima mundi*, or the Apeiron, which is the Whole whose process becomes luminous only in the trail of equivalent experiences and symbolizations in man's consciousness.

Therefore, there is no independent "length of time" in which things happen which would allow their meaning to be discerned by a "System of science." There is only the process of the Whole. Voegelin explains that the various strata of reality participate in one another through the foundation of the higher levels by the lower and the organization of the lower by the higher levels of reality. In this way the different time dimensions of their lasting form a hierarchy of times in which no time is independent of the rest. Thus, not even the lasting of the astrophysical universe can be considered an external "length of time" because it is not independent of the other strata of reality and their times. Moreover, the universe cannot be identified with the lasting of the Whole because in his consciousness man experiences his constitution through the presence of divine reality, thus making transparent the creative constitution of all reality from the divine ground. The universe and everything in it happens in the eternity of God, and the philosopher can now articulate this mystery as the structure of reality. "Once the fallacies are removed, the hierarchy of being comes into view, not as a number of strata piled one on top of the other, but as movement of reality from the apeirontic depth up to man, through as many levels of the hierarchy as can be discerned empirically, and as the countermovement of creative organization from the divine height down, with the Metaxy of man's consciousness as the site where the movement of the Whole becomes luminous for its eschatological direction."[43]

41. Ibid., p. 332.
42. Voegelin, "Equivalences of Experience and Symbolization in History," pp. 227–33.
43. Voegelin, *Order and History*, 4:335.

VI

The foregoing quotation summarizes the philosopher's response, in the contemporary context, to the problem of articulating the experience of the transfigurative process of reality. It consists in the recognition that "the Mystery of the historical process is inseparable from the Mystery of a reality which brings forth the universe and the earth, plant and animal life on earth, and ultimately man and his consciousness."[44] No element, no matter how dramatic, can be separated from the process of the whole in which it occurs. The philosopher must develop a thoroughly balanced account of the process of reality, preventing even his own illumination from being considered in isolation from its place in the whole. Voegelin illustrates this in the concluding pages of *The Ecumenic Age* where he demonstrates how the noetic revelation of the soul in tension toward the divine ground, can illumine not only the nature of man and society, but also the order of history and the process of reality as a Whole.

On Voegelin's own admission, however, the order of reality is not something apprehended within the revelatory experience, which directly concerns only the relationship between the soul and God. The larger order of reality in which it occurs can only be known indirectly, by extrapolation from the revelatory core, and must be symbolized by means of a "likely" description in the form of a myth. Yet his discussion does not go much beyond asserting the essential requirements for a balanced view of the whole and offers little indication of the possible character of a contemporary construction of the myth. He recognizes the importance of myth but does not suggest any detailed conception of its nature in a modern symbolization of order. While admitting that myth is the only way in which the comprehensive order of reality can be articulated, he does not appear to fully accept that the philosopher must become its creator, or face the alternative of leaving the field open to the proponents of ideological myths proclaiming the destruction of man.

Voegelin does correctly identify the need for a new symbolization of the whole, as arising from the problem of Christianity's excessive emphasis on the transfiguring goal of reality and the consequent neglect of an articulation of the transfiguring process that is already going on within reality. The balance must be restored by the introduction of the classic symbolization of structure in reality, both in man and the cosmos, so that the order of immanent reality can be explicated by means of the mythic expression of its tension toward the divine ground. Nevertheless, Voegelin seems reluctant to explore such developments any further and confines himself to a rather cursory treatment of Christianity which emphasizes the negative side of the danger of disorder,

44. Ibid.

rather than the positive aspect of its potential for the creation of order. He recognizes the utterly transfiguring encounter with the Spirit of Christ as the essential experience of Christianity, but has given little detailed consideration, in his published writings, to the way in which this experience can be integrated into a balanced view of reality as a whole. The possibility that the differentiated fullness of Christ's death and resurrection might itself contain the spiritual depth to redress any of the imbalancing strains in its first articulation is nowhere clearly acknowledged within his work. It is a puzzling silence which can, perhaps, be explained only by his desire to avoid all doctrinal forms, and his suspicion that mythico-religious symbolisms lend themselves most frequently to misinterpretation as descriptions of merely external objects and events.

His reticence on this question of the restoration of myth has also lessened his sympathy for the intentions of the modern thinkers, many of whom were concerned with recovering the meaning of man and immanent reality in the context of the whole. It was unfortunate that their response to the lacunae of the Christian symbolism was allied with a decline or rejection of the Christian experience and a substitution of the autonomous rational individual as the source of order in reality. In spite of this major qualification, however, they did succeed in indicating some of the directions which a modern formulation of the myth of the whole would have to assume. The speculations of the Renaissance religious thinkers and of the German Romantics and Idealists, for example, showed how the relationship between God and the world would have to be symbolized as a process within God himself, that immanent reality is the self-expression of God through which he unfolds his self-revelation. And if the transfiguration of man and nature is to have a real meaning in the present, it must signify the divine image already present in man and nature which urges it on and eventually brings about a final transformation. Admittedly, the return to such a mythic symbolization is fraught with dangers for the Christian achievement of differentiation, since the expression of consubstantiality in the myth may eclipse the transcendence of God that is experienced in the revelation of Christ. But in what other way can the balance of the whole be symbolized, in which immanent reality too has its origin in the divine being?

Although Voegelin does not show us the way in detail, the broad lines for such a restoration of the order of the whole have been clearly defined by him. They emerge from his analyses which are in continuity with the spectrum of man's experiences of the divine-cosmic order which reach back to the oldest cosmogonic symbolizations. That is, his articulation of the structure of reality as it becomes luminous in the process of history, is based on the symbolisms that have been created to express such experiences of reality. This is the empirical basis in which Voegelin's work is firmly rooted, and his recovery of the fundamental symbolisms of order has meant that the broad lines of his analysis are not likely to be overturned. Improvement of the empirical knowledge of the materials of history can be expected to greatly expand and deepen the symbolization of order, but it is unlikely to entail a radical revision of the insights gained by Eric Voegelin. It is his mark as a philosopher to have articulated the fundamental horizon within which we think and in relation to which even his own work must be judged. Every attempt to symbolize the structure of reality as it becomes luminous in man's search for order must follow the example of his work, which is, as he has intended, "an act of open participation in the process of both history and the Whole."[45]

45. Ibid.

ERIC VOEGELIN'S THEORY OF REVELATION

Eugene Webb

In view of the intensity and the frequently nonrational character of both political and religious commitments, a writer who would attempt to explore these areas and to raise reflection on them to the level of genuinely theoretical understanding would have to be courageous—willing to endure unreasoned reactions, as well as to face clearly and take account of reasoned criticism. That Eric Voegelin's studies of the history of order in several of the major civilizations of the world, both ancient and modern, should have given rise to controversy was to be expected. What is interesting in the controversy that has developed is that some very serious criticisms of Voegelin's positions have arisen among scholars fundamentally sympathetic with his work—especially since the publication of *Anamnesis* (1966) and the long-awaited fourth volume of *Order and History*, *The Ecumenic Age* (1974), with its brief but provocative treatment of Christian thinking and experience as represented in the writings of St. Paul.[1]

I would like in this essay first to note a few of the more significant criticisms that have been voiced recently, then to show how Professor Voegelin's controversial positions are consistently intelligible in the light of the basic principles of his thought, and finally to identify what seem the major points of divergence between his interpretation of the Israelite-Christian revelation and those of traditional theology. In doing so, I hope to act as an intermediary between Voegelin and his critics, and especially between Voegelin and orthodox Christian theology, and I hope to formulate the points of divergence as important challenges to both sides.

This essay first appeared in *The Thomist* 42 (1978):95–110, and is reprinted here by permission.

1. Eric Voegelin, *Anamnesis: Zur Theorie der Geschichte und Politik* (Munich: R. Piper & Co., Verlag, 1966). Voegelin, *Order and History*, 4 vols. to date (Baton Rouge: Louisiana State University Press, 1956–), Vol. 4, *The Ecumenic Age* (1974).

I

The most extensive set of particular criticisms of Voegelin's treatment of Christianity is in Gerhart Niemeyer's recent article on *The Ecumenic Age*.[2] Niemeyer's basic complaint is that by dismissing the question of the facticity of the "historical Jesus," by treating the "Pauline Vision of the Resurrected" (the title of Voegelin's chapter on Paul) as "the entire 'speculation' of St. Paul as analyzed by Voegelin," and by leaving out of consideration the possibly miraculous encounter on the road to Damascus, Voegelin has neglected— indeed ruled out—the uniqueness of the Christian revelation; he has put St. Paul "into the same category with Plato, with St. Paul's performance receiving a grade of 'superior,' and on the other hand with Hegel, who comes out worst." Voegelin has, in other words, treated the Christian revelation as part of a continuum of revelation that becomes clear in varying degrees among different philosophical thinkers and among various religious traditions. Moreover, says Niemeyer, "Voegelin's exegesis of St. Paul would not have to be changed if one removed Jesus Christ from it altogether. Voegelin allows that man is a creature in whom God can incarnate himself. St. Paul, however, reflects on what it means that God did incarnate himself in one particular man at one particular time." With regard to Voegelin's interpretation of the Resurrection as a "vision" on the part of St. Paul, Niemeyer says that Voegelin "would have to concede the application to himself of his own remarks that 'critical doubts' about the life, death, and resurrection of Jesus Christ 'would mean that the critic knows how God has a right to let himself be seen. . . .'"[3] Voegelin, that is, has both dismissed traditional Christian claims regarding the historical Incarnation and Resurrection and interpreted the Incarnation in Jesus as part of a continuum of Incarnation realized in varying degrees in universal mankind, a position that parallels his position on revelation as described above. "It seems that this once," says Niemeyer, "Voegelin has approached a great spiritual reality from a standpoint extraneous to it." If this is the case, it is a serious charge; an analysis of the particulars of the issue, however, will have to wait until later.

The other principal theme of complaint among Voegelin's recent critics has had to do with his conception of the relation between reason and revelation. Before the publication of *The Ecumenic Age*, Dante Germino, in an article on *Anamnesis*, said Voegelin had not yet treated "in any range or depth the entire thorny question of the relationship between philosophy and theology, reason and revelation, nature and grace" and suggested that "perhaps Voegelin's reticence or ambiguity on this entire range of topics may well re-

2. Gerhart Niemeyer, "Eric Voegelin's Philosophy and the Drama of Mankind," *Modern Age* 20, no. 1 (Winter 1976):28–39. See especially pp. 34–35.
3. Ibid., quoting Voegelin, *Order and History*, 4:243.

flect on [sic] *aporia* in his inquiry."[4] Since Voegelin does not attempt to deal with theology as such, but with "man's consciousness of his humanity as it differentiates historically" by treating "the history of experiences and their symbolization," it is not surprising that he does not deal directly with the nature of theology or of grace.[5] The topic of revelation, on the other hand, is central to his subject matter as he has defined it, and in *The Ecumenic Age* he tackles it directly, speaking of "the dichotomy of reason-revelation" as a fundamental misconstruction of thought deriving from the Stoic deformation of philosophy into doctrine subsequently perpetuated in Christian theology to the present.[6] Thomas J. J. Altizer, writing more recently, has expressed reservations about what he calls Voegelin's "herculean effort" to unite the Hellenic and Israelite-Christian breakthroughs "into one revelation and one theophany."[7]

Clearly Voegelin's treatment of revelation, both of particular traditions of revelation and of revelation as such, has placed him in conflict with prominent traditional and modern schools of thought. What is surprising about this, however, is only that his critics should not have seen developing long ago, *in germine*, the positions they would later be surprised and disturbed by. Whether or not one might agree with his conclusions, the complexities and controversial points of Voegelin's thought are clearly intelligible when one understands the basic principles according to which his analyses proceed. Since the first responsibility of any reader of a thinker as important and as challenging as Eric Voegelin is to understand him in the full range and subtlety of his thought, it will be worthwhile to consider briefly the theoretical foundations from which the larger structure of his philosophy of revelation unfolds.

II

In *The New Science of Politics*, which offered a preliminary sketch of the enterprise that was to develop into *Order and History*, Voegelin indicated that his goal was to raise the human and social sciences once again to the level of genuine theory. What he meant by theory he defined concisely as "an attempt at formulating the meaning of existence by explicating the content of a definite class of experiences."[8] He went on to say that the argument of theory "is not arbitrary but derives its validity from the aggregate of experiences to which it must permanently refer for empirical control." The experiences in question are experiences of actual existential order as they are known in the

4. Dante Germino, "Eric Voegelin's *Anamnesis*," *Southern review*, n.s. 7 (1971):85.
5. Voegelin, *Order and History*, 4:302, cf. 242; and ibid., 2:159.
6. Ibid., 4:48, 236.   7. See p. 188, this volume.
8. Voegelin, *The New Science of Politics: An Introduction* (Chicago: University of Chicago Press, 1952), p. 64.

inner life of one whose character is formed by them, a person such as Aristotle called the *spoudaios*, the mature man. That these are not simply the experiences of a self-enclosed world-immanent entity, but "experiences of transcendence" is made clear subsequently in that book and in *Order and History*.[9] He also indicated in *The New Science of Politics* one aspect of the solution to the problem of the relation of reason and revelation when he spoke of such an insight into actual existential order, brought "to the ultimate border of clarity," as being that experience "which by tradition is called revelation."[10] This is not an exhaustive definition of what Voegelin means by revelation, but it does indicate that revelation is a form of what Voegelin means by theoretical insight and that it lies along a continuum of such insights.

Connected with his conception of theory as the explication of concrete experiences is what he terms "the principle of correlation between theory and the maximal experiential differentiation."[11] The constant substratum of experience in a concrete human life contains within it a range of differentiable features, some of which may be noticed and thereby raised into consciousness, and some of which may remain unnoticed and consequently obscure. Whether they are noticed or not, they are always present within the fundamental experience. As Voegelin stated it in *Israel and Revelation*, "the range of human experience is always present in the fullness of its dimensions," although, "the structure of the range varies from compactness to differentiation."[12] Experience may, in other words, become more or less conscious and articulate, depending on one's ability, and also willingness, to notice its full range of implicit contents. The process of differentiating in which man articulates his existence to himself does not take place in the lifetime of a single individual or even of a society or civilization, "but extends through a plurality of societies,"[13] and in doing so constitutes what Voegelin means by history, i.e., "a process of increasingly differentiated insight into the order of being in which man participates by his existence."[14]

Implicit in Voegelin's analysis is a distinction between major and minor types of articulation of experience. For the most part he confines his use of the term "differentiation" to the major types; that is, he does not usually use it to refer to the articulation of elements within a given area of experience of which one is already conscious in a general way, but to signify the emergence into consciousness of whole new areas of experience.[15] The most important differentiations of this type constitute what he calls "leaps in being," epoch-

---

9. Ibid., p. 80.
10. Ibid., p. 79.
11. Ibid., p. 80.
12. Voegelin, *Order and History*, 1:60.
13. Ibid.
14. Ibid., 4:1; see also ibid., 1:130, 2:2, 4:6, 226, 303, 332–35.
15. An example of his relatively rare use of the term to refer to distinctions within a given area of experience may be seen in *Order and History*, 3:167, in his reference to Plato's *Statesman* as offering "a more differentiated classification of types [of men]" than did *The Republic*.

making advances in consciousness which are not only cognitive but also qual-
itative in that they affect the soul ontologically by restructuring it in its existential order.[16] The continuity of the fundamental substratum of experience,
however, remains the same; whatever becomes differentiated out of it was always contained within it. It will be helpful, therefore, to consider the constant contents of this core of experience as analyzed by Voegelin.

It is, to begin with, an experience of existence, of participation in being:
"Whatever man may be, he knows himself a part of being."[17] It is also an
experience of movement or change, especially of lasting and passing;[18] because man is not being itself, but only participates in being, he experiences
himself as one who has come into existence and may also fall out of it. More
fundamentally still, it is an experience of tension, of attraction *toward* being.
This "tension of existence" may express itself in various ways—not only as a
fear of perishing, but also as a questioning unrest, a desire to know and
thereby to participate more fully in real being: "The movement that draws
man into existential participation is a movement toward a more eminent degree of reality. . . ."[19] The differentiation of experience is itself a movement
toward greater participation in being, since in man the participation takes the
form of consciousness. It is important to remember, Voegelin says, that consciousness is not something that looks at reality from a standpoint outside,
but is itself reality: "Das Bewußtsein aber ist die Realität menschlichen Par-
tizipierens. . . ."[20] The attraction toward eminent reality has the character of
an attraction toward the sacred in the full sense of that word, since it is an
attraction toward an inexhaustible *mysterium* that is both *tremendum* and *fas-
cinans*.[21] This is one reason Voegelin frequently speaks of this fundamental
attractive force that motivates man in his existential strivings as a tension toward "the divine ground" (beside the fact that this is the terminology of the
classical philosophers who first articulated the tension).[22]

It is the reality of participation that constitutes what Voegelin calls the "In-
Between" or Metaxy character of human existence: man is in between lim-
itedness as such and fullness of being. He has a fundamental *eros* or tension
toward unlimited being but can never reach it without ceasing to be a finite
existence—though the tension of not reaching it is difficult to endure and
may tempt him to try to overleap the limits of the human condition through
some form of Gnosis, the attainment of a certain and definitive grasp of being
itself through knowledge. Voegelin represents the open, non-Gnostic striv-

16. Voegelin, *Order and History*, 1:10.
17. Ibid., 1:3.   18. Ibid., 1:3, 4:74.
19. Voegelin, "Reason: The Classic Experience," *Southern Review*, n.s. 10 (1974):241; *Order and History*, 4:271.
20. Voegelin, *Anamnesis*, pp. 304, 306.
21. Voegelin, *Order and History*, 1:2, 4:330, 233, 271.
22. See, e.g., Voegelin, "Reason: The Classic Experience," p. 243.

ing toward cognitive participation in being by the symbol of "the Question";
he says that "there is no answer to the Question other than the Mystery as it
becomes luminous in the acts of questioning. Any attempt to find an answer
by developing a doctrine concerning spatio-temporal events will destroy the
"In-Between structure of man's humanity."[23]

One of the major difficulties in clearly conceptualizing the primary or fundamental experience of existence (the substance of the later differentiations)
is that its mode of being is nonobjectifiable: "the subject-object dichotomy,
which is modeled after the cognitive relation between man and things in the
external world, does not apply to the event of an 'experience-articulating-
itself'."[24] Thus the concept of the Metaxy is not an item of information about
man as an objective (i.e., quasi-external) entity, but a symbolization of the
fundamental tension that is a constant feature of human existence in actual
experience. For man this tension in the soul is the bedrock of existential reality accessible to him in his attempts to raise into consciousness his participation in the mystery of being. It is the core experience from which his movements of searching and striving proceed and which he can never leave behind
and it will always remain a mystery which he can represent and communicate
only through symbols.

The *telos* or goal of the tension is also a nonobjectifiable mystery, and it too
is present in the fundamental existential experience. It can be symbolized but
must not be hypostatized into an object separate from the concrete relationship of participation. One must not forget that when one says, "Man, in his
existence, participates in being," the subject and predicate "are terms which
explicate a tension of existence, and are not concepts denoting objects."[25] It is
this mutual participation of being and existence in one another within the
compact core of human experience that serves as the key to the intimate relationship between reason and revelation in Voegelin's thought. The core experience that eventually differentiates is not self-enclosed, nor is the soul that
becomes constituted by the process of differentiation; rather, both open out
beyond themselves into ultimate mystery. Or to put it another way, in the
terms that Voegelin uses in his analysis of the *Apocalypse of Abraham*: "Since
God is present even in the confusion of the heart, preceding and motivating
the search itself, the divine Beyond is at the same time a divine Within."[26]
This divine reality, present within the core of experience as the being in
which existence participates, is the moving force that attracts the soul, elicit-
ing the movement of the soul by which the contents of the experiential
ground of thinking are differentiated and raised into consciousness to constitute man's conscious existence as a soul in movement toward its transcendent
goal. Because it is the divine reality of being itself that is the moving force in

23. Voegelin, *Order and History*, 4:330.
24. Ibid., p. 186; see also *Anamnesis*, p. 300.
25. Voegelin, *Order and History*, 1:2.   26. Ibid., 4:324.

this, and because the movement is a movement *toward* being and in the process is a disclosure *of* being, the process of differentiation always has a revelatory or theophanic character, whether its emphasis is on the noetic (in the case of Philosophy) or on the spiritual or pneumatic (in the case of what is usually termed religious Revelation).

It is in this sense that Voegelin speaks of "the constitution of reason through revelation": "The life of reason . . . is firmly rooted in a revelation . . ." because ". . . the God who appeared to the philosophers, and who elicited from Parmenides the exclamation 'Is!', was the same God who revealed himself to Moses as the 'I am who (or: what) I am,' as the God who is what he is in the concrete theophany to which man responds." [27]

In the earlier volumes of *Order and History* Voegelin tended to use the terms "Reason" and "Revelation" for the disclosures of being to the Hellenic philosophers and the Israelite religious thinkers respectively. [28] In *The Ecumenic Age*, however, he shifted to different terms for these two leaps in being, thereby making clearer that both are theophanic events and have the character of ontological disclosure: "noetic" and "pneumatic" differentiation. In the case of the noetic differentiation, the discovery of reason, both Plato and Aristotle were aware, he says, that *noesis* was not an autonomous human project (as the later concept of "natural reason" would have it): "Participation in the noetic movement is not an autonomous project of action but the response to a theophanic event (the Promethean light exceeding bright, the Socratic *daimonion*) or its persuasive communication (the Platonic *Peitho*). To this revelatory movement (*kinesis*) from the divine ground, man can respond by his questioning and searching, but the theophanic event itself is not at his command." [29] Although the process of noetic differentiation was complex and required the contributions of several generations of Hellenic "mystic-philosophers," [30] it may be described concisely as "the adequate articulation and symbolization of the questioning consciousness." [31] The Nous, once differentiated, can be applied to the investigation of world-immanent ("natural" in the conventional sense) reality, but it is not itself reducible to the status of a world-immanent ("natural") entity. Rather, the very fact that it is existent reality participating in being itself gives reason a transcendent dimension: "Obviously, the Aristotelian nous is more than the intellect that becomes active in the sciences of world-immanent objects. The nous as the *theiotaton* [the divinest part in man] is the region in the soul where man transcends his mere humanity into the divine ground." [32]

27. Ibid., pp. 228–29.   28. E.g., ibid., 2:204.
29. Ibid., 4:217.
30. For a good summary of the process and its results see ibid., 4:177–78.
31. Voegelin, "Reason: The Classic Experience," p. 241.
32. Voegelin, *Order and History*, 3:306. Defining the terms *immanent* and *transcendent*, Voegelin says in *Anamnesis*, p. 300: "Immanent und transcendent sind die räumlichmetaphorischen Indizes, die wir in der post-noetischen Dispensation den Realitätsbereichen zuteilen, die

The continuity between noetic differentiation and pneumatic "Revelation" (in the traditional terminology) is a function of the fact that "the structure of a theophanic experience reaches from a pneumatic center to a noetic periphery."[33] This is itself, of course, simply another way of stating the basic principle discussed earlier that the core experience that becomes differentiated in varying degrees, the experience of participation in being, is "always present in the fullness of its dimensions." In the noetic differentiation focal awareness (to borrow Michael Polanyi's terminology for the moment) is directed to the Nous, the questioning consciousness, while the pneumatic center, that level of reality in the depths of the soul at which it is experientially united with being itself, remains in comparative obscurity. In both differentiations, what is raised into consciousness from the depths of experience is the inner structure of human existence itself, in both its immanent and transcendent dimensions. A revelatory or theophanic event, in Voegelin's analysis, whether it is noetic or pneumatic in its emphasis, never provides information about the world; rather, it renders explicit what was always implicit in the substratum of experience.[34]

For this reason, revelation cannot be something arbitrary or "subjective" in the pejorative sense; the test of the truth of its content always remains its grounding in experienced reality. If a person makes a claim to have received through revelation any kind of informational knowledge, whether of rational truths, of miraculous occurrences (past, present, or future), or of political or military policies preferred by God (as in the case of Isaiah's urging King Ahaz to renounce military defense),[35] he is simply miscontruing the nature of revelation.

Informational understanding is to be had only through the necessary procedures of rational inquiry, the patient activity of the questioning consciousness as it carefully and critically raises its questions and considers the data of experience in the light of them. Any attempt to bypass this necessary process is in effect to try to overleap the human condition; it is to deviate into some form of Gnosis, intellectual, emotional, or volitional.[36] Because the Israelite

---

respektive zur Welt der Dinge in Raum und Zeit und zum göttlichen Sein des Weltgrundes jenseits von Raum und Zeit geworden sind."

33. Voegelin, *Order and History*, 4:244.

34. Cf. ibid., 2:283: "The mystic-philosopher has no information to tender; he can only communicate the discovery which he has made in his own soul, hoping that such communication will stir up parallel discoveries in the souls of others." Cf. also ibid., 3:84, on Plato's conception of inquiry (*zetema*) as exegesis of the depths of the soul. For some modern interpretations of the nature of revelation that are fundamentally in accord with this position, see H. Richard Niebuhr, *The Meaning of Revelation* (New York: Macmillan Co., 1941), and John Macquarrie, *Principles of Christian Theology* (New York: Charles Scribner's Sons, 1966).

35. Voegelin, *Order and History*, 1:477.

36. For a discussion of Isaiah's speculation on the divine plan of history as a form of incipient Gnosis, see ibid., 1:451. For the nature of the Gnostic temptation as a general human problem

revelation was focused on the pneumatic center rather than on the noetic periphery, the tradition deriving from it was always especially susceptible to such deviations; reason was not sufficiently articulated to be able to serve as a consistently adequate critical control on thought.[37]

III

The discussion of pneumatic differentiation, in distinction from noetic, brings us at last to Voegelin's interpretation of Revelation, in the traditional sense, as constituted by the Israelite leap in being and its subsequent history in the Christian tradition. It will be worth tracing the pneumatic differentiation historically, since it took place over a far longer period than the noetic and, due to the lack of adequate noetic control, gave rise to more tendencies to derailment. Although Moses, in the symbol of the "I am who I am," was the first, according to Voegelin, to articulate the "compact experience of divine presence so as to express the essential omnipresence with man of a substantially hidden God,"[38] he accepts the tradition that the first movements of spiritual revelation took place in Abraham as an "inrush of divine reality into his soul" which gave rise to an expectation of future fulfillment: "In the case of Abram's experience this 'future' is not yet understood as the eternity under whose judgment man exists in his present. To be sure, Yahweh's berith is already the flash of eternity into time; but the true nature of this 'future' as transcendence is still veiled by the sensuous analogues of a glorious future in historical time." This futuristic component in the early experience remained a continuing influence, lasting throughout Israelite and later Judaic history and issuing into the apocalyptic literature. At the time, however, it led to comparatively little because it did not become socially effective: "The new domain of Yahweh is not yet the political order of a people in Canaan; at the moment it does not extend beyond the soul of Abram."[39]

The order of Israel as a people had its origin in Moses, and the order in the soul of Moses had its origin in his response to a further divine revelation, the next advance of pneumatic differentiation. This became a collective, as compared with a strictly individual, reality when Moses communicated the substance of the leap in being more or less effectively to the Israelites and thereby constituted them as a people directed toward transcendence: "To the skepti-

("The temptation to fall from a spiritual height that brings the element of uncertainty into final clarity down into the more solid certainty of world-immanent, sensible fulfillment . . ."), see id., *Science, Politics, and Gnosticism: Two Essays*, trans. William J. Fitzpatrick (Chicago: Henry Regnery Co., Gateway Edition, 1968), pp. 114, 107–109. For a discussion of the range of possible varieties of Gnosis—intellectual, emotional, and volitional—see id., *The New Science of Politics*, p. 124.

37. Voegelin, *Order and History*, 1:240, 327.
38. Ibid., p. 411.   39. Ibid., p. 194.

cal sons of Israel Moses will have to say: '*Ehyeh* [I am] has sent me to you' ([Exod.] 3:14). The people thus will break the bondage of Egypt and enter the present under God, once they have responded to the revelation of God's presence with them."[40]

The spiritual order thus founded subsequently had its famous ups and downs. It is not necessary to go into them in detail here. It will suffice to say that the downs took three principal forms. One was an immanentizing tendency deriving from the residual compactness of the experience: a tendency to equate the transcendent goal of the tension of Israel's existence with some form of worldly success, such as a kingdom of Solomonic grandeur in Canaan. Another was a tendency to retreat from conscious existence in the immediate presence of God by reintroducing mediating existences: the Davidic king conceived of as "Son of God," the reconceiving of the living Word of God as sacred Scripture, and the fictional invention of the Deuteronomic Moses as Lawgiver and author of Scripture.[41] The other was the recurrent temptation among the prophets to develop what Voegelin calls "metastatic" tendencies, to attempt to escape from the tension of existence by overleaping the human condition, "to make the leap in being a leap out of existence into a divinely transfigured world beyond the laws of mundane existence," as in the various expectations of a coming age in which Israel will no longer have to defend herself with arms, the lion will lie down with the lamb, holy men will be able to have direct insight into the intentions of God, and so on.[42]

The one really significant advance that was made in the later history of Israel, on the other hand, was closely related to this last pattern of deviation. The metastatic tendencies were a confused outgrowth of an inchoate further step in the process of pneumatic differentiation. This was the realization "that there are problems of order beyond the existence of a concrete society and its institutions," that the *terminus ad quem* of the prophetic movement, and of history itself, is ultimate transcendence.[43] Voegelin speaks of this "third procreative act of divine order in history" as "the Exodus of Israel from itself," and he sees it as culminating in the representative suffering of Deutero-Isaiah. This was the high point of pneumatic differentiation in Israel, but it came almost simultaneously with the major defection of Israel into the Deuteronomic legalism and scripturalism, which Voegelin considers the major point of demarcation between the history of Israel and that of Judaism.[44]

His comment on Israel's defection is significant because it indicates the character of the crucial problem of "religion" as such, a problem that Christianity was going to have to confront centuries later, especially after the Council of Nicaea: ". . . it looks as if in Deuteronomy we were touching the genesis of 'religion,' defined as the transformation of existence in historical

40. Ibid., p. 407.
41. Ibid., pp. 397, 367, 364.
42. Ibid., p. 452.
43. Ibid., p. 491.
44. Ibid., p. 372.

form into the secondary possession of a 'creed' concerning the relation between God and man."[45] That this should have happened, he says, is understandable, almost inevitable, because

> the prophets, philosophers, and saints, who can translate the order of the
> spirit into the practice of conduct without institutional support and pres-
> sure, are rare. For its survival in the world, therefore, the order of the spirit
> has to rely on a fanatical belief in the symbols of a creed more often than on
> the *fides caritate formata*—though such reliance, if it becomes socially pre-
> dominant, is apt to kill the order it is supposed to preserve.[46]

The crucial conflict, then, is between the immanentizing, virtually Gnostic,
closing of faith into dogmatism and the opening of faith into actual participation in its transcendent goal, between the reduction of faith to opinion and
the flowering of faith in *caritas*.

The movement toward the latter, the realization of Israel's final Exodus
from itself, was not taken up again until the time of Christ. At that time it
manifested itself in various ways, but the most important was in the concrete
experience of certain individuals, among whom the central figure was Jesus
of Nazareth. It is here, of course, that Voegelin's area of greatest difficulty
begins. In *The New Science of Politics*, where he did not have to go into this
area in any detail, he could speak of "the appearance of Christ" as the "acme"
of a giant cycle of spiritual development that "culminated in the maximum of
differentiation, through the revelation of the Logos in history."[47] When he
came to a direct and detailed treatment of the theophanic events from which
Christianity arose, however, he had, if he was to operate in accord with his
basic theoretical principles, to investigate the revelation on the level of concrete experience.

In view of this fundamental requirement of Voegelin's own process of noetic inquiry, it should be understandable why he chose Paul rather than Jesus
as his major point of focus. Paul left writings that speak directly of his experience, whereas the experience of Jesus comes to us only through the mediating interpretations of other writers. It should also be understandable, in
the light of his basic conception of revelation, why he concentrated on the
Pauline "vision of the resurrected" as a symbolic expression of the actual
event of pneumatic differentiation within Paul himself, and not on any sort of
external miraculous manifestation. For such an external manifestation could
not possibly, on Voegelin's terms, amount to revelation. Revelation, after all,
according to Voegelin's conception, does not provide information about what

---

45. Ibid., p. 375.   46. Ibid., pp. 376–77.
47. Voegelin, *The New Science of Politics*, p. 164. Cf. id., *Order and History*, 1:345: "With
the appearance of Jesus, God himself entered into the eternal present of history." Cf. also id.,
"The Gospel and Culture," in D. Miller and D. G. Hadidian, eds., *Jesus and Man's Hope*, 2 vols.
(Pittsburgh: Pittsburgh Theological Seminary Press, 1971), 2:93.

is *outside* experience; rather it is a process of differentiation *within* experience. The most that an external miraculous appearance of Jesus could offer to an observer would be an indication of the power of God to restore a human person to life after he has died. From the traditional Christian point of view this sort of evidence of divine omnipotence and graciousness to man is not negligible; for those who have little capacity for conscious, differentiated spiritual experience, it may be a valuable means of orientation toward the transcendent God whose presence they can know only through inference. Even a staunch traditionalist, however, will have to admit that to make the mode of understanding of the spiritually ungifted into a norm or standard and to restrict the authoritative spokesmen of the faith, such as Paul, to so narrow a standard would be to reduce Christianity to a travesty of itself. If Paul's revelation were limited to the viewing of an external physical body and the hearing of physical sounds, he would have no spiritual authority; he could speak of evidence for the existence and beneficent intentions of an external God, but he could not tell us, as he so frequently does in his letters, that men can now enjoy the happiness of spiritual communion with that God. The question, Voegelin might say in response to Niemeyer, is not how God has a right to reveal himself, but how revelation in the fullest sense can actually take place. A miraculous manifestation could *indicate* something about God, but it would not actually *reveal* him. It would only point in the direction of the divine reality; it would not bring the soul into immediate relationship with it.

It may be helpful with respect to this issue to take notice of a distinction that St. Thomas Aquinas makes between two levels of faith, *fides informis* and *fides formata*, a distinction Voegelin is well aware of.[48] *Fides informis* is faith without its proper form, i.e., without its vital principle or "soul." It is simple belief of the sort that infers a reality external to itself, and its relationship to the reality that is its object remains purely extrinsic. *Fides formata*, formed faith, on the other hand, is faith that has *caritas*, the divine love, as its vital principle: ". . . charity is called the form of faith, in as much as it is through charity that faith is brought to completion and given its form."[49] Since the divine essence itself is *caritas*, and since the virtue of *caritas* created in the soul by grace is a participation in the divine life and unites the soul to God immediately, *fides caritate formata* is intrinsically, not extrinsically, related to its object.[50] Unformed faith is valuable as a preparation for formed faith, but it is rudimentary and has no authority grounded in experience by which to speak of God or of the life of the spirit.

48. Voegelin, *The New Science of Politics*, p. 79; id., *Order and History*, 1:377. For Aquinas's discussion of the distinction, see *Summa Theologica*, II–II, q. 4, a. 3–6, q. 6; q. 23, a. 6, a. 8. This work will be hereinafter abbreviated as *ST*.

49. *ST*, II–II, q. 4, a. 3. Cf. q. 23, a. 6, ad 2: "Faith works by love, not instrumentally, as a master by his servant, but as by its proper form."

50. *ST*, II–II, q. 23, a. 2.

From this it should be clear why Voegelin would not choose to focus his discussion on the miracle of Jesus' rising from the dead and appearing to Paul on the road to Damascus. Looking at the issue in the light of Aquinas's distinctions, even the orthodox Christian who accepts the miracle as a true event must acknowledge that, wonderful as it is, it pertains to an elementary level of faith. *Fides caritate formata*, on the other hand, is faith on its most mature level. It is also the culmination of the spiritual process of differentiation that Voegelin has chosen as his subject of study. As Voegelin analyzes it and as the orthodox Christian who locates Voegelin's point of focus will have to agree, the story Paul tells of the death, resurrection, and transfiguration of Jesus becomes, when Paul is speaking of his own *inner* experience of the presence of Christ, a mythic language by which to articulate and communicate an experienced spiritual reality. One of the major challenges for Christianity in the modern world, says Voegelin, is to find a way to explain to a literalizing or psychologizing public that myth can serve as "an objective language for the expression of a transcendental irruption, more adequate and exact as an instrument of expression than any rational system of symbols."[51] The extent to which the vocabulary of that myth is drawn from prior experience of external events is a question that both Voegelin and the orthodox Christian can agree amicably to set aside, since it is not directly pertinent to the analysis of a pneumatic differentiation.

The Pauline differentiation, says Voegelin, was a substantial advance over such earlier ones as that presented in the Platonic myth of the Demiurgic presence of God in man, society, history, and the cosmos. Plato's myth was "carefully devised so as to make the tale of divine presence in reality compatible with the existential truth of man's tension toward the divine ground," but Paul's vision carried him "beyond the structure of creation to its source in the freedom and love of divine creativity."[52]

This led to three important new insights. Paul, says Voegelin, differentiated the ordering process in existence to the point that "the transcosmic God and his Agape were revealed as the mover in the theophanic events which constitute meaning in history." He also "differentiated fully the experience of the directional movement by articulating its goal, its *teleion*, as the state of *aphtharsia* [immortality]. . . ." And finally he "fully differentiated the experience of man as the site where the movement of reality becomes luminous in its actual occurrence," so that man becomes revealed as "the creature in whom God can incarnate himself with the fullness (*pleroma*) of his divinity, transfiguring man into the God-man (Col. 2:9)."[53]

51. Voegelin, *From Enlightenment to Revolution*, ed. John H. Hallowell (Durham, N.C.: Duke University Press, 1975), 22.
52. Voegelin, *Order and History*, 4:249–50.
53. Ibid., 251.

It is important to note that in all of this Paul is not, says Voegelin, presenting a doctrine, but "articulating his experience of the God who enters him
through the vision and by this act of entering transfigures him."[54] Doctrine is
a secondary symbolism that develops in both philosophy and theology when
the original experiential insights have been lost. It literalizes and reifies or
hypostatizes the primary symbols engendered by the theophanic events and
then elaborates itself as an intellectual game with concepts that have lost their
substance. In the Patristic period the openness of the theophanic field was
substantially preserved, according to Voegelin's estimate, for almost three
centuries until the Council of Nicaea in 325 A.D. The subsequent history of
Christian theology, however, has been largely a process of deformation of experiential symbols into doctrine. Doctrine is not an entirely negative phenomenon, he acknowledges, since it can help to protect "an historically
achieved state of insight against . . . disintegrative pressures" under conditions of cultural turmoil, but it can also impede efforts to restore substance to
religious thinking.[55] Thus, "the prestige of the deformation is the source of
the constant tension between dogmatic and mystic theology."[56] That tension
of this sort should develop is inevitable in view of the fact that experiential
insights can be expressed only through symbols and that "the possibility of
literalist or hypostatizing derailments" is "inherent to all symbolization."[57]
This problem can be more or less acute, however, and in Voegelin's opinion it
has become especially so in our own period: "In our time, the inherited symbolisms of ecumenic humanity are disintegrating, because the deforming
doctrinalization has become socially stronger than the experiential insights it
was originally meant to protect." This is why he says that we have lost the
reality of man's existence in the Metaxy behind a mass of accumulated symbols, secondary and tertiary, and that his own purpose in *Order and History* is
"to raise this obstacle and its structure into consciousness, and by its removal
to help in the return to the truth of reality as it reveals itself in history."[58]

IV

This should serve to set forth the basic pattern of Voegelin's thought on the
subject of revelation. We can now turn to consider some of the points of difference between Voegelin's analysis and more traditional theological thinking. Many of Voegelin's major challenges to theology have already become
clear. Far from having neglected the question of the relation of reason and
revelation, he has explored it in great depth and in the process has formulated

54. Ibid., 256.   55. Ibid., 43–44.
56. Ibid., 48.
57. Ibid., 147. Cf. id., "Immortality: Experience and Symbol," *Harvard Theological Review*
60 (1967):235–36.
58. Voegelin, *Order and History*, 4:58.

what seem sound criteria by which to evaluate the authenticity and theoretical adequacy of theological analysis. He has pointed out, for example, the danger of a loss of substance to thinking that forgets its experiential roots. He has also developed a clear theoretical grasp of the nature of human experience as existence characterized by a constant tension, from which man is continually tempted to flee into impossible metastatic dreams or into Gnostic certainties. "Uncertainty is the very essence of Christianity," as Voegelin said in *The New Science of Politics*, and the Christian critic who would find fault with him for insufficient interest in the question of "the historical Jesus" must not forget to ask himself if his own interest in that question is related to a desire to turn faith into certainty through some form of intellectual Gnosis. Or if he wishes to defend the importance of dogma regarding this or other matters, Voegelin reminds him that he must be on guard against making *fides informis* into an absolute norm that would impede both authentic rational inquiry and the further movement of the soul into *fides formata*. To the pietist, on the other hand, who might wish to dispense with theoretical formulations altogether, Voegelin offers the warning that Gnostic deviations can take emotional and volitional forms as well as intellectual.[59]

Could an orthodox Christian critic, nevertheless, address any challenging questions to Professor Voegelin? Let us consider some possibilities. For one thing there is the matter of the need for at least a certain amount of *fides informis* in the life of the Church. There will probably always be many among the faithful who will be incapable, at least in this life, of sharing in the conscious spiritual experience that is the vital principle of religion and that engenders its primary symbols. Lacking experiential insight of their own and consequently incapable of evaluating claims to it in others, such people will probably always feel strongly dependent on what they think of as "objective" evidence in the form of external miraculous signs. If the ecclesiastical statesman, who needs some means of orienting such people toward the divine reality in the hope that they may enjoy its vision in the life to come, has external signs of this sort that he can use for this purpose, he has good reason to be grateful for them. Whether such signs have been granted, of course, must remain a matter to be decided through rational inquiry on the basis of historical evidence carefully tested for its reliability. To decide apart from such inquiry that such signs could not be granted, on the other hand, would be to place limitations on both the divine power and the divine generosity.

Voegelin is, in fact, well aware of the need for statesmanship that can shepherd those who lack insight of their own—in the religious sphere as well as in the political. He has high praise for Plato's treatment of this issue in *The Laws*, for example, and regarding the dispute between Comte and Littré over Comte's desire to substitute a Religion of Humanity for that of the Christian

59. Voegelin, *The New Science of Politics*, pp. 122, 124.

Church, Voegelin says that Littré simply did not understand the need for some form of institutionalization of the spirit.[60] Voegelin's own statements regarding "religion," on the other hand, have tended to have a rather negative tone.[61] Why this should be so ought to be quite clear by now; we have already sufficiently explored the grounds for his distrust of dogmatism. There is more to religion than dogmatism, however, and if as Voegelin says and as the churchman must agree, "precautions of meditative practice" are needed to foster "the process of experiential reactivation and linguistic renewal" that the doctrinization of symbols is liable to interrupt,[62] one must also recognize that for the average person the only form of meditative practice normally available to him is his participation in the worship of an organized religious community. It is true, and the orthodox churchman should acknowledge it to his shame, that the Church's practice of its *magisterium* has often tended to promote dogmatism and *fides informis* over meditation and *fides formata*, but it has not done so exclusively, and the thoughtful theologian remains aware that the Church is *semper reformanda*—both in need of reform and capable of it.

There is a further question related to this issue, however. It has to do with the ultimate prospects of those not now capable of actually realizing the goal of meditative practice. As Voegelin himself has said, "meditation requires more energy and discipline than most people are able to invest," and even when a person does engage in it, "the theophanic event itself is not at his command."[63] Much, perhaps too much, of the Church's teaching is based on the assumption that spiritual experience of the mysteries of the faith will be realized for many only in the life to come. But what indeed *can* one hope for in the way of a life to come—for anyone? The traditional Christian hope of a future life is definite, but Professor Voegelin's thinking on the subject is difficult to get a precise picture of. On the one hand, he takes the idea of immortality very seriously, speaking of it as "a fundamental human experience" that may rise "to the lucidity of consciousness in which it becomes clear that the divine can be experienced as immortal because the experiencing soul shares or participates . . . in the divine."[64] But on the other hand, he is wary about allowing this experience to be turned into a doctrine of immortality,[65] and his frequent references to Anaximander's dictum that all things must perish once again into the *Apeiron* (the Boundless) from which they came must make the reader wonder whether Voegelin's own idea of what awaits the soul after death is a complete dissolution of the individual existent back into absolute being. To attempt to believe with certainty that the human person will con-

60. Voegelin, *From Enlightenment to Revolution*, p. 143.
61. Voegelin, *Order and History*, 1:376; 4:43–48.
62. Ibid., 4:56.
63. Voegelin, "Immortality: Experience and Symbol," p. 236; id., *Order and History*, 4:217.
64. Voegelin, *Order and History*, 2:206.
65. See, e.g., "Immortality: Experience and Symbol," p. 236.

tinue in individual existence after death would be to speculate beyond experience, and it is obvious why Voegelin would wish to avoid this; but the Christian faith in the risen life to come is not, at its most lucid and authentic, an intellectual speculation, but rather an act of trust in the divine generosity. This act of trust is itself rooted in concrete experiences of the soul—both the experience of the profound longing of the individual for continuing life and the experience of the generosity of the God who draws the soul to himself and discloses himself to it in the theophanic events. Professor Voegelin has not addressed himself directly to this issue in his writings, but there is no reason why the position of faith, when formulated in this way rather than as a speculative doctrine, would not be compatible with his theoretical principles. If the legitimacy of such faith should be admitted, however, the concern of the ecclesiastical statesman with the possibilities the next life may hold for those who now remain spiritually ungifted must seem reasonable, even a necessary corollary of the *caritas* which is the soul of faith. What to make of a situation in which it is the spiritually ungifted themselves who try to play the role of statesman, on the other hand, is perhaps an issue best left in silence.

Of the criticisms by Niemeyer of Voegelin's approach to Christianity, two important ones remain to be discussed. These had to do with the questions of the uniqueness of the Christian revelation and of the uniqueness of the Incarnation of God in Jesus. Niemeyer said that whereas Voegelin discusses man as a creature in whom God can incarnate himself, St. Paul reflected on what it means that God did incarnate himself in one particular man. Both from Voegelin's point of view and also from St. Paul's, the Incarnation is not something limited to Jesus, unless one wishes to find some other interpretation for the many references in Paul to the idea that Christians are baptized into Christ's life, "have the mind of Christ" (1 Cor. 2:16), "have fullness of life in him" in whom "the fullness of the divine reality dwells bodily" (Col. 2: 9–10), and are indeed so intimately one with Christ that he can say "it is no longer I who live, but Christ who lives in me" (Gal. 2:20).[66] Similarly the actual participation of the faithful in Christ and in the divine life itself was a constant theme of Patristic and Medieval theology.[67] This is, after all, simply

66. The passage from Colossians is one Voegelin himself has referred to (*Order and History*, 4:251), as mentioned above. Whether or not Colossians may be considered to have been written by Paul himself, it is at least a very early document and is unquestionably from Paul's circle; see Wayne A. Meeks, ed., *The Writings of St. Paul: A Norton Critical Edition* (New York: W. W. Norton & Co., Inc., 1972), p. 114, for a discussion of the authorship of this letter. Paul's authorship of 1 Corinthians and Galatians is undisputed.

67. For a modern expression of this theme, cf. Georges Florovsky's statement that "the core of the conception of catholocity (*Sobornost'*)" is the idea that each member of the church "is in direct and immediate union with Christ and His Father," in "The Church: Her Nature and Task," p. 53, quoted in Peter A. Chamberas, "Some Aspects of the Ecclesiology of Georges Florovsky," in *The Heritage of the Early Church: Essays in Honor of the Very Reverend Georges Vasilievich Florovsky*, ed. David Neiman and Margaret Schatkin (Rome: Pont. Institutum Studiorum Orientalium, 1973), pp. 430–31.

an aspect of the question discussed earlier regarding *fides caritate formata* as effecting immediate union of the soul with God.

For most of its history, however, the orthodox Christian tradition has assumed that although each of the faithful is united with God through grace, there remains something unique in an absolute sense about the union of humanity and divinity in Jesus. Aquinas's approach was to distinguish between what he called habitual grace, which Christians share with Christ, and the grace of union, which belongs to Christ alone. As Aquinas formulated the issue, it was a question of whether the union of the two natures in Christ took place by grace.[68] One objection to the idea that it was by grace, he said, could be that since every saint is united to God by grace, if Christ was also, it would seem that he was God no more than other holy men. The supposition of the additional *gratia unionis* solved the problem. Or did it? Professor Voegelin could reasonably claim here that this is a classic example of the process of the deformation of primary symbols into doctrine: that Aquinas, following an uncritical tradition, simply literalized the scriptural symbol of the "only son" (*monogenes*) and did so by the invention of a verbal concept with no reference to experience.[69] It would obviously be difficult for a defender of the tradition to take Aquinas's side here, since clearly neither he nor Aquinas himself, according to their own premises, could have any clear grasp of the supposed reality to which the phrase *gratia unionis* refers. To play such a game with an opponent as critically acute as Voegelin would be like inviting him to join one in admiring the Emperor's new clothes.

Is orthodoxy necessarily locked into such a position, however? There is another way of formulating the underlying issue that never occurred to the earlier tradition, and that is to ask if the union of man and God in Christ is to be interpreted as unique in kind or in degree. There is no need to try to settle that issue here; it is sufficient to identify it as a possible approach to show that the conflict between Voegelin's position and that of orthodoxy may not be a complete impasse. This very question has, in fact, been taken up in recent times by theologians who grow out of the orthodox tradition and intend fidelity to it but who do not interpret orthodoxy as such as requiring the more customary interpretation.[70] It is worth remembering that, as Alan Rich-

68. *ST*, III, q. 2, a. 10, "Utrum unio incarnationis sit per gratiam." For a further indication that Aquinas thought the union of God and man in Jesus to be absolutely unique in kind, consider also ibid., q. 7, a. 3, which says that Jesus did not have the virtue of faith, because he had no need of it.

69. For a discussion of the *monogenes* in John, see Raymond E. Brown, *The Gospel According to John* (I–XII) (Garden City, N.Y.: Doubleday & Co., Inc., 1966), pp. 13–14. For the ancient Near Eastern background of the symbolism, see Voegelin, *Order and History*, 1:390; Voegelin traces it ultimately to Egyptian coronation rites.

70. See, e.g., D. M. Baillie, *God Was in Christ: An Essay on Incarnation and Atonement* (New York: Charles Scribner's Sons, 1948), and W. Norman Pittenger, *The Word Incarnate: A Study of the Doctrine of the Person of Christ* (New York: Harper & Brothers, 1959). I wish to

ardson said in his *Creeds in the Making*, the Chalcedonia Definition did not prescribe a theory of how Godhead and manhood were united in Christ but contented itself with insisting on the mere fact of their union in him. "Thus," he says, "it permits the formulation of theories provided that the principle is safeguarded in them."[71] Voegelin's interpretation of Incarnation in terms of continuity and universality would not in any way contradict this principle; rather, it is one possible theoretical approach beginning from it.

This can be seen from Voegelin's own interpretation of the Definition of Chalcedon which was stated as follows:

> In the light of these implications, then, the symbolism of Incarnation would express the experience, with a date in history, of God reaching into Man and revealing Him as the Presence that is the flow of presence from the beginning of the world to its end. History is Christ written large. This last formulation is not in conflict with the Platonic 'Man written large.' To be sure, the two symbolisms differ, because the first one is engendered by a noetic experience in the context of Hellenic philosophy; but they do not differ with regard to the structure of the reality symbolized. In order to confirm the sameness of structure expressed in different symbolisms, I shall quote the essential passage from the Definition of Chalcedon (A.D. 451), concerning the union of the two natures in the one person of Christ: "Our Lord Jesus Christ . . . truly God and truly man . . . recognized in two natures . . . the distinction of natures being in no way annulled by the union, but rather the characteristics of each nature being preserved and coming together to form one person and subsistence."

This valiant attempt by the Patres to express the two-in-one reality of

---

make clear that in suggesting a conception of the Incarnation of God in Jesus as unique in degree, by its incomparable fullness, while denying that it is absolutely unique in kind, I do not intend to suggest what might be called a "humanistic" theory of Incarnation—as though participation in divinity were a natural property of man as an independent, world-immanent entity. Such a "humanistic" conception, moreover, would be the farthest thing from Voegelin's intentions as well. Voegelin has consistently opposed the concept of a world-immanent, autonomous human nature. For him, humanity is not a universal, "merely natural" quality all men share; rather it is constituted through experiences of transcendence, and these come only by divine grace. (See *Anamnesis*, pp. 290–91; *Order and History*, 3:358, 4:304–5; and "Reason: The Classic Experience," p. 252.) To put it another way, humanity in the full sense of the term is a possibility that existing human beings realize in actuality only to varying degrees, and then only through the divine gift that makes them sharers in the life that was incarnate in its fullness only in Jesus. Cf. Voegelin's comment on Matt. 16:17 and John 6:44 in "The Gospel and Culture," p. 91. "The divine Sonship is not revealed through an information tendered by Jesus, but through a man's response to the full presence in Jesus of the same Unknown God by whose presence he is inchoatively moved in his own existence."

71. *Creeds in The Making* (London: SCM Press, 1951), pp. 84–85. For a more extensive theoretical discussion of the same idea, see Bernard J. F. Lonergan, "The Origins of Christian Realism," in *A Second Collection* (Philadelphia: Westminster Press, 1974), pp. 239–61, 251–53, 259.

God's participation in man, without either compromising the separateness of the two or splitting the one, concerns the same structure of intermediate reality, of the *metaxy*, the philosopher encounters when he analyses man's consciousness of participation in the divine ground of his existence. The reality of the Mediator and the intermediate reality of consciousness have the same structure.[72]

With regard to the question of the uniqueness of the Christian revelation, whether, as Niemeyer put it, Paul can legitimately be placed on a continuum of revelation with non-Christian thinkers, the spokesman for the orthodox position might reasonably claim that the miracle of Christ's resurrection, rationally inferred from historical testimony such as that of St. Paul in 1 Cor. 15, gives Christianity a special basis for hope that all who put their trust in God may share in that risen life. The reason why Voegelin would not consider an external manifestation of that sort to be revelation in the proper sense of the word, however, has already been made clear, as has the fact that even the orthodox believer himself must admit that a miracle is not a direct disclosure of the divine reality but only an indication of it. That actual revelation, in the full sense, should be interpreted as continuous with genuine spiritual insight wherever it occurs cannot be said, moreover, to be a necessarily unorthodox position, since numerous representatives of orthodoxy, including Aquinas himself, have held it.[73] The implication, even of the orthodox position, is that where the Christian revelation may be said to be unique in kind is only in the lower region of revelation, that of external indication, while in the area of actual disclosure of divine reality it is unique only in degree—unless one wishes to claim that never except among professing Christians has there been actual *caritas* or even genuine wisdom. This is, of course, a position not unknown among spokesmen for orthodoxy, but it involves inferences about the experience of non-Christians that by their very nature would be impossible to support from evidence and that would place very narrow limits on God's action. It amounts to a doctrinaire exclusivism that cannot accord well with the fundamental Christian belief in God's providential care for all of mankind.[74] On this point Voegelin challenges Christianity to live up to its calling to realize fully the inherent universality that is of its essence.

72. Voegelin, "Immortality: Experience and Symbol," p. 263.

73. Consider Justin Martyr, I *Apologia*, xlvi, and II, xiii, in Henry Bettenson, ed. and trans., *The Early Christian Fathers*, (London: Oxford University Press, 1956), pp. 60, 63–64, and Clement of Alexandria, *Stromateis*, I, v (28, 1), in Bettenson, pp. 168–69. For Aquinas, see *ST*, III, q. 8, a. 3, "Utrum Christus sit caput omnium hominum." Cf. also *ST*, II–II, q. 23, a. 2, ad 1: "The Divine Essence Itself is charity, even as it is wisdom, and goodness. Therefore, just as we are said to be good with the goodness which is God, and wise with the wisdom which is God (since the goodness by which we are formally good is a participation of Divine goodness, and the wisdom by which we are formally wise, is a share of Divine wisdom), so too, the charity by which formally we love our neighbor is a participation of Divine Charity."

74. Cf. Lonergan, *A Second Collection*, p. 155: ". . . it is not Christian doctrine that the gift

A final challenge Professor Voegelin offers to the potential defender of orthodoxy is to be clear about the nature of his loyalty to the tradition he defends. If Voegelin is distrustful of doctrinal formulations, it is because they so easily can lose their experiential substance and degenerate into empty words. To maintain his own authenticity of faith the orthodox interpreter must always remember that his primary loyalty is not to the formulae of tradition, but to the spiritual intention that gave rise to them. He must be willing to go behind the words, "to deconstruct the concept," as Paul Ricoeur puts it,[75] in order to recover his living communion with that intention—which is itself the mind of Christ. He must remember, as Georges Florovsky has said, that "tradition is not a principle striving to restore the past, using the past as a criterion for the present. . . . Tradition is the constant abiding of the Spirit and not only the memory of words."[76]

---

of God's love is restricted to Christians." Cf. also id., *Philosophy of God and Theology* (Philadelphia: Westminster Press, 1973), p. 20, to the effect that supernatural revelation and supernatural grace, to use the traditional terminology, are present in all religions and among all mankind. Karl Rahner has said, "Just because grace is free and unmerited, this does not mean that it is rare (theology has been led astray for too long already by the tacit assumption that grace would no longer be grace if God became too free with it)," *Nature and Grace* (London and New York: Stagbooks, 1963), p. 31, quoted in Alan Richardson, *Religion in Contemporary Debate* (Philadelphia: Westminster Press, 1966), pp. 117–18.

75. *The Conflict of Interpretations: Essays in Hermeneutics*, ed. Don Ihde (Evanston, Ill.: Northwestern University Press, 1974), p. 270.

76. *"Sobornost'*," p. 63, quoted in Chamberas, "Some Aspects of the Ecclesiology of Georges Florovksy," p. 425.

A NEW HISTORY AND A NEW BUT ANCIENT GOD? VOEGELIN'S *THE ECUMENIC AGE*

Thomas J. J. Altizer

The first volume of Voegelin's monumental work, *Order and History*, was published in 1956 under the title of *Israel and Revelation*. This book may someday be perceived as the most important work of Old Testament scholarship ever written in the United States, and it is noteworthy that it was written by a political scientist and philosopher, and one who oddly chose the seemingly unpromising ground of the Old Testament as the foundation of a new and fundamental inquiry into the meaning of the order of being in history. The second and third volumes of *Order and History* were published in 1957 under the titles of *The World of the Polis* and *Plato and Aristotle*. These volumes embodied the virtues of one who was at once a Greek scholar of first rank and a philosophical mind equal or superior to any in America today. Eric Voegelin may well be historically unique in having mastered the worlds of both Athens and Jerusalem: *Order and History* is surely unique in its project of unveiling the coinherence of noetic understanding and biblical faith as the primary and indispensable ground of Western civilization. Originally *Order and History* was to comprise six volumes, the third to be followed by *Empire and Christianity*, *The Protestant Centuries*, and *The Crisis of Western Civilization*, the last to be published in 1959. Not until 1974 did the fourth volume of *Order and History* appear, entitled *The Ecumenic Age*, and this long delay was occasioned by what Voegelin calls the breakdown of the original project. Breakdown is not a light word for a philosopher of order, and this breakdown may well signify the end of what we have known as history.

What ultimately broke the project, Voegelin declares, was the impossibility of aligning the empirical types of order and symbolization in any time sequence at all that would permit the structures actually found to emerge from a history conceived as a "course." Indeed, Voegelin is now persuaded that the conception of history as a meaningful course of events on a straight line of time was not the discovery of Israel, but was rather a symbolic form devel-

This essay and the accompanying response were originally published in the *Journal of the American Academy of Religion* 43, no. 4 (1974): 757–72, and are reprinted by permission. Published as "A Review Essay," Altizer's article has been retitled.

oped by the end of the third millennium B.C. in the empires of the Ancient Near East. One of the original theses of *The Ecumenic Age* is that the unilinear construction of history (here called *historiogenesis*) is an ancient symbolic form not differing in principle either from Ancient Near Eastern mythopoesis or from the Ionian speculation on the ground and beginning of all being. Not only has historiogenesis persisted until our own day, it has even displayed a tendency to swallow up all other types of mytho-speculation: "It is the symbolism by which the cosmological style of truth survives most obdurately in social fields whose style of truth is informed by philosophy and revelation" (p. 91). Yet historiogenesis had a historical beginning, and perhaps it is now undergoing a historical end. It begins with a crisis of empire, its motivation discernible as an anxiety aroused by the recent impact of irreversible events: "Historiogenesis implacably places events on the line of irreversible time where opportunities are lost forever and defeat is final" (p. 65). For example, the Sumerian King List (2050 B.C.) is here understood, following Thorkild Jacobsen, to have reached its unilinear history of Sumer only by having abolished the parallel histories of the city-states that it conquered, and thereby their histories are absorbed into an imaginary, unilinear history of empire. Historiogenesis is an ancient imperial creation, its intention being to sublimate the contingencies of imperial order in time to the timeless serenity of the cosmic order itself.

Voegelin states at the end of the Introduction to *The Ecumenic Age* that the purpose of *Order and History* is to help us return to the truth of reality as it reveals itself in history, and to do so by recovering in consciousness our inherited but now disintegrating symbolisms. What establishes his as a radical project is that these symbolisms achieve a new form if not a new meaning in his reconstruction. Voegelin, like Ricoeur, is radical and reactionary at once and altogether, thus baffling all who attempt to employ him either for political or theological ends. One fundamental question to be asked of Voegelin is whether his work issues in a truly new symbolism, one which is perhaps the reflection of a new "leap of being" in our history, or whether its novelty simply derives from its truly being a recovery, a recovery which can be realized only by "deconstructing" the darkness of the modern mind. Certainly our historical consciousness is an integral component of a uniquely modern darkness, and Voegelin intends to go both beyond and before that consciousness by a new kind of historical thinking. We have long known that our inherited symbolisms are the historical product of what Voegelin calls the Ecumenic Age, a historical period extending from the rise of the Persian to the fall of the Roman Empire. But we have not apprehended the Ecumenic Age as an integral historical entity, and thereby we have falsely differentiated its components. Above all we have created a false dichotomy between Athens and Jerusalem, between reason and revelation, between *civitas terrena* and *Civitas*

Dei. The seed of this dichotomy is already present in Paul, receives a total expression in Gnosticism, and is reborn with devastating historical consequences in the ideologies of the nineteenth century.

At this point *The Ecumenic Age* is in full continuity with the preceding volumes of *Order and History*, but it deepens the earlier and primary thesis by giving it a new historical context. The earlier volumes commonly seemed to ignore the apparently overwhelming differences between the language of the Bible and the language of ontological understanding. Thus, in the first sentence of the Introduction to *Israel and Revelation* Voegelin declares: "God and man, world and society form a primordial community of being." Thereby, too, Voegelin was forced to condemn the prophetic faith of the Old Testament, for it seems to demand a leap out of existence. He even coined a term, *metastasis*, to signify the change in the constitution of being envisioned by the prophets. While the category of metastatic faith is still present in *The Ecumenic Age*, it assumes a fuller and now positive meaning, for Israel's exodus from pragmatic history can here be understood as a spiritual exodus culminating in Second Isaiah's vision of a reconstituted Israel as the center of an ecumenic mankind under Yahweh. So likewise Plato and Aristotle are given a more universal identity, so much so that our historical distance from them threatens to disappear. Can that be a primary intention of this volume? Is Voegelin's understanding of historiogenesis as an imperial creation intended to deliver us from linear and chronological time? Already in an early page of this volume Voegelin can state: "History is not a stream of human beings and their actions in time, but the process of man's participation in a flux of divine presence that has eschatological direction" (p. 6).

Fundamental to Voegelin's enterprise is what he calls the cosmos of the primary experience, a cosmos that is the whole, *to pan*, of an earth below and a heaven above, and a cosmos full of gods. In cosmological empires, the understanding of history is dominated by this primary experience of the cosmos. But this cosmos is not a thing among others. It is rather the background of reality against which all existent things exist, and it has reality even in the mode of nonexistence. The ground of the primary experience, for Voegelin, is the fundamental tension of all experienced reality: the tension of existence out of nonexistence. Lying at the center of the primary experience of the cosmos is the experience of a cosmos existing in precarious balance on the edge of emergence from nothing and return to nothing. And the balance is truly precarious, being maintained in the pre-ecumenic world only because there the tension in reality between existence and nonexistence, though experienced as real, does not become actually articulate. Here, what Voegelin terms the "In-Between" of cosmic reality encloses in its compactness the tension of existence toward the ground of existence. That compactness is disrupted with the dawn of the Ecumenic Age:

The compression of the tension into the In-Between of cosmic reality becomes critically untenable when the astrophysical universe must be recognized as too much existent to function as the non-existent ground of reality,
and the gods are discovered as too little existent to form a realm of intracosmic things. In the hierarchical order of realities that governs the symbolization of kingship there become visible the lines along which the cosmological style will crack until the cosmos dissociates into a de-divinized
external world and a world-transcendent God. At this point, however, one
must be careful not to overstate the results of differentiation and dissociation. What cracks is the cosmological style of truth as far as it tends to conceive all reality after the model of In-Between reality; and what dissociates
is the cosmos of the primary experience. But neither of these consequences
of differentiation affects the core of the primary experience, i.e., the experience of an In-Between reality. On the contrary, it is still with us. (p. 77)

While it may still be with us, it surely is heard or spoken by few. Eric Voegelin is one of those few.

Or is he alone? Voegelin must be very lonely as one who is at once a historical and an ontological thinker. Perhaps he is not so lonely as a religious
thinker. Interestingly enough, he not only repudiates the word "religion,"
but he also forcefully negates any theological categories or distinctions that
cross his path. And if he is forced again and again to coin words and phrases,
that is only because he is attempting to establish a new mode of understanding, a mode that obviously cannot stand upon our common language. Voegelin's prose style is tantalizing, for it is clear and obscure at once, and its clarity
is indistinguishable from its obscurity. So much is this the case that it gradually becomes apparent that the actual subject of *Order and History* is a mystery. In the conclusion of this volume we learn that what happens "in" history
is the very process of differentiating consciousness that constitutes history.
What, then, Voegelin asks, is the relation of the process of differentiation to
the lapses of immanent time? He answers that to formulate the problem
means practically to resolve it: "The divine-human In-Between of historically
differentiating experience is founded in the consciousness of concrete human
beings in concrete bodies on the concrete earth in the concrete universe"
(p. 333). For there is no "length of time" in which things happen; there is
only the reality of things which has a time-dimension. Finally, things do not
happen in the astrophysical universe: "The universe, together with all things
founded in it, happens in God" (p. 334).

Is God, then, the actual subject of *Order and History*? Certainly not if
by God one means the God of our theological understanding. The subject of
Order and History is a "process of the Whole," a process of which the In-
Between reality with its process of history is no more than a part, although

the very important part in which the eschatological movement of the total process becomes luminous. Here, eschatological movement is not only a forward movement, but a movement which is at once cosmic, noetic, and divine. Consciousness not only records this movement, but it also embodies it, and it does so in the structurally equivalent symbolisms of myth and philosophy.

> What becomes visible in the new luminosity, therefore, is not only the structure of consciousness itself (in classical language: the nature of man), but also the structure of an "advance" in the process of reality. Moreover, the site of the advance is not a mysterious entity called "history" that would exist independent of such advances; the site rather is the very consciousness which, in its state of noetic luminosity, makes these discoveries. The theophanic events do not occur *in* history; they constitute history together with its meaning. The noetic theophany, finally, reveals consciousness as having the structure of metaleptic reality, of the divine-human Metaxy. As a consequence, "history" in the sense of an area in reality in which the insight into the meaning of existence advances is the history of theophany. (p. 252)

The Metaxy, for Voegelin, is the concrete psyche of concrete human beings in their encounters with divine presence. This psyche is finally one (the "universal humanity"), just as theophany is finally one. And the core of the theophany is the revelation of God as the Nous both in the cosmos and in man.

It was Plato who most fully discovered the noetic theophany, thereby revealing the intelligible structure in reality as divine. But the noetic theophany that is present in Plato and Aristotle is structurally equivalent to the Israelite experience of revelation, whereby man has acquired his consciousness of historical immediacy under God. The God of Plato and the God of Moses are one God, and this God is both the historical and the ontological ground of our universal humanity, a humanity that was the discovery of the Ecumenic Age. Most fully, it is in the Macedonian conquest that the conception of a Homonoia of mankind emerges, but this does not continue the cosmological form of the older empires; rather, it moves on the line from the Platonic-Aristotelian to the Pauline Homonoia. One of Voegelin's most striking and most forceful theses is that pragmatic conquest and spiritual exodus are so closely related in the Ecumenic Age. It is Second Isaiah who first reveals a preestablished harmony between the universality of a spiritual exodus and the establishment of an ecumenic field through conquest. This occurs when Second Isaiah names Cyrus as Yahweh's Messiah, thereby revealing that in the transition from cosmological to ecumenic rule, the empire that keeps in bondage is the empire that sets free; this experience of a connection between conquest and exodus will later recur in the Pauline-Augustinian connection between Roman Empire and Christianity. For the age of ecumenic empire is also the age of spiritual outbursts that Jaspers has named the "axis-time" of mankind. Nevertheless, there is a conflict, until Voegelin theoretically unresolved, between the meaning which Jewish, Stoic, and Christian thinkers again and again discern in the convergence of conquest and exodus, and the historical nonfinality of every attempt at ecumenic finality.

Voegelin resolves this conflict by way of his ontological understanding of history and his noetic understanding of revelation. Spiritual exodus from pragmatic reality is a movement within reality, as Plato and Aristotle make manifest. But this same movement is also and equally manifest in the eschatological and biblical vision of an ultimate transfiguration of reality. Yet this movement can be consciously manifest and historically real only by means of a balance between existence in the lasting cosmos and the truth of transfigured reality. Plato and Aristotle established this balance, both in historical fact and as a postulate of reason, and this is one of the principal events in the history of mankind, for it has determined the life of reason in Western civilization up to our own time and is also a primary source of order in history. That order now threatens to disappear, and the source of our crisis is our historical failure to unite Athens and Jerusalem. Our greatest failure, theologically, is that we have failed to understand either the nature or the identity of revelation. Israel failed in its creation of Scripture, thereby deforming original revelatory symbols by a doctrinization of the Word. Christianity failed by identifying the transfiguring incarnation with the historical and dogmatic Christ: "Transfiguring incarnation, in particular, does not begin with Christ, as Paul assumed, but becomes conscious through Christ and Paul's vision as the eschatological *telos* of the transfiguring process that goes on in history before and after Christ and constitutes its meaning" (p. 270). Above all Christianity failed by establishing a dualistic distinction between *civitas terrena* and *Civitas Dei*. Thus historical Christianity has closed itself to what Voegelin calls the Paradox of Reality or the Exodus within Reality.

Christianity has not failed simply because of its Christocentrism. On the contrary, in the epiphany of Christ, the formation of humanity in history has become transparent for its meaning as the process of transformation (p. 17). Although Voegelin does not say so in so many words, it is clear that he believes that the primary failure of Christianity is its misidentification, its misreading, of Christ. The Incarnate Word is not a man; it is rather the eschatological movement of the Whole, of reality itself. Our consciousness, including most particularly our historical consciousness, has issued from a split between the subject and the object of consciousness. The total reality that was once manifest as a process of transfiguration has evaporated in the hypostatized subject and object of our historical consciousness. Then the luminosity of noetic consciousness is deformed into an "anthropology" of intramundane man and a "theology" of a transmundane God, and the theophanic event is destroyed. The death of God, then, originates in Christianity, and it originates precisely in Christian faith in the transcendent God. So likewise, the modern revolt against God, the modern murder of God, is simply a development of the Christianity against which it is in revolt. May we not then conclude that it is the Christian Christ, the Christian Word, which is the most fundamental source of our crisis today?

While Voegelin insists that he is not dealing with problems of theology, and writes in such a manner as to make a theological exegesis of his work a virtual impossibility, it would be difficult to deny that his primary quest is to unveil the identity of God. Moreover, he seeks that identity in the reality which reveals itself in history. That reality is finally a reality moving towards its own transfiguration. And it is in the Incarnation that a transfiguring reality is most luminous: "The transfiguring exodus within reality achieves the full consciousness of itself when it becomes historically conscious as the Incarnation of God in Man" (p. 302). Do not these words have a familiar ring? Are they not, indeed, a paraphrase of Hegel? Yet Hegel is the great villain of *The Ecumenic Age*. He looms so large in these pages as to be a virtual Antichrist, for Hegel is the real creator of modern ideology. Only Plato, Aristotle, and Paul are treated more fully here than Hegel, for Hegel is here understood as having effected a total reversal of noetic understanding, and Hegel is also understood, in part at least, as an authentic descendent of Paul. The violence of Voegelin's assault upon Hegel is almost without limits, for here our modern darkness is fully incarnate. Voegelin even coins a word in his wrestling with Hegel, *egophany*, signifying the pathos of thinkers who exist in a state of alienation and libidinous obsession. Perhaps the following is Voegelin's most violent and most revealing attack upon Hegel:

In the experience of existential tension toward the divine ground, the poles of the tension are symbolized as "God" and "man," while the In-Between of existence is expressed by such symbols as *methexis, metalepsis,* or *metaxy*. In the closed existence of the alienated speculator, the structure of the Metaxy remains the same, but the thinker must now, in Nietzsche's phrase, extend grace to himself. He must develop a "divided self," with one self acting the role of "man" who suffers the human condition and the other self acting the role of "God" who brings salvation from it. The Metaxy becomes, in Hegel's language, the state of *Zerrisenheit* (diremption) or *Entfremdung* (alienation); the elaboration of the speculative system becomes the act of salvational *Versoehnung* (reconciliation); and the man who performs the feat combines in his person the two natures of God and man in the sense of the Definition of Chalcedon; he is the new God-man, the new Messiah. The structure of reality does not disappear, however, because somebody engages in libidinous revolt against it. While the structure remains the same, the revolt results, personally, in the destruction of existential order and, socially, in mass murder. (p. 255)

Ideology is self-deification, wherein the subject of consciousness becomes the ground and source of all, and it ultimately issues in the tyranny and mass murder of the twentieth century.

Is Hegel the antipode of Voegelin? Or the dialectical twin? In some sense Hegel surely lies behind Voegelin, for it was Hegel who created a philosophy uniting ontological and historical understanding, and Hegel also created a philosophy wherein the subject of consciousness, and of modern consciousness, is a self-realization of both the mind and the object of Greek noetic understanding. While Hegel's understanding of Israel was deeply scarred by his own rebellion against the Bible and orthodox Christianity, it is nevertheless true that he reached an understanding of the New Testament and Christianity wherein the Christian Word is both the symbolic expression of absolute truth and the Word or negativity which is the source of all meaning, movement, and activity. Indeed, it is the Incarnate Word which is the center and ground of Hegel's "system." For Voegelin, Hegel's *Geist* is simply his ego. But this is an absurd and grotesque interpretation. One could just as easily say the same of Aristotle's *Nous*. May we not with far more justice say that Voegelin's hatred of Hegel is an attempted Oedipal murder of his father? And we can see it as such because it doesn't succeed. Certainly the Voegelin who believes that what happens in history is the very differentiating consciousness that constitutes history is a clear descendent of Hegel. Voegelin can even directly follow Hegel in identifying the problem of an "absolute epoch" as the central issue in a philosophy of history; for Voegelin, too, an absolute epoch is understood as the events in which reality becomes luminous to itself as a process of transfiguration. Hegel's philosophy of history is grounded in his identification of the absolute epoch as being marked by the epiphany of Christ. Voegelin refuses to identify the absolute epoch with the epiphany of Christ as a particular event or historical process, identifying it rather with a universal humanity as embodied in the great spiritual outbursts and the universal empires of the Ecumenic Age.

Nevertheless, as we have seen, for Voegelin, too, the transfiguration of reality only realizes a full consciousness of itself when it becomes historically conscious as the Incarnation of God in Man. Like Hegel, too, Voegelin presents a largely negative portrayal of Hinduism and Buddhism as undifferentiated and nonhistorical expressions of consciousness in quest of a precosmic totality. At this point, only his penultimate chapter on the Chinese Ecumene seems to distinguish him from Hegel. But does it do so in a decisive sense? True, Voegelin now affirms that there are two ecumenic ages, a Western and a Far Eastern, both unfolding parallel in time. But the Chinese Ecumene failed to culminate in a radical break with cosmological order, and thus it is an incomplete breakthrough: it failed to realize a full "leap in being." It is difficult to see how Voegelin's wrestling with China has had any real effect upon his conception of history. It doesn't in the least affect his persuasion that history is a forward-moving theophany or that the core of the theophany is the revelation of God as the Nous in both the cosmos and man. Perhaps what it truly and decisively affected was Voegelin's earlier conception of history as a meaningful course of events on a straight line of time. Here lies a decisive difference between Voegelin and Hegel, for Voegelin seems to surrender any conception of history as a singular or linear course. This is important, but is it possible to abandon a unilinear conception of history even while conceiving the process of history as an eschatological movement in time?

At this point it is instructive to compare *The Ecumenic Age* with the earlier volumes of *Order and History*. The analysis of the first three volumes proceeds chronologically and systematically and it seems to lie within our established conception of history. But, as Voegelin himself notes, the analysis of *The Ecumenic Age* moves backward and forward and sideways, in order, as he believes, to follow empirically the patterns of meaning in history as they reveal themselves in the self-interpretation of persons and societies in history. While the new volume retains the thesis that there is a fundamental historical advance from compact to differentiated consciousness, there no longer seems to be a unilinear development of either society or consciousness. There also appears to be a diminution of historical meaning itself. There is nothing in *The Ecumenic Age* which has the historical power and authority of the earlier treatment of the history of Israel or of Homer and Aeschylus, or the philosophical power of the earlier analysis of Parmenides, Heraclitus, Plato, and Aristotle. True, we are given a series of fascinating and enlightening historical exegeses of such subjects as Philo, Stoicism, Cicero, Hesiod, Herodotus, Polybius, Paul, Mani, and Alexander. But in *The Ecumenic Age* the power of historical analysis is overshadowed by the pervasive and dominant presence of speculative thinking and polemical assault. One is reminded of the older Hegel, but this is not just a question of age, for Voegelin's mind is as vigorous as ever. Has Voegelin undergone a fundamental turn which is a movement away from anything we can recognize as historical meaning? Or has he discovered a new order of history which is baffling precisely because of its singular uniqueness?

If Voegelin differs decisively from Hegel in his refusal of a unilinear meaning of history, he also does so in his attempt to unite cosmos and history as two poles of one order of meaning, and in his insistence upon maintaining a balance of consciousness between both time and eternity and humanity and God. That balance was established for all time in the ancient world. For there has been only one real noetic breakthrough, and that was established by Plato and Aristotle. So likewise there has been only one purely spiritual revelation, and that occurred in Israel. Voegelin's greatest project is his herculean effort to unite these breakthroughs into one revelation and one theophany. But does this very project inevitably lead him into his violent assault upon the modern world? Our real time and world are present in these volumes only in a negative form. While Voegelin does fully employ modern critical and historical studies, one will look in vain in these volumes for the positive presence or influence of twentieth-century philosophical thinking, just as he will be aware that the modern revolutions in literature, art, and science are present here only in their all too significant absence. Is this the price that must be paid for a contemporary affirmation of God and cosmos? It is also noteworthy that the interior never appears or is manifest on these pages. Is this because Voegelin's work reflects a truly postmodern world? And is that world in some fundamental sense a return to the cosmic world of premodernity? And a return to God? To the God whom we have lost? To a God who is no longer recognizable as God to us? Only a thinker of first rank could force us to ask such questions.

RESPONSE TO PROFESSOR ALTIZER'S "A NEW HISTORY AND A NEW BUT ANCIENT GOD?"

Eric Voegelin

Dear Professor Hart

Professor Altizer was kind enough to send me his essay-review of *The Ecumenic Age*. In my lengthy response to his courtesy I thanked him for his perceptive and brilliant study of my work, and I tried to clarify some points that seemed to worry him. When he communicated this letter to you, the three issues raised in it appeared of sufficient interest to you to have my answer published together with the review, provided my brief intimations of the problems were elaborated somewhat, but not too much, to become intelligible to a wider body of readers. In order to fulfill this condition, we agreed on the form of a letter to you which indeed does no more than spell out intimations which needed no spelling out in a private correspondence between scholars who know each other well. Well, here is the letter.

The first of the issues arises from the conflict between Altizer's admirable perspicacity in discerning the subject-matter of my study and the difficulty he experiences in relating it to "the common language" of theology and philosophy. He characterizes my prose style as tantalizing, "for it is clear and obscure at once, and its clarity is indistinguishable from its obscurity"; I am writing in such a manner, he says, as to make a theological exegesis of my work a virtual impossibility, though one cannot deny that my "primary quest is to unveil the identity of God"; he attributes this character of my language to the fact that the actual subject of my study is "a mystery"; and he assumes a conflict between my inquiry into the "mystery" and the Christianity of the Church. He goes even as far as to find implied in my study the belief "that the primary failure of Christianity is its misidentification, its misreading of Christ."

Let me repeat my admiration for Altizer's perspicacity in discerning the issues, before I make the qualifications which I deem necessary.

I am using the neutral language of issues raised by my study, because I am not a theoretical activist who raises them wantonly; rather, I am forced to

raise them by the extensive study of the sources offered by the historical sciences. I am indeed attempting to "identify" (though I do not consider this the
mot juste) the God who reveals himself, not only in the Prophets, in Christ,
and in the Apostles, but wherever his reality is experienced as present in the
cosmos and in the soul of man. One can no longer use the medieval distinction between the theologian's supernatural revelation and the philosopher's
natural reason, when any number of texts will attest the revelatory consciousness of the Greek poets and philosophers; nor can one let revelation begin
with the Israelite and Christian experiences, when the mystery of divine presence in reality is attested as experienced by man, as far back as ca. 20,000
B.C., by the petroglyphic symbols of the Palaeolithicum. The modern en-
largement of the ecumenic horizon to globality, and of the temporal horizon
by the archaeological millennia, has made a revision of the traditional "common language" indeed ineluctable.

The revision is necessary. But I do not believe that the contemporary reluctance to face this problem can be imputed as a guilt to "Christianity" without
careful qualifications. Professor Altizer, if I understand him correctly, identifies "Christianity" with the Christian dogma and is therefore inclined to attribute to my pursuit of "the mystery" an originality which I must modestly
decline. There were always Christian thinkers who recognized the difference
between experiences of divine reality and the transformation of the insights
engendered by the experience into doctrinal propositions. The tension between *theologia mystica* and *theologia dogmatica* goes as far back as the Patres.
It dominates the work of Origen; and its dynamics is the living force in such
noteworthy successors as Augustine, Pseudo-Dionysius, Scotus Eriugena,
Anselm of Canterbury, and the mystics of the fourteenth century. It is definitely an intra-Christian tension.

As far as my own vocabulary is concerned, I am very conscious of not relying on the language of doctrine, but I am equally conscious of not going beyond the orbit of Christianity when I prefer the experiential symbol "divine
reality" to the God of the Creed, for "divine reality" translates the *theotes* of
Col. 2:9. The *theotes*, a neologism at the time, is a symbol arising from experiential exegesis; its degree of generality is so high that it can be applied, not
only to the specific experience of divine reality becoming incarnate in Christ
and the Christian believers (the experience analyzed in Col. 2), but to every
instance of *theotes* experienced as present in man and forming his insight into
his nature and its relation to the divine ground of his existence. Moreover, I
am very much aware that my inquiry into the history of experience and symbolization generalizes the Anselmian *fides quaerens intellectum* so as to include every *fides*, not only the Christian, in the quest for understanding by
reason. Even this expansion of the *fides*, however, to all of the experiences of
divine reality in which history constitutes itself, cannot be said to go beyond

"Christianity." For it is the Christ of the Gospel of John who says of himself: "Before Abraham was, I am" (8:58); and it is Thomas Aquinas who considers the Christ to be the head of the *corpus mysticum* that embraces, not only Christians, but all mankind from the creation of the world to its end. In practice this means that one has to recognize, and make intelligible, the presence of Christ in a Babylonian hymn, or a Taoist speculation, or a Platonic dialogue, just as much as in a Gospel. I cannot admit, therefore, a conflict with "Christianity"; I can admit only that the Thomasic declaration, included as accepted doctrine in Denzinger's *Enchiridion*, has aroused hardly any response among theologians and philosophers in their work on the process of revelatory experiences in history.

Having brought the larger range of Christian thought to attention, I can now heartily agree with Professor Altizer in his attribution of a guilt to "Christianity." It is the guilt of Christian thinkers and Church leaders of having allowed the dogma to separate in the public consciousness of Western civilization from the experience of "the mystery" on which its truth depends. The dogma develops as a socially and culturally necessary protection of insights experientially gained against false propositions; its development is secondary to the truth of experience. If its truth is pretended to be autonomous, its validity will come under attack in any situation of social crisis, when alienation becomes a mass phenomenon; the dogma will then be misunderstood as an "opinion" which one can believe or not, and it will be opposed by counteropinions which dogmatize the experience of alienated existence. The development of a nominalist and fideist conception of Christianity is the cultural disaster, with its origins in the late Middle Ages, that provokes the reaction of alienated existence in the dogmatic form of the ideologies, in the eighteenth and nineteenth centuries. The result is the state of deculturation with which we are all too familiar from our daily talks with students who are caught in the intellectual confusion of a debate that proceeds, not by recourse to experience, but by position and counter-position of opinion. Once truth has degenerated to the level of true doctrine, the return from orthodoxy to "the mystery" is a process that appears to require as many centuries of effort as have gone into the destruction of intellectual and spiritual culture.

The second issue arises from Professor Altizer's accusation that I am "attacking" Hegel, and interpreting him in "an absurd and grotesque" manner, while in fact I am his descendant. The accusation culminates in the suggestion that "Voegelin's hatred of Hegel is an attempted Oedipal murder of his father."

Again I must admire Altizer's sensitivity for the central problems of my study before engaging in a few emendations.

Above all, I do not "attack" Hegel but submit key passages of his work to philologically and theoretically the same type of analysis to which I submit the work of other thinkers. If the result is less positive than in the case of my studies on Aeschylus or Heraclitus, which Altizer praises for their philosophical forcefulness, one might perhaps consider the possibility that the difference of spiritual stature between the thinkers mentioned has something to do with the matter. When I read Altizer's outburst, I was reminded of similar accusations on occasion of my various analyses of Marxian ideas; when my recent volume *From Enlightenment to Revolution* came out, I even was accused of falsifying the quotations from Marx. The German *Ich-Philosophie*, and the prestige of Hegel and Marx, has become so much a part of the "climate of opinion," if I may use Whitehead's term, that the mere confrontation with the texts, as well as their treatment by ordinary methods of analysis, will cause surprise and hurt sensibilities. Of course, there are sensibilities of all kinds. In a recent review of *The Ecumenic Age*, for instance, I was taken to task for my German bias, caused by my German origins, in according Hegel such a prominent rank among modern philosophers. Well, one has to bear it, even if sometimes with a sigh rather than a grin. But now let us return from the opinions to reality.

There is a story to my relation to Hegel: for a long time I studiously avoided any serious criticism of Hegel in my published work, because I simply could not understand him. I knew that something was wrong, but I did not know what. There was a thinker whom I admired for the political acumen of his study on the English Reform Bill of 1831, and for his qualities as a German man of letters which he displayed in his essay-review of *Hamanns Schriften* (1828), a thinker whom I consulted at every step in my own work because of his vast historical knowledge and his powerful intellect, and who at the same time baffled all my efforts at following the thought process of his dialectics or at understanding the experiential premises of his system.

The first relief in this frustrating state came through my study of Gnosticism and the discovery that by his contemporaries Hegel was considered a Gnostic thinker. Baur's *Christliche Gnosis* (1835) proved of considerable help at this stage. I became aware at last of Hegel's explicit declaration that he wanted to advance beyond philosophy, beyond the mere love of wisdom, toward real knowledge, a passage which I had read many times in the *Phänomenologie* without grasping its import. The discovery of the Gnostic component, however, did not dissolve all that was obscure to me in Hegel's thought. I had yet to become aware of the origins of his dialectics in Neoplatonism, and especially in the triadic dialectics of Proclus, as well as of Hegel's self-interpretation of his work as the fulfillment of the Proclian intentions in the *Geschichte der Philosophie*. In the further pursuit of this factor, Diderot's article on *Eclectisme* in the *Encyclopédie Française* proved of great help for understanding the connection between Neoplatonism and encyclopedism; Hegel's *Enzyklopädie* lost much of its strangeness as a work of modern thought when it could be placed in succession to the Neoplatonic encyclopedism of the Enlightenment *philosophes*. A third find was Hegel's self-declaration of the *Phänomenologie* as a work of Magic. As in the case of Gnosticism, I had read the passages on the "magic words" and the "magic force" in the *Phänomenologie* many a time without becoming aware of their implications, though I should have remembered the warning of Jacob Boehme, in his *Mysterium Magnum*, against precisely the type of *magia* that Hegel was to pursue. The new awareness was stimulated, and materially supported, by a closer study of Kojève's *Introduction*. The results of my inquiry into Hegel's Magic, its principles and techniques, I have published in my essay "On Hegel: A Study in Sorcery" (1971). I should perhaps add that I found Malinowski's definition of magic, developed for the case of the Trobriand islanders, also to fit the case of Hegel's Neoplatonic *Zauberei*.

Since the publication of this essay, things have begun to fall into place. Thanks to the work of Frances Yates on *Giordano Bruno* (1964), I can now relate the Hegelian Magic to the Neoplatonists of the fifteenth century. Marsilio Ficino's formulation, in the Introduction to his translation of the *Corpus Hermeticum*, that the Divine Mind "may glow into our mind and we may contemplate the order of all things as they exist in God," comes as close to Hegel's declaration of his *Logik* as written from the position of the Logos before the creation of nature and the mind of man as it can come without being identical. The attainment of this knowledge is for the Neoplatonists the basis for magical operations on reality, and especially on the future of mankind in history. Hegel's program of Magic, I would now say, belongs to the continuous history of modern Hermeticism since the fifteenth century. Festugière, by the way, in his *Hermès Trismégiste*, has classified Hermeticism as the optimistic variety of Gnosticism.

A still wider horizon opens with Mircea Eliade's *The Forge and the Crucible: The Origin and Structure of Alchemy* (1956; English paperback 1971). With his vast empirical knowledge as the basis, he assigns to Alchemy its place in a history of man's belief in his ability magically to transform reality that extends from the metallurgists of the Neolithicum to the ideologists of the nineteenth and twentieth centuries A.D. In order to clarify a point that seems to me not sufficiently clear in Eliade's work, I want to stress that the growth of a nonmagical natural science in the modern centuries has affected the areas of science in which Alchemistic beliefs are still socially permissible. In our contemporary world, Alchemist magic is primarily to be found among the ideologists who infest the social sciences with their efforts to transform man, society, and history. This statement, however, is not meant to detract from Eliade's observation that Alchemistic conceits survive also in the inspiration of the natural sciences, recognizable in such phenomena as the technological dreams of a new world, or in the biological dreams of producing a *homunculus*.

In the present context, I cannot elaborate on these intimations. It must be enough to state their obvious implication: the contemporary disorder will appear in a rather new light when we leave the "climate of opinion" and, adopting the perspective of the historical sciences, acknowledge the problems of "modernity" to be caused by the predominance of Gnostic, Hermetic, and Alchemistic conceits, as well as by the Magic of violence as the means for transforming reality.

There remains the task of determining with precision the point at which Hegel went wrong. What exactly is that disorder of existence that moves a thinker of the undoubted rank of Hegel to become a magician? Again I can rely on Professor Altizer's philosophical astuteness to have seen the crucial issue. Immediately preceding the passage on the "Oedipal murder" I have committed, he formulates it succinctly by the critical charge that I consider Hegel's *Geist* simply to be his ego. "But this," Altizer continues, "is an absurd and grotesque interpretation. One could just as easily say the same of Aristotle's *Nous*." Professor Altizer is right, one could indeed do that. And as a matter of fact, it has been done, quite easily, though not by me, but by Hegel himself. Hegel's self-declaration of his system of science as the final realization of Aristotle's noetic intention is the great bang at the end of the *Enzyklopädie*. The last paragraph of Hegel's dialectical exposition is followed by the quotation from Aristotle's *Metaphysics* XII, 7, which is supposed to show the sameness of noetic intention in the two works by confronting the reader who just has finished the *Enzyklopädie* with Aristotle's yet imperfect identification of the divine with the human Nous. I for my part consider the confrontation a failure; Hegel's assumption concerning the meaning of the passage is a gross misunderstanding, for the reasons I have given elsewhere. Still, the confrontation is of importance, because it indicates the spiritual disorder that induced it.

At the core of Hegel's difficulties lies his misconstruction of the relation between Being and Thought, which he needs for his misconstruction of "Christianity," which he needs for his misconstruction of history, which he needs if he wants to place himself at the climax of history as the fully revealed and revealing Logos who completes the Revelation that was left incomplete by the Logos who was Christ. Since Hegel is a conscientious thinker, he carefully states the principle that pervades the series of misconstructions. In his *Geschichte der Philosophie* he calls it the "Protestant Principle" of relocating the divine intellect in the mind of man, so that "one can see, know, and feel in one's own consciousness everything that formerly was beyond" (quoted in *Ecumenic Age*, p. 173).

The principle is not altogether wrong. Its solid part is Hegel's effort to get rid of the hypostatic Beyond of a purely doctrinal God, so that the poor in spirit can return to the "mystery" of the divine reality experienced as present in the "heart" of man, i.e., in his concrete existence as a human being. For Hegel, Christ is the image of "the identity of the *Geist* with God for the heart"; but he is an image given on the level of perception (*Anschauung*). From this image of the identity of God with man, however, from the symbolism of the Son, man must advance to the self-consciousness of the Spirit that will internalize the image in the concreteness of his existence. But from the old Christianity of the Son to the new Christianity of the Spirit, "there is a long way." For man must realize that "the absolute Being" is not a "beyond of finite consciousness." He must abandon the hypostatic distinction between an infinite Being and a finite man, so that he can come to know both God and man to have the same nature of self-conscious *Ich*. Ontologically, there is no separate God but only "the absolute Being, i.e., *Ich* = *Ich*, thinking self-consciousness"; nor is there a separate man but only the "*Ich*, i.e., everybody who thinks" as a "moment" in the existence of absolute Being. Repellent as this constructivist language may appear to many, and untranslatable as it is into the language of common experience, there can be no doubt about Hegel's honest effort to reestablish an understanding of man's existence in the divine-human In-Between, in the *metaxy* in the Platonic sense. Moreover, in the construction of "the absolute Being" (*das absolute Wesen*) there can be discerned the experience of the reality that comprehends both God and the Creation, the experience of the cosmic Whole as a process in which there occurs the subprocess of reality becoming luminous to itself in the In-Between of consciousness. With so large a block of solid experience to be acknowledged, what then is the defect of thinking that leads to its deformation in the odd construction of the cosmic Whole as the *Ich* = *Ich*?

The defect is the magician's transformation of the *fides quaerens intellectum*, which belongs to the In-Between reality of existence, into a thought-process that can penetrate the comprehensive reality of the cosmic Whole. The luminosity of consciousness is expanded to a luminosity of the Whole in which it occurs; and in order to make this expansion tenable, the Whole must be construed as consciousness, as the *Ich* = *Ich*, in the Hegelian sense. Through this magic expansion of consciousness, the order of the Whole becomes a knowable and manageable reality in "the heart of man," "in every man who thinks," in the concrete case in the consciousness of Hegel. The experienced mystery of divine presence in reality has been transformed into the mastery of real knowledge concerning the Whole that comprehends both God and man. Philosophy, the loving search of the divine *sophon*, has come to its end in the absolute knowledge of Hegel's System.

The transformative expansion of consciousness is rationally impermissible, because it ignores the limits set by the structure of reality to any "quest of understanding." In his *Proslogion*, Anselm of Canterbury has taken cognizance of this limit and explored it. In the first part of his work, he pushes the quest to the limit of the argument that later has come to be called the ontological proof for the existence of God. In the second part, in *Proslogion XIV*, he acknowledges that the God found by the truth of reason is not yet the God whom the seeker experienced as present in the formation and re-formation of his existence. He prays to God: "Speak to my desirous soul what you are other than what it has seen, that it may clearly see what it desires." And in *Proslogion XV* he formulates the structural issue with classic exactness: "O Lord, you are not only that than which a greater cannot be conceived, but you are also greater than what can be conceived." This is the limit of conception disregarded by Hegel. One should note that in the section on Anselm of Canterbury, in his *Geschichte der Philosophie*, Hegel deals extensively and competently with the ontological proof, but does not mention the second part of the *Proslogion* with its analogical exploration of the divine light beyond human reason. This neglect, however, must not be imputed as a guilt exclusively to Hegel, for by his time the concentration on the syllogistical merits and demerits of the ontological proof, to the neglect of the divine mystery beyond reason, had already become standard practice among Western thinkers. Set against this background, one rather would have to acknowledge Hegel's philosophical perceptiveness which moved him to recognize the issue by deforming it. In our time, this barbaric destruction of intellectual and spiritual structures is in the process of being repaired. I mention only the fine study on *Fides Quaerens Intellectum* (1931) by Karl Barth, which prepared its author for the revision of his *Dogmatik*. This renewed attention, accorded by a leading Protestant theologian to Anselm's balance of mystery and reason, might also cause some second thoughts whether Hegel's principle is quite as "Protestant" as he believed it to be.

The destruction of the fundamental structure of knowledge and truth invalidates Hegel's System as a work of philosophy, but it does not invalidate the vast range of historical materials and theoretical problems embraced by his truly imperatorical mind. The great representative of modern magical thought cannot be ignored. But since he cannot be ignored, it is not permitted to ignore the manner in which his Magic affects his language and its use. When the thinker breaks through the barrier of reason, he can give to the magical results of his expansion of consciousness an appearance of rationality only by playing magical con-games with the common language. I have analyzed a representative example, the case of Hegel's play with the terms *Geist* and *Wesen*, in *Ecumenic Age*, pp. 262–66. As this type of con-game has become an all-pervasive phenomenon in our "climate of opinion," the analysis of the tricks a magician plays with language is not a wanton "attack" on anybody, but the duty of the philosopher, if he wants to understand the contemporary disorder, and of the educator, if he wants to help the young in the intellectual and spiritual misery caused by their exposure to the formidable pressure of these con-games in their environment.

I can be brief on the third issue. It is raised by Professor Altizer's observation that I neglect the thought and science of the twentieth century. Whether this observation is correct depends on what kind of thought and science one considers representative of our times. I consider representative, by the side of the work in theoretical physics, the magnificent work of the historians. They have brought to light the background of modernity in Gnosticism, Hermeticism, Alchemy, and Magic; they have restored our knowledge of ancient and medieval philosophy; they have provided a solid basis for our understanding of the Israelite-Judaic-Christian experiences; they have extended our knowledge to the Indian, Chinese, pre-Columbian, and African societies; and they have expanded our historical horizon by the prehistoric millennia. This vast amount of historical knowledge accumulated has by now the historic effect of letting the ideological systems of the eighteenth and nineteenth centuries, to say nothing of their epigonal aftermath, appear as pitifully inadequate and obsolete interpretations of reality, for reasons both empirical and theoretical. On the other hand, Professor Altizer would be right if he meant to observe that the marvelous advance of science which characterizes the twentieth century has not yet affected the notorious "climate of opinion" which dominates the public debate. But I do not believe that the end of the world has come, if it does not come to the end the ideologists have projected for it. The world will go on, and the restoration of intellectual and spiritual culture in the sciences will ultimately affect an ideological climate that by now has become a reactionary force. To assist in this process is one of the motives of my work.

In conclusion of this long letter, let me thank Professor Altizer once more for the sympathetic and generous review which provoked my answer, and you, my dear Professor Hart, for this opportunity of elaborating the response for a wider public.

> With my warmest regard, I am,
> Sincerely yours,
> Eric Voegelin

EPILOGUE

Eric Voegelin

The organizer of the Symposium, Professor Ellis Sandoz, wants me to respond to the present volume with an epilogue. The request is not unjustified as my work provided a strong motive in the meeting of minds and as I participated in the discussions. But the response must not violate the spirit of the meeting, a spirit that was cooperative, not adversarial. It was a Symposium indeed—a meeting of likeminded men, all equally burdened with the intellectual confusion of the age, all equally determined to work their way out of utopian phantasies and reductionist methodologies, all equally attempting to find again the common ground of reason and reality that has been lost in the dominant climate of opinion. It would be in conflict with my function as a participant in a common effort, if I were to engage in a critical evaluation of the essays or, worse still, in the pedantry of taking issue with this or that particular statement. The essays resulting from the Symposium, and contained in this volume, are written by competent scholars who know what they are talking about; the authors do not promote unfounded opinions but engage in well-reasoned argument; the essays do not need my commentary but speak for themselves to the reader. I shall confine myself, therefore, to a brief remark about the general structure of the Symposium and the difficulties which the effort to regain reality is still encountering.

By its language of communication, the structure of the Symposium is topical, not analytic. The overall subject is denoted by the topic "thought," leaving it to the reader to place its meaning somewhere in the range from noetic analysis, through ideas and doctrines, to occasional thoughts-about and idiosyncratic opinions. The first essay uses a musical title, leaving the reader to guess what the constant theme in a man's life might be that will justify the metaphors of prelude and variations. The subsequent essays deal, under the topical head of "contribution," with the manner in which the "thought" might affect the present state in such topical, specialized fields of science as political science, philosophy, theology, and philosophy of history, leaving the reader to wonder how to place a fellow who appears to be talking about everything in the topically familiar field of contemporary specialized science.

These observations sound critical, but their criticism is not directed against the structure of the Symposium. They criticize an intellectual situation which imposes the topical pattern of communication on any noetic effort at analysing man's experience of reality, as well as the reality of his experience, in our time. In the study of man's humanity, the *peri ta anthropina* in the Aristotelian sense, the modern revolt has practically expelled from public consciousness the philosophers' language of noetic experience together with the deformation of its meaning through a decadent dogmatism of theology and metaphysics that was the target of the revolt. I apologize for the banality of the baby thrown out with the bath. The modern study of man has become questionable because the revolt against dogmatic obscurantism, while gaining new horizons of experience, has not regained the philosopher's noetic experience, but has uncritically imposed on the new freedom the heritage of dogmatic form as its own form of truth. The old dogmatism was exchanged for a new one. The great dogmatomachic conflicts and wars of the sixteenth and seventeenth centuries were followed, after a brief interlude of exhaustion, by the dogmatomachies, ideological and methodological, of the nineteenth and twentieth centuries, culminating in the contemporary murderous grotesque of world-wars, liberations, brainwashing, terrorism, and the threat of annihilation by the atom bomb. As far as the study of the *anthropina* is concerned, this ambiguity of the modern revolt has resulted, in our time, in the confrontation of a vast horizon of experiential knowledge, daily enlarging by the empirical freedom of the historical sciences, with a welter of dilettantic, dogmatic misconstructions of noetic symbols, misconstructions that go under the topical name of "theory." The intellectual situation to which I referred, thus, is characterized by the conflict between the freedom of the empirical horizon and the dominance, on the theoretical level, of fundamentalist constructs that are regrettably unfit to be used in the interpretation of the empirical materials.

On the nature and the types of the fundamentalist constructs I do not have to enlarge on this occasion. The varieties of reductionist and metastatic misconstructions are by now well known and the struggle with the theoretical detritus that has accumulated fills the pages of this volume. If any criticism be allowed, it could only be that the Symposium does not range far enough over the various fields. An essay on the detritus in the theory of evolution, for instance, would have been helpful. I have dealt with this area of problems in my monograph on the *Rassenidee* (published in 1933 but soon withdrawn, under Nationalsocialist pressure, by the publisher from circulation), and I mention it now, because the problems analysed on that occasion have recently again become a public issue in the silliness of demanding equal time for creationist and evolutionist "theories" in high-school textbooks. The protagonists in the case are theological and biological fundamentalists. The theologists, as far as I can judge from what has penetrated in the media reports, do not know what a cosmogonic myth is and that, whatever it is, it is not a "theory" of anything; and the biologists appear to be just as unfamiliar with the limits of a "theory" of evolution that have been analysed by Kant in the *Kritik der Urteilskraft*. Moreover, as neither of the two parties is aware of the noetic defects in the opponent's position, a rational discussion between them is impossible. The case is interesting because it illuminates the process in which the dilettantic fundamentalism of an older generation is imposed, by means of the educational system, on the generations to come.

The task of clearing up the antinoetic mess that has accumulated over the centuries in the contemporary science of man is enormous. It is not to be discharged by one generation of scholars who "think," and still less so by one man alone. Reading the essays in their finished form I had sometimes the feeling that my fellow symposiasts, perhaps in a state of enthusiasm engendered by the sense that something is done after all, underrate the magnitude of the task, a feeling fostered by the recurrent complaints about my failure to have dealt sufficiently with the complex of problems they comprehend under the topical head of "Christianity." The complaint, with its admonition to deliver the goods, implies the confidence that I can do everything that is supposed to be done. Flattering as this confidence is, and as it appeals to my sense of humor, a word of caution may be in place neverthess.

Fortunately this concluding word can be brief because the editor had the good idea of including in the volume Professor Altizer's review of my *Ecumenic Age* as well as my answer to the review. This exchange, together with the essay on "Revelation," in which certain problems of "Christianity" have become thematic, gives the answer to the complaint. If the published part of my studies on "Christianity" is less comprehensive than desired, the quite unmysterious reason is the quantity of the historical materials that have to be submitted to noetic analysis. Moreover, the topic "Christianity" is theoretically even more inadequate, if that is possible, than such other topics as "philosophy," "theology," "history," "religion," or "science," for it covers under its broad wing no less than the pneumatically formative force of the Western and Eastern *Christianitas* for the better part of two millennia, in both the Church formations and the sectarian movements, not to mention the successor movements of the modern ideologies. A study of "Christianity" is inextricably involved in the study of Western civilizational order since antiquity, in its phases of ecumenic, national, and ideological imperialism; and about this involvement I have had to say quite a bit in the course of my publications. The modernist topicality of "Christianity" as a "religion" among others, a topicality determined by a variety of polemical motives, may have been so dominant in the mind of the critics that it has obscured the fact of my dealing all the time with problems of "Christianity" when dealing with aspects of order which also may appear to fall under other topics. The exchange with Altizer will illuminate the range and the complications of these involvements in civilizational order. But more is yet to come. In the meanwhile, if anybody is dissatisfied with the results hitherto published, or cannot wait for more, he is heartily invited to take a hand at the task himself.

THE CONTRIBUTORS

THOMAS J. J. ALTIZER is professor of English and religious studies at the State University of New York at Stony Brook. He is the author of *The Dialectic of the Sacred*, *The New Apocalypse*, *The Descent Into Hell*, *The Self-Embodiment of God*, and *Total Presence*.

JÜRGEN GEBHARDT is professor of political science at the Friedrich-Alexander-Universität Erlangen-Nürnberg. He formerly taught at the University of Munich and Western Reserve University and has held a visiting appointment at the University of Virginia. He is the author of *Politik und Eschatologie* and *Die Krise des Amerikanismus*.

DANTE GERMINO is professor of government and foreign affairs at the University of Virginia. He is presently spending a sabbatical year in Rome with the help of a National Endowment for the Humanities Fellowship for Independent Study. He is the author of *Beyond Ideology*, *Modern Western Political Thought*, and *Political Philosophy and the Open Society*.

WILLIAM C. HAVARD, JR., is professor of political science and chairman of the department at Vanderbilt University. A former editor of the *Journal of Politics*, he has published a dozen books and monographs, as well as numerous articles, on political philosophy and politics, including several essays and reviews on the work of Professor Voegelin.

ELLIS SANDOZ is professor of political science at Louisiana State University. He is the author of *Political Apocalypse*, *Conceived In Liberty*, and *The Voegelinian Revolution*.

GREGOR SEBBA retired in 1973 as emeritus professor of liberal arts from the Graduate Institute of Liberal Arts at Emory University. His most recent publication is a monographic essay on history, modernity, and Gnosticism in the Festschrift for Eric Voegelin (*The Philosophy of Order*), which he edited with Peter J. Opitz.

ERIC VOEGELIN retired in 1969 as emeritus professor of political science from the University of Munich to return to the United States as Henry Salvatori Distinguished Scholar at Stanford University's Hoover Institution on War, Revolution, and Peace, a position he held until 1974. Among his numerous publications are *The New Science of Politics*, *Order and History*, and (most recently) "The Magic of the Extreme: A Meditation on Truth," *Southern Review*.

DAVID J. WALSH is assistant professor of government and philosophy at the University of South Carolina at Sumter. A native of Ireland, he earned his Ph.D. at the University of Virginia and previously taught at the University of Florida. He is the author of *Jacob Boehme and the Mysticism of Innerworldly Fulfillment* and "The Scope of Voegelin's Philosophy of Consciousness," *Philosophical Studies*.

EUGENE WEBB is professor of comparative religion and comparative literature at the University of Washington and chairman of the Comparative Religion Program. He is the author of four books, including *The Dark Dove: The Sacred and Secular in Modern Literature* and *Eric Voegelin: Philosopher of History*.

INDEX

DATE DUE

DEMCO 38-297